FootprintAsia

Thailand Islands

Andrew Spooner

Listings

Introducing the region

About the region

Bangkok

Eastern coast

Gulf Coast

Gulf Islands

Phuket & North Andaman Coast

South Andaman Coast & Islands

Practicalities

Contents

About the author

Andrew Spooner is a feature, travel and sports writer and photographer. As well as being the author to Footprint's Thailand, Cambodia and Southeast Asia handbooks, his work appears regularly in the Independent on Sunday, the Independent, CNN Traveller, the Guardian and Bike. He has also taught Media and Journalism, part time, at the University of East London. In his previous life, Andrew travelled through the underbelly of Europe with various punk rock bands and still likes loud music, played badly. After travelling to Thailand in 1989, Andrew developed a compelling fascination with the country and now shares his time between Bangkok and London.

Acknowledgements

Andrew Spooner would like to thank all at Britbike Triumph dealership in Phuket, Claude at Cape Panwa, the staff at Sri Panwa, Roger Moore, Nanthida Rakwong, Craig Douglas, Ben Sudhikam and Six Senses staff, TAT London and Bangkok and Alan Murphy and all at Footprint.

About the book

The guide is divided into four sections: **Introducing the region**; **About the region**; **Around the region** and **Practicalities**.

Introducing the region comprises: **At a glance**, which explains how the region fits together by giving the reader a snapshot of what to look out for and what makes this area distinct from other parts of the world; **Best of Thailand Islands & Beaches** (top 20 highlights); **A year in Thailand Islands & Beaches**, which is a month-by-month guide to pros and cons of visiting at certain times of year; and **Thailand Islands & Beaches on screen & page**, which is a list of suggested books and films.

About the region comprises: **History**; **Art & architecture**; **Thailand today**, which presents different aspects of life in the region today; **Nature & environment** (an overview of the landscape and wildlife); **Festivals & events**; **Sleeping** (an overview of accommodation options); **Eating & drinking** (an overview of the region's cuisine, as well as advice on eating out); **Entertainment** (an overview of the island's cultural credentials, explaining what entertainment is on offer); **Shopping** (the island's specialities and recommendations for the best buys); and **Activities & tours**.

Around the region is then broken down into five areas, each with its own chapter. Here you'll find all the main sights and at the end of each chapter is a listings section with all the best **sleeping, eating & drinking, entertainment, shopping** and **activities & tours** options plus a brief overview of public **transport**.

Sleeping price codes
$$$$ over US$100 per night for a double room
      in high season
$$$ $46-100
$$ $20-45
$ under $20

Eating & drinking price codes
$$$$ over US$30 per person for a 2-course
      meal with a drink, including service
      and cover charge
$$$ US$20-30
$$ US$10-20
$ under $10

Picture credits

Alamy: page 226: Andrew Woodley; page 96: Dan Vincent; page 194: Paul Christoforou; page 97: Whitehead Images.
Alex Robinson: page 10.
Andrew Spooner: pages 13, 15, 17, 18, 20, 21, 28, 29, 30, 32, 34, 35, 36, 37, 38, 39, 40, 42, 43, 46, 48, 51, 52, 53, 54, 55, 59, 60, 62, 63, 80, 88, 92, 105, 113, 115, 117, 118, 119, 175, 183, 186, 187, 193, 210, 220, 221, 224, 233, 262, 263, 264, 267, 268, 270, 272, 273, 274, 279.
Caroline Sylger Jones: pages 65, 126 & 127.
Charm Churee Villa Rustic Resort & Spa: page 162.
DUSIT THANI PATTAYA: page 98.
Fotolia: page 137: Joakim Leroy; page 64: pailoolom; page 195: simon gurney; pages 2, 9, 108: sojies.
istock: page 123: Alexander Bischoff; pages 1, 230: laughingmango.

Metropolitan Hotel: pages 79, 276.
Monsoon Books: page 23.
Nick Nostitz & White Lotus: page 23.
Shutterstock: page 71: aaleksander; page 237: Alexander Chaikin; page 134: Andreas Nilsson; page 146: Andy Heyward; page 77: Andy Lim; page 124: Artur Bogacki; page 68: ATIKARN MATAKANGANA; page 177: Bruce Amos; pages 69, 74, 277: Bryan Busovicki; page 156: Charles Taylor; page 107: Colman Lerner Gerardo; pages 2, 24: David Quixley; pages 94, 104, 180: Dmitry Kushch; page 166: DPiX Centre; page 179: Eniko Balogh; page 190: Eric Lundberg; pages 3, 9, 216: F Rae; pages 218, 247: Gina Smith; pages 106, 150, 152, 228: Holger Mett; page 91: isaxar; pages 76, 121, 225, 227: javarman; pages 142, 148, 149, 154: Johan1900; page 143: John Blake; page 57: John Carnemolla; page 235: karnizz; page 58: Kjersti Joergensen; pages 3, 258: LIN,JING-CHEN; pages 2, 9, 66, 75: Luciano Mortula; page 110: Mark Burrows; pages 2, 6: Mateo Pearson; pages 223, 256: Mikhail Nekrasov; pages 3, 9, 172: MR.LIGHTMAN; page 93: OLIVES JEAN-MICHEL; page 236: Pang Chee Seng Philip; page 22: Pieter Janssen; page 174: prapass; page 16: reihe13; page 26: Surabky; page 261: Thor Jorgen Udvang; page 259: Timur Kulgarin; page 155: Tomasz Otap; page 2, 9, 86: Tusia; page 219: Uroš Medved; page 111: William Casey; page 144: Xavier Ye; page 14: ZQFotography.
Superstock: page 103: Prisma; pages 119, 181, 192: Robert Harding Picture Library.
Tierney/seafocus.com: pages 19, 44, 148, 149, 196, 197, 265.
TIPS Images: pages 188, 189: Andrea Pistolesi; page 90: Angelo Cavalli; page 41: Arco; pages 122, 136, 182, 185: Luca Invernizzi Tettoni; pages 2, 9, 89, 140, 278: Photononstop.

Contents

Long tail boat, Maya Bay, Koh Phi Phi Ley.

Introducing the region

Introduction

The Islands and Beaches of Thailand is a territory that spans thousands of miles of coastline, untold beaches and hundreds of islands. Everything from the most remote, wild and tropical isle through to full-blown overdeveloped resort towns are available. Breathtaking sunsets, jawdropping sunrises, all-night parties and calm serenity; opulent resorts, rickety bungalows and community-friendly homestays; locally sourced seafood, curries, pad thais, cheeseburgers, chips and pizzas; all this is vying for your attention, seeking to draw you in.

Start at the Eastern Coast at rainforest-clad Koh Chang travelling past Chantaburi and the white sands of Koh Samet. Then comes flamboyant Pattaya, eccentric Koh Si Chang, and enthralling Bangkok. Keep heading south down the Gulf Coast past the royal resort town of Hua Hin, the beaches of Prachuap, Chumphon and Nakhon. Learn to scuba dive at Koh Tao, meditate on Phangan and luxuriate on Samui. Head back west via the forests of Khao Sok to rain-drenched Ranong's hot springs before taking in more beaches at Khao Lak.

Phuket is next with its high class hotels and dynamic nightlife. Nearby Phangnga bay is simply spectacular, while Krabi is the best hub for budget travel in the region. The islands of Phi Phi and Lanta are now stuffed full of resorts though have never lost their beauty while Trang excites the tastebuds and makes for another excellent hub.

Finally, tucked away in the southwestern corner is Tarutao, mysterious, exotic and the definitive tropical idyll. If you've made it this far it will certainly have been worth the journey.

Koh Phi Phi.

At a glance

A whistle-stop tour of Thailand Islands & Beaches

Tropical white sands, beset by swaying palms and lapped by ebbing clear, blue seas. Delicious, exotic flavours, bright, rich fruits and pungent spicy tastes. Friendly locals, charming smiles and luxurious spas, massage, yoga and meditation. The beaches and islands of Thailand offer all this.

Yet, the ancient Kingdom of Siam also offers anarchic, vibrant culture, edgy and lost in the dynamic energies of modernity. Buddhism and Islam, Nokia and Prada, uprisings and temples, serene beaches and heaving cities, layer after layer of contrast. And, if you're up for it, you can enjoy every aspect of this invigorating region.

Bangkok

The Thai capital, known locally as Khrungthep - the City of Angels – is one of the most bewildering and engaging cities on earth. Begin in Bangkok's heart, at the gaudy excess of the Grand Palace and work your way through the temples, shopping centres, street food and nightlife. Take in the *khlongs* (canals) – Bangkok was once riven with them, hence the moniker, Venice of the East – and the markets, the luxury accommodation and the endless sensory pleasures and you'll soon get to grips with this dynamic city.

Before the royal Thai court moved here from Ayutthaya in the late 18th century Bangkok was a small trading post, known more to foreign sailors then indigenous Thais. These days it's home to 16-million-plus citizens and the seemingly endless urban sprawl keeps pushing outwards, gobbling up more of Thailand's vast central plain.

It's the nation's transport hub and main entry point and love it or loathe it most visitors are sure to pass through it. The trick is to make like the locals and indulge yourself as best you can. That way the traffic jams, smog and overwhelming cacophony are at least bearable.

Eastern Coast

If time is short and you've been overwhelmed by the scale of Bangkok, the easiest route out is eastward. In fact, if they're after a slice of beach this is where most Bangkokians will head. The nearest island of any note is Koh Si Chang, an eccentric place not known for divine beaches or sumptuous resorts. Instead, you'll get authentic island life, weird Chinese temples and great seafood.

Next up is sinful Pattaya, filled with dubious bars, pretty decent hotels and some of the best western food in the country. The highlights for the more discerning traveller will be ladyboy cabaret and the more family-orientated beach at Jomtien.

Koh Samet, an island so beautiful it has inspired poetry, is fringed by picture-perfect white sands and is supposed to be a protected national park. Yet, at weekends it resembles a giant nightclub catering to the needs of students.

The east coast's remote, most far-flung corner plays home to emerging Koh Chang. Twenty years ago the islands here were almost completely uninhabited. Now they are home to one of the fastest growing tourist destinations in Thailand. Don't worry, the beaches are still fantastic and the seas turquoise and sun-drenched. There are even rain forests and tropical waterfalls should everything else become a drag.

Gulf Coast

The stretch of Gulf Coast immediately south of Bangkok also marks the historical beginnings of Thailand's tourist industry. Here, at Hua Hin, at the

The lowdown

Money matters
Visitors staying in the reasonable hotels and eating in decent restaurants will probably spend at least ฿3000 per day, conceivably much much more. Tourists staying in cheaper a/c accommodation and eating in local restaurants will probably spend about ฿1000-1500 per day. Backpackers staying in fan-cooled guesthouses and eating cheaply, should be able to live on ฿300 per day.

Opening hours & holidays
Banks: Monday-Friday 0830-1530. Exchange: daily 0830-2200 in Bangkok, Pattaya and Phuket; shorter hours in other places. Government offices: Monday-Friday 0830-1200, 1300-1630. Shops: 0830-1700, larger shops 1000-1900/2100. Tourist offices: 0830-1630.

Tourist information
Tourist Authority of Thailand (TAT), 1600 New Phetburi Rd, Makkasan, Ratchathewi, T02-2505500, tourismthailand.org; also at 4 Rachdamnern Nok Av (intersection with Chakrapatdipong Rd), Monday-Friday 0830-1630; in addition there are two counters at Suvarnabhumi Airport, in the Arrivals halls of Domestic and International Terminals, T02-134 0040, T02-134 0041, 0800-2400. Local offices are found in most major tourist destinations in the country. UK, T0870-900 2007, tourismthailand.co.uk. USA, T461-9814, tatla@ix.netcom.com.

start of the 20th century the first resort-style hotels were built to accommodate the Thai aristocracy and their associated hangers-on. These days Hua Hin is still the weekend destination of choice for Bangkok's elite and is also the regular haunt of the present Thai king.

Head further south down the Isthmus of Kra and you'll soon reach Prachuap Khiri Khan. Nearby is one of southern Thailand's best kept secrets – the elegant and unspoilt beach at Ao Manao.

Chumphon is next, providing a well-known jump-off point to Koh Tao and the Gulf Islands, yet, once again, you'll find relatively unknown beaches to the north of the town, bereft of the usual clamour of mass tourism.

The venerable town of Surat Thani, set on a grand sweeping river and offering beguiling markets and friendly down-to-earth locals, is one of the most important conurbations on this stretch of coast. A hub for travel to the nearby Gulf Islands few visitors now stop here, preferring instead to book through-travel to the piers. Luckily, if you do visit, this means you'll have the place pretty much to yourself.

Finally, Nakhon Si Thammarat, home to a venerated temple and, allegedly, important elements of the Thai mafia, is a unique and engaging place where few travellers venture. The national parks, jungles, nearby hills and the beaches to the north at Khanom are all relatively undiscovered.

But there is much more to the island than that, with some gorgeously secluded spots that allow for endless days of lazy hammock dwelling, gazing at the gently lapping ocean…

Gulf Islands
The three Gulf Islands of Kohs Tao, Phangan and Samui are a destination all of their own. You could easily have a perfectly wonderful extended two-month winter break here and never venture to the mainland.

The largest, Samui, is busiest of the three and is now firmly on the mass-tourist circuit, with charter and scheduled flights making frequent arrivals at the island's new airport. Some of Thailand's finest resorts are found on Samui and there are plentiful beaches, good dining and lively nightspots.

Phangan is internationally renowned for the wild parties held every full moon on Mae Rim beach. But there is much more to the island than that, with some gorgeously secluded spots that allow for endless days of lazy hammock dwelling, gazing at the gently lapping ocean.

Although it is the smallest of the three, Koh Tao is in many ways probably the most attractive. It's

relative remoteness means that it is unlikely to ever overdevelop, while it's still large enough to soak up the people who do make it here – you should be able to find a quiet spot even in the midst of the high season. Tao is also a fantastic place to learn to scuba dive (make sure you pick your school with caution – plenty cut corners with safety to save money), giving yourself an easily accessible activity to distract yourself with should all that hammock lazing get too much.

Phuket & North Andaman Coast
For the last twenty years Phuket has been the veritable boom-town of the Thai tourism industry. Splendid beaches, verdant interior, ease of access and some fantastic hotels and resorts have pulled the punters in by the million.

Whilst Phuket may now be considered at the leading edge of overdevelopment it is one of the few destinations along Thailand's coast that has maintained any historical integrity – the Sino-Portuguese mansions of the island's former tin mining barons found in Phuket City's old quarter being the highlight.

Just off the east coast of Phuket is Phangnga Bay. Filled with hundreds of limestone karst towers it is often considered the most striking stretch of ocean along the many thousands of miles of Thai coastline – watching the sunrise or set over the bay is truly spectacular. The bay is also home to the welcoming islands of Koh Yao Yai and Yao Noi – the latter being home to a Muslim community that runs a world class homestay programme.

Despite the devastating tsunami of 2004 that decimated several communities, the stretch of coast that heads north from Phuket is re-emerging as a fashionable destination. The beaches of Khao Lak are certainly beguiling while the Similans – a group of islands a couple of hours offshore – are the biggest scuba-diving draw in the region.

Pressed up by the Burmese border is Ranong, home to hot springs and streets filled with handsome Sino-Thai architecture. The nearby isles and beaches of Kohs Chang and Phayam offer tranquillity and splendid isolation.

The White Sand Beach Resort, Khao Lak.

South Andaman Coast & Islands

Krabi Town, a long-time hub for budget travellers, marks the start of the Southern Andaman coast. You can connect by boat, plane and bus to much of the rest of southern Thailand from here and stay in some pretty nice surroundings while waiting to do so.

Just outside Krabi Town are the beaches of Ao Nang and Rai Leh – both celebrated destinations for mass tourists of differing descriptions (package tourists and backpackers) who are rightly attracted to the area for it's breathtaking location with limestone karsts and dramatic cliffs rising out of the sea.

A short boat hop from Krabi pier are the sweet tropical islands of both Koh Phi Phi and Koh Jum. Phi Phi, with its dreamy beaches and crystal clear seas is now a firm fixture on most travellers' itineraries even if, at times, it can seem completely overrun with people all searching for the perfect island getaway. Koh Jum, with less natural beauty is far more modest yet you'll find some genuine charm and serenity here.

The biggest island in these parts is Koh Lanta with almost the entire western coast rimmed with sandy beaches, bungalows and up-market resorts. For many years Lanta was a sleepy backwater but with flights landing at nearby Krabi airport the place has been transformed.

The last major town southbound is earthy Trang, another hub and served by direct sleeper trains from Bangkok. Trang is most famous for its tasty roast pork but you can also use it as the jump-off point to nearby islands and beaches.

Finally, dropped into the Andaman Sea right at the far southwestern reaches of Thailand is the Tarutao National Park. Home to an archipelago of definitive tropical islands you're likely to find the sand and corals of the ancient Sea Gypsy home of Koh Lipe divine while Koh Tarutao itself is mysterious, wild and sultry.

Best of Thailand Islands & Beaches

Top 20 things to see & do

❶ Bangkok – Grand Palace & Wat Po
The fulcrum of the city – the Grand Palace – began life in 1782 and is now a spectacular collection of golden stupas, gilded throne halls and gaudy statues. The highlight of the Grand Palace complex is Wat Phra Kaeo – Temple of the Emerald Buddha which houses the most venerated Buddha image in Thailand. Head next door to the neighbouring temple compound of Wat Pho, home to a huge reclining Buddha figure and you'll find the perfect way to unwind – medicinal Thai massage.

❷ Bangkok – Chinatown & the river
Weird food, labyrinthine back-streets and a frenetic atmosphere greet the visitor to Bangkok's Chinatown. Come in the evening and engage in some of the best streetfood in the city not forgetting to dip in and out of the arcane Taoist temples. Nearby is the river; haggle with a long-tail boat owner for a tour, taking in the *khlongs* (canals) and old city of Thonburi, set just over the water.

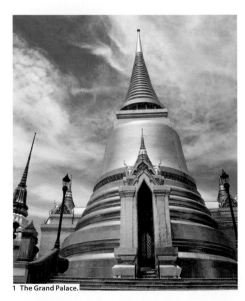
1 The Grand Palace.

❸ Koh Si Chang –
Chinese temple & seafood
The nearest island getaway to Bangkok, Si Chang, without fashionable beaches and resorts, tends to get overlooked by many visitors. The ones who do make it here can take in the honeycomb of caves and weird shrines that are the Chaw Por Khaw Yai Chinese Temple, one of the most important in Thailand, and the island's incredible seafood – Si Chang is noted for its fine squid.

❹ Pattaya – Ladyboy cabaret
Probably the most notorious destination in Thailand, Pattaya is not for everyone. Despite this it still manages to maintain an atmosphere that is distinctly Thai. One of the most unusual nights out you'll have here is a visit to a Ladyboy (transsexual) Cabaret, where men on their way to becoming women dress in the wildest outfits and high-kick their way through the evening. Head to one of the most famous cabarets at Tiffanys and they even have a gun range in the basement should you want to let off steam post-show.

❺ Koh Chang – Wild interior of the island
Set in the remote far eastern corner of the Gulf of Thailand, Koh Chang is rightly popular for its beaches. Yet the island is also home to a national park with 75% of the island being covered in pristine rainforest, providing the setting for all manner of beasties, plants and thick jungle. There are numerous waterfalls and also some great walking paths throughout the island. The Jungle Way guesthouse (see page 101) offers treks through the interior.

❻ Hua Hin – Tea at the Railway Hotel
The oldest beach resort destination in Thailand is also home to one of the country's oldest hotels – the Railway Hotel. Built in 1923 by a Thai prince who was then head of Thailand's state railways, it is the archetypal Asian colonial era hotel and has been used in various films, most famously in *The Killing Fields*. These days the name has been changed to the Sofitel Central Hua Hin but it's still a

8 A tending spirit house at Hat Thung Wua Lean, Chumphon.

perfect place to imbibe a colonial afternoon tea, complete with cakes and sandwiches.

❼ Prachuap Khiri Khan –
Ao Manao beach & seafood
Linked to Bangkok by the southern railway, many travellers pass through Prachuap without stopping. What they are missing out on is a friendly, down to earth fishing town, famed for its seafood and home to one of the Gulf coast's best beaches at nearby Ao Manao. Set on a military base, Ao Manao is strictly controlled, making it clean and unfettered by much of the development you'll experience in other places.

❽ Chumphon – Hat Thung Wua Laen Beach
Another place that travellers pass through eager to reach more crowded destinations, Chumphon is an easy jump-off point to a run of quieter beaches just to the north of the town. Hat Thung Wua Laen is the highlight, with a huge stretch of gorgeous sand, some decent guesthouses and good places to eat. It does have a sandfly problem but is still a perfect secluded spot for dazzling sunrises.

9 Fire dancer on the beach.

heaviest rainfall in the kingdom. You can also pick up boats to the slowly-being-discovered idyllic islands just off the coast here of Koh Chang and Koh Phayam.

⑫ Similans – Diving

For experienced divers there is only one place in Thailand that is essential and that is the Similans. Cast deep into the Andaman Sea, the Similans themselves are relatively untouched with stunning beaches and clear seas. Most divers visit here on live-aboard cruises, enabling them to reach such legendary dive sites as Koh Bon and Richelieu Rock. Come at the right time of year (February to April) and you might even get to glimpse the magnificent whaleshark.

⑨ Koh Phangan – Full Moon Parties

If you're coming to Thailand to party, the likelihood is that you will be heading to Koh Phangan and the beach at Hat Rin to indulge in one of the legendary Full Moon Parties. Here you'll find sound systems pumping out outrageously loud beats, fire jugglers of every description and some pretty nice spots to kick back in afterwards.

⑬ Phuket – Vegetarian Festival

Quite possibly one of the wildest festivals in Thailand the visceral Vegetarian Festival belies its compassionate title and serves up a riot of insane piercings, fire walking and other acts of self mutilation. You'll need a strong stomach and your camera for this Chinese celebration of the Taoist goddess of the sea and queen of the heaven Mazu's return to earth. The date moves but it's usually held in September or October – see phuketvegetarian.com for details.

⑩ Koh Tao – Learn to scuba dive

A lack of currents but shallow waters and some decent coral gardens set in good visibility have made Koh Tao one of the planet's busiest scuba dive training spots. There are dozens of schools – remember not to compromise on safety – offering the standard PADI Open Water qualification. During the months of March and April more experienced divers should head to the nearby Chumphon Pinnacle where they could encounter a whaleshark.

⑭ Phuket – Phuket Old Town

The 19th century Sino-Portuguese mansions built for wealthy tin barons, some sophisticated places to stay and eat and an historic atmosphere lost in most Thai towns is still available in Phuket Old Town. Come in mid-December for the Old Phuket Town Festival and many of the illustrious mansions throw their doors open to public. Government House, Sala Phuket and the old red light district Soi Romanee offer up the most charming examples of a bygone age.

⑪ Ranong – Hot springs and nearby islands

Tucked up against the Burmese border on the most northern point of the Andaman Coast, eccentric Ranong is home to sultry hot springs, one of Thailand's oldest Chinese communities and the

⑮ Phangnga – Koh Yao Noi homestay and bay

Forested with limestone karsts set amid a turquoise ocean, the bay at Phangnga is one of the most beautifully evocative images you'll encounter on any part of Thailand's coastline. While there, factor in a visit to the Muslim island of Koh Yao Noi and sample one of the best-run homestay programmes in Southeast Asia. The fishermen and women on this island are exceptionally friendly and the seafood is out of this world.

⑯ Krabi – Rai Leh & climbing
If the white sand beaches, the turquoise seas or the myriad sub-aquatic wildlife don't grab you then the climbing on offer around Krabi and Rai Leh might. The limestone karst towers that pepper the seas around these parts are certainly pretty but they are also excellent climbing sites – on some of the lower runs you don't even need ropes as you will fall directly into the sea. There are several climbing schools in the area and it's a great place to experience the sport for the first time.

⑰ Koh Phi Phi – Boat tours & Phi Phi Le
The natural beauty of Thailand's Koh Phi Phi island is world-renowned. Much of it has now been colonised by mass tourism but some stunning spots remain, not least the uninhabited neighbouring island of Phi Phi Le, famed for being used for the location of the film, The Beach. Rent a long-tail boat from Ton Sai on the main island and set yourself up with a memorable day combining a visit to Le with some exceptional snorkelling.

⑱ Lanta – Koh Lanta Town
While everyone is heading to the beach on Koh Lanta, the place on this tourist island that easily maintains the most atmosphere is Ban Koh Lanta. Here old wooden houses, a proper living community, great food and a couple of sweet places to stay combine to create a neat alternative to the gung-ho tourism everywhere else.

⑲ Trang – Roast pork
Rootsy Trang town makes a great hub from which to visit many of the region's best islands and beaches. For Thais it is famous for one thing – its roast pork. Trang's community is mostly Hainan Chinese and when they immigrated here in the 19th century they brought with them some time-honoured recipes. Visit one of the day-time pork restaurants and you won't leave disappointed.

⑳ Tarutao – National Park
There are few islands in Thailand that can now genuinely claim to have preserved their natural habitat and created a long-term tourist industry. Koh Tarutao in the Tarutao National Park is one of them. The only accommodation on this wild, green island rimmed with gorgeous beaches, is provided by the National Park – everything is strictly controlled. Tarutao's bizarre history of pirates and political prisoners only adds to the effect.

20 Tarutao.

Month by month

A year in Thailand Islands & Beaches

Boat to Pak Bara.

The swirl of tropical weather that moves across Thailand affects different parts at different times – while it's sunny on one side of the country it's likely to be monsoonal on the other. That doesn't mean rainy moments are to be avoided. Amazing bargains can be found when things are quieter, with up to 70% reductions. The only place that really escapes the machinations of the various monsoons and weather patterns is Koh Samet – one of the driest spots in Thailand.

We've broken our month by month guide into three distinct regions – each of these encounters different climatic conditions at different times, having a large input on the kind of travel experience you are likely to have.

Bangkok & the Eastern Coast

January to March

After the Christmas tourist influx and with temperatures lower than usual, the first few weeks of the year can be the perfect time to visit Bangkok and the Eastern Coast. In February prices will start to lower. By the end of March things will begin to get extremely hot and the rains will slowly start to emerge. Diving is still good around Koh Chang.

April to June

With the April heat – which can be completely debilitating in Bangkok – comes Thailand's biggest national public holiday, Songkran, held officially on the 13th to 15th of that month. Expect prices to skyrocket around this time on the beaches and often be fully booked out. April is also the height of the mango season. May and June stay hot with more frequent rainy spells, though the humidity can be quite oppressive. Prices will be low everywhere though.

July to September

These are the wettest months for this region and the monsoon will be in full effect. With the rains come floods and parts of Bangkok will usually be temporarily underwater so expect some delays. The seas will be choppier so swimming is not great either. Koh Chang will be very quiet with several places closing down – expect prices to be very low.

October to December

October marks the final weeks of the rains and the movement into the final, driest part of the year and the beginning of the tourist high season. As the weather improves prices move upwards and places fill up. In Bangkok the King's Birthday (5 December) is a spectacular event. Xmas is celebrated to a degree in Thailand and more so in Bangkok – it's not a public holiday though.

Gulf Coast & Islands

January to March

The weather along the 360 miles of Gulf Coast from Hua Hin to Nakhon Si Thammarat is based on the same monsoonal movements that afflict the Eastern Coast. Everything arrives a little bit later the further south you travel. So while Hua Hin is dry in January, Nakhon is wet. The Gulf Islands will still be a little wet for the first few weeks but by February things are pretty dry everywhere and the dive season begins. March is also a time to sight whalesharks. Prices will be quite high during this period.

Khao Lak.

Nam Mao beach near Krabi.

April to June

Diving in the Gulf is still excellent during April – when you might still be able to spot whalesharks – and May but by now the weather can begin to be very hot. There are fewer tourists and prices are a little lower than the peak periods earlier in the year. This can be a good time to visit the Gulf Islands with pretty good swimming conditions while the mainland is still reasonably dry as well. Expect a few storms but these are sporadic.

July to September

As this is the European school holidays many travellers will head to the Gulf Islands even though these are not the best months to visit. Prices will climb a little throughout the region due to the influx but this is still not considered high season. The monsoon will start to build during July and August with more frequent downpours. By September the weather should be in complete transition – bring an umbrella and expect localised flooding.

October to December

In the far south of the Gulf Coast the monsoon will persist through these months bringing quite serious deluges that can often cause floods. The seas can be quite choppy with high winds – November is the best month for kite-surfing around Chumphon. This is about the worst time for swimming and diving with poor visibility and general bad conditions. Everything will calm down by December and the weather can be quite benign in Hua Hin even though there are still downpours in Nakhon. The high season starts in mid-December with prices skyrocketing on the islands.

Andaman Coast & Islands

Tarutao.

January to March

Much like other parts of Thailand's coastline the first three months of the year tend to be reasonably dry along the Andaman Coast with the first serious outbreaks of rain beginning to move north from the far southern corner in late March. Phuket, Krabi and Khao Lak are often very busy at the start of the year when prices will peak. Diving is good at this time with the possibility of sighting whalesharks.

April to June

By the start of April the monsoon will begin to blow in from the southwest affecting the southern reaches of the Andaman Coast first. Islands in the Tarutao archipelago will start to be affected quite dramatically and from mid-April boats may be delayed or cancelled altogether. Yet it can still be a nice time to travel, particularly at the beginning of April. It will be getting increasingly hotter and muggier through May into June by which time monsoon weather will start to really come into play. By this point Koh Tarutao is likely to be closed and won't open until the weather calms again in October or November.

July to September

The monsoon carries on throughout this period until it begins to slowly dissipate at the end of September. If you do manage to make it on to one of the more remote islands like Koh Lipe you may get stranded for several days if storms are passing through. At times large weather systems might pass over the region, particularly in the deep south and flooding may occur. The seas are not great for swimming or diving. On islands such as Koh Lanta many places will be closed and real bargains can be had.

October to December

By October the monsoon starts to run out of energy and many of the Andaman Sea's beaches and islands start to come back to life. Most places that were closed re-open and the seas and weather begins to calm. With November comes the beginnings of a return to high-season prices, which carries on through to December. At the end of the year places such as Phuket will be running on full steam and rammed full of tourists. Diving is also excellent with many live-aboards heading for the Similans.

Screen & page

Thailand Islands & Beaches in film & literature

James Bond island.

Films

Bangkok Dangerous
Pang brothers, 1999

The riotous tale of a deaf-mute hitman on the dark and terrible streets of Bangkok. Was remade in 2008 by the same directors, starring Nicholas Cage.

The Beach
Danny Boyle, 2000

Directed by the maker of *Trainspotting* and *Slumdog Millionaire* and starring Tilda Swinton and Leonardo di Caprio, the film was based on Alex Garland's famous book. This production allegedly did plenty of damage to remote Koh Phi Phi Le during filming.

Southern Thailand as a film set

The coastline of Thailand has provided rich pickings for film directors – particularly those looking for stand-in locations. Here's our pick of the best…

Man with the Golden Gun (1974) Phangnga Bay
The Killing Fields (1984) Hua Hin and Phuket (as Phnom Penh and Cambodia)
Casualties of War (1989) Phuket (as Vietnam)
The Beach (2000) Koh Phi Phi Le
Stars Wars Episode 3 (2005) Krabi province (as Wookie homeworld of Kashyyyk)
Blackbeard (2005) Surat Thani and Nakhon Si Thammarat (as Caribbean).

Ong Bak
Prachya Pinkaew, 2003

Martial arts epic featuring Tony Jaa – it's famed for its lack of special effects relying almost completely on the Muay Thai skills of its actors.

Tears of the Black Tiger
Wisit Sasanatieng, 2000

The first Thai film selected for competition at Cannes, this is a surrealist tinged tale of love and Thai cowboys.

Literature

Fiction
The Beach
Alex Garland, 1997

A notorious fictionalised account of young travellers coming unstuck in their search for the perfect island idyll in southern Thailand. Was also made into a film in 2000.

The King Never Smiles
P M Handley, 2006

Banned in Thailand, this book charts the untold history of the present day king. Highly controversial, many Thais consider Handley's book to be almost blasphemous.

Private Dancer
Stephen Leather, 2008

The story of a young traveller drawn into the seedy Bangkok nightlife of the 1990s. The protagonist, Pete, succumbs to the charms of a stunning bargirl with dramatic consequences.

Non-fiction
Very Thai
Phil Cornwel-Smith, 2007

Brilliant excavation of the intricacies of Thai popular culture rendered in a chatty, down to earth style. Some nice photography as well.

Tearing Apart the Land
Duncan McCargo, 2008

A thorough dissection of southern Thailand's recent Islamic insurgency and the roots and causes of the violence. Unlikely to be greeted by the generals in Bangkok.

Red v Yellow; Thailand's Crisis of Identity
Nick Nostitz, 2009

This photo-led book is the first part of photo-journalist Nic Nostitz's account of the recent political troubles gripping Thailand. Nostitz gives a perspective that is likely to be viewed as the defining historical document of these events.

Contents

About the region

Sukothai, the ancient capital of Thailand.

History

Sukothai historical park.

Early history

Evidence of civilization in Thailand stretches back 1000s of years – discoveries at archaeological sites in the northeast, north and west of Thailand have revealed early agriculture (possibly 7000 BC), pottery (3500 BC) and metallurgy (2500 BC).

The first major civilisation, the Dvaravati Kingdom, lasted from the sixth to the 11th centuries; but virtually nothing of the Dvaravati period remains though there are some examples of sculpture at the National Gallery in Bangkok. In the south of Thailand the powerful Srivijayan Empire, with its capital at Palembang in Sumatra, extended its control from the seventh to the 13th centuries. Probably the best examples of what little remains of Srivijayan architecture in Thailand are Phra Boromthat and a sanctuary at Wat Kaeo, both in Chaiya (see page 118).

Of all the external empires to impinge on Thailand before the rise of the Thai, the most influential was the Khmer. The peak of the Khmer period in Thailand lasted from the 11th to the 13th centuries, corresponding with the flowering of the Angkorian period in Cambodia; many towns in central Thailand are Khmer in origin.

The Thai did not begin to exert their dominance over modern Thailand until the 12th and13th centuries when they took control of Lamphun in the north, founded Chiang Mai, established the Sukhothai Kingdom in the Yom River valley, and gained control of the southern peninsula. From the 13th century onwards, the history of Thailand becomes a history of the Thai people.

Sukhothai

The Sukhothai Kingdom, focused on the northern edge of the central plain, evolved in the 13th century but it wasn't until the reign of its most famous king, Ramkhamhaeng (c1279-1298) that it took centre-stage. When Ramkhamhaeng ascended to the throne in 1275, Sukhothai was a relatively small kingdom. When he died in 1298, extensive swathes of land came under his control. The kingdom promoted Theravada Buddhism (see page 36), sponsoring missionary monks to spread the word. In 1298, Ramkhamhaeng died and was succeeded by his son Lo Thai. His father's empire began to wane and by 1321 Sukhothai had become a small principality among many competing states.

Ayutthaya

In the middle of the 14th century, Sukhothai's influence began to be challenged by another Thai kingdom, Ayutthaya. Located over 300 km south on the Chao Phraya River, in 1351, a Thai lord took control of the area and founded a new capital. He called the city Ayutthaya – after the sacred town of Ayodhya in the Hindu epic, the Ramayana. This kingdom would subsequently be known as Siam. From 1351, Ayutthaya began to extend its power south as far as Nakhon Si Thammarat, and east to Cambodia. During the Ayutthayan period, the basis of Thai common law was introduced, the administration centralized and the kingdom extended over 500,000 sq km.

Yet Ayutthaya was continually attacked by the Burmese and by 1766 the city fell, being reduced to ashes by the Burmese army who enslaved tens of thousands of Ayutthayans.

Bangkok & the Rattanakosin period

After the sacking of Ayutthaya, General Taksin moved the capital 74 km south to Thonburi, on the other bank of the Chao Phraya River from modern day Bangkok. From Thonburi, Taksin successfully fought Burmese invasions, until he was forced to abdicate in 1782 and was replaced by one of his generals, Chao Phya Chakri, marking the beginning of the current Chakri Dynasty. Worried about the continuing Burmese threat, Rama I (as Chao Phya Chakri is known) moved his capital to the opposite bank of the Chao Phraya River and founded Bangkok.

Mongkut set about modernizing his country and was succeeded by his 15-year-old son Chulalongkorn who showed himself to be a reformer like his father, managing to keep the colonial powers at bay.

19th century

The 19th century was a dangerous time for Siam. Southeast Asia was being methodically divided between Britain, France and Holland as they scrambled for colonial territories. The same fate might have befallen Siam, had it not been blessed with two brilliant kings: King Mongkut (Rama IV – 1851-1868) and King Chulalongkorn (Rama V – 1868-1910). Mongkut set about modernizing his country and was succeeded by his 15-year-old son Chulalongkorn who quickly showed himself to be a reformer like his father, managing to keep the colonial powers at bay.

20th century

Rama VI, King Vajiravudh (1910-1925), son of Chulalongkorn, was educated at Oxford and Sandhurst Military Academy and seemed well prepared for kingship. However, he squandered

Pridi Pamonyong's statue at Thammarat University.

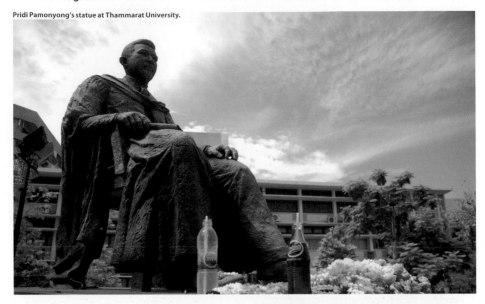

much of the wealth built up by Chulalongkorn and died at 44, leaving an empty treasury.

Like his older brother, King Prajadhipok (Rama VII – 1925-1935), was educated in Europe, but he never expected to become king and was thrust on to the throne at a time when the country was being seriously affected by the Great Depression. With the economy in crisis a clique of soldiers and civilians staged a *coup d'état*. This episode is often called the Revolution of 1932, but it was orchestrated by a small elite, essentially for the elite. However, King Prajadhipok had great difficulty adapting to his lesser role and abdicated in favour of his young nephew, Prince Ananda Mahidol, in 1935. The prince at the time was only 10 years old so two princes were appointed to act as regents.

Phibun Songkhram & Pridi Panomyong

While the monarchy receded from view, two key men began to dominate Thai politics – the fascist-leaning army officer Phibun Songkhram and the left-wing idealist lawyer Pridi Panomyong.

When Prime Minister Pridi Panomyong tried to introduce a socialist economic programme in 1933, pushing for the state control of the means of production, he was forced into exile in Europe. Phibun Songkhram became prime minister in 1938 and his enduring influence makes him the most significant figure in 20th-century Thai politics. Under his direction, Siam became more militaristic, xenophobic, as well as 'religiously' nationalistic. As if to underline these developments, in 1939 Siam adopted a new name: Thailand.

Second World War

During the Second World War, Phibun sided with the Japanese who he felt sure would win while Pridi, with the help of the British and Americans helped to organize the Thai resistance – the Free Thai Movement. As the tide of the war turned in favour of the Allies, so Prime Minister Phibun was forced to resign. He spent a short time in gaol in Japan, but was allowed to return to Thailand in 1947.

Post-war Thailand

In 1946 Pridi Panomyong, who had gathered a good deal of support due to the role he played during the conflict, became PM. However, in the same year King Ananda was mysteriously found shot dead in his royal apartments and Pridi was implicated in a plot – he was forced to flee Thailand. With King Bhumibol now secure on the throne, Phibun's fervent anti-communist stance quickly gained support in the USA. Phibun was eventually deposed and by 1963 another extreme rightwing General – Thanom Kitticachorn – had taken power. With the war in Indochina escalating, Thanom allowed US planes to be based in Thailand, but the political situation began to slowly deteriorate.

1973 October Revolution

It was Thailand's students who precipitated the tumultuous events of 1973. By June 1973 they began to demonstrate against the government calling for the resignation of Thanom. After a series of demonstrations, Thanom lost the support of the army and was forced to resign and flee the country. The October Revolution ushered in a period of turbulent democratic government in Thailand: radical scholars, students, labour unions and leftist politicians could make their views known. The middle classes began to feel that things were going too far. The fall of Vietnam, Cambodia and Laos to communism left many Thais wondering whether they would be the next 'domino' to topple. Fascist groups began to garner support, and anti-communist organizations like the Red Gaurs and the Village Scouts gained in influence.

October 1973 Uprising monument.

October 1973 massacre monument.

Thammasat University Massacre

The trigger for the appalling events of October 1976 was the return of former Prime Minister Thanom from exile. He was visited by members of the royal family and the students took this as royal recognition of a man who had led the country into violence. Demonstrations broke out in Bangkok and newspapers printed pictures apparently showing the crown prince being burnt in effigy by students at Thammasat. Fascist groups, along with the police and the army, advanced on the university on 6 October and an orgy of killing ensued. With the situation rapidly deteriorating, the army stepped in and imposed martial law.

Stability returns

Things calmed down and by 1980 the ascendancy of Prem Tinsulanond ushered in a relatively stable period. He finally resigned in 1988, and by then Thailand – or so most people thought – was beginning to outgrow the habit of military intervention. Chatichai Choonhaven won general elections in 1988, by which time the country was felt to be more stable and prosperous.

From massacre to crisis: 1991-1997

In February 1991, with the prime minister daring to challenge the armed forces, General Suchinda Kraprayoon staged a bloodless *coup d'état* and ousted Chatichai's democratically elected government. A series of huge demonstrations ensued until in 1992 Suchinda called in the army and scores of people were killed.

Three days after the massacre, King Bhumibol ordered both Suchinda and demonstration leader Chamlong to his palace where television cameras were waiting to witness Suchinda and Chamlong prostrate themselves on the floor while the king lectured them. Immediately afterwards, the army and the demonstrators withdrew from the streets. Less than one week after the killing began, Suchinda Kraprayoon fled the country.

New elections were won by the Democrats and Chuan Leekpai was appointed prime minister – his government lasted more than 2½ years, making it, at that point, the longest serving elected government in Thai history.

The Chart Thai Party, led by 62-year-old Banharn Silpa-Archa won the next election. Yet, Banharn's Chart Thai was closely associated with the military junta and was viewed as incorrigibly corrupt. This finally caught up with Banharn and in September 1996 he announced his resignation.

The elections of 17 November 1996 were close, with Chaovalit Yongchaiyudh's – an old-style patronage politician who depended on his links with the army and on handing out lucrative concessions to his supporters – New Aspirations Party (NAP) just managing to win the largest number of seats.

Bust, boom & bust

Until July 1997 the kingdom's economy was expanding at close to double-digit rates, a 'miracle' economy, and Asian 'tiger.' Of course there were those who questioned the rapidity of the country's development, and the social, economic and environmental tensions and conflicts that arose. While the elite few breezed from boutique to club in their air-conditioned Mercedes, around one million people were living in slum conditions in the capital. This was viewed by many analysts as a side effect of healthy economic growth.

Economic crisis

Then everything went horribly wrong. The local currency, the baht, went into freefall, the stockmarket crashed, unemployment more than doubled, and the economy contracted. Chaovalit resigned and Chuan Leekpai, his successor, struggled to put things to rights but after two years at the helm was trounced in a general election in early 2001 by telecom billionaire Thaksin Shinawatra.

Thaksin Shinawatra takes over

With the rise of Thaksin Shinawatra and the Thai Rak Thai party, for probably the first time in Thai history, was a man with an unprecedented democratic mandate to rule. The Thai electorate grabbed at Thaksin's pledge to grant one million baht (US$23,200) to each of Thailand's 70,000 villages, a debt moratorium for poorer farmers and cheap medical care – things he quickly delivered.

While the elite few breezed from boutique to club in their air-conditioned Mercedes, around one million people were living in slum conditions in the capital.

Liberal authoritarian

As his first term progressed Thaksin revealed an authoritarian side that was increasingly alarming. In 2003, a war against drugs was declared that involved the extra-judicial murder of thousands of suspected drug dealers and drug addicts. During this period of Thaksin's rule, Thailand's restive Muslims in the deep south began to wage a low level insurgency. This rapidly escalated after an incident in October 2004 in the small town of Tak Bai when more than 80 Muslim demonstrators died. The insurgents began targeting teachers and government officials and by September 2005 the death toll had reached 1000.

Second term

The December 2004 tsunami came to overshadow many of the events in the south. Thaksin's handling of this disaster was seen by most to be efficient and statesman-like. An election was called soon after in February 2005 and Thaksin's TRT won a landslide victory.

Early in 2006, and fuelled by an alleged tax-avoidance scam by the Shinawatra family, a protest movement, the Peoples' Alliance for Democracy (PAD) took to the streets of Bangkok.

With deadlock in the capital, Thaksin called a snap election yet his opponents, led by the Democrat Party, realizing they could never beat Thaksin at the ballot box, boycotted the election. This led to a constitutional crisis that created a political stalemate.

Democracy monument, Ratchadamuoen Klang Rd.

Military coup

September 2006 changed everything. On the morning of the 19 September (UK time) the BBC was reporting that Thaksin's government had been replaced by an army council – a full scale military coup had taken place.

Within a few weeks a new prime minister, General Surayud Chulanont, was installed and the constitution shredded. New elections and a rewritten constitution were mooted for later in 2007 and a civilian cabinet was put in place. A mini stock market crash then transpired and several bombs exploded in Bangkok on New Year's Eve, killing nine people. By the middle of 2007 a great deal of uncertainty had crept back into Thai society and a badly drafted and anti-democratic new constitution was forced on the Thai people.

In December 2007 a general election was called, and with Thaksin's TRT party officially dissolved the new Thaksin-inspired People's Power Party (PPP) took power. The prime minister, Samak Sundaravej, had 233 MPs to draw from in the new 480 seat parliament while the opposition, the Democrat Party led by British-born ex-Etonian Abhisit Vejjajiva, managed to secure only a third of available seats – a huge failure. In effect, Thailand was back were it started before the 2006 coup – with Thaksin's people firmly back in control.

Crisis year: 2008

Thaksin returned to Thailand in February 2008 to a mixture of jubilation and outright hostility. By May 2008 the PAD were back out on the streets but this time they had transformed from a popular movement into an extremist vanguard.

In August the yellow-shirted PAD (yellow is the king's colour) seized Government House, the home of the Thai cabinet, facilitated strikes and briefly occupied Krabi and Phuket airports.

As the rhetoric and ranting became increasingly hysterical, PM Samak was removed from his position by a military appointed court.

Samak's replacement was the mild-mannered Somchai Wongsawat (Thaksin's brother- in-law), The PAD were not placated, extended their platform to get around the 'failings' of 'democracy' and demanded a 70% unelected parliament filled with appointed army officers and bureaucrats. Then in late November, the PAD, with popular support draining, and while clutching portraits of the king, occupied both of Bangkok's main airports in what they termed 'Operation Hiroshima'.

Thailand's tourism industry ground to a complete halt. Hotels and resorts stood empty as no flights could take off or land through the nation's main entry points. What was incomprehensible for outsiders was the way in which the PAD had so easily taken over important facilities such as Bangkok's main airports. On 2 December the constitutional court dissolved the PPP (and coalition members Chart Thai and Matchima) and so, with all hint of Thaksin's influence now absent from government the PAD departed the airports and claimed outright victory. Many commentators quite fittingly called this a 'judicial coup.'

A new era?

With reports of MP's being bought for millions of baht and army commander-in-chief, General Anupong, meeting with potential Democrat-coalition partners to 'advise' them what to do, a shiny, handsome, alternative rock-loving Democrat PM Abhisit was installed. A new era of accountability and democracy was promised yet a huge clampdown on free speech was implemented with over 4000 websites closed. It didn't end there. A story that several hundred Burmese refugees – from an ethnic Muslim group known as the Rohingya – were murdered at the hands of the Thai military began to circulate in the international press. The Democrat Party-led government's reaction was to blame the media. And it wasn't all quiet on the home front either. The red-shirted National United Front of Democracy Against Dictatorship (UDD), who'd formed out of a broad coalition of pro-Thaksin, anti-2006 coup and anti-PAD activists, took to the streets.

Songkran 2009

By the beginning of April 2009 UDD demonstrations were growing to 200,000, making the Redshirt protests some of the largest in Thailand's history. With passions running high PM Abhisit headed to Pattaya to host the important ASEAN heads of state meeting. In what proved to be terribly humiliating for both PM Abhisit and Thailand a demonstration of Redshirts stormed the hotel where the heads of state were due to meet forcing them to flee by helicopter.

Emboldened, the Redshirts took to the streets of Bangkok in huge numbers, occupying and barricading themselves in on several streets.

With the city slipping out of control and Thaksin calling for revolution, events during the Songkran holiday of 2009 in Bangkok reached fever pitch. Then Abhisit declared a State of Emergency and personally took charge of orchestrating a 10,000 strong army assault on the UDD's barricades. Within 24 hours the Redshirts had been cleared from the streets, the leadership arrested and all UDD TV stations, websites and radio programmes were taken off the air. Within 48 hours, just as everything started to die down another extraordinary event transpired on Bangkok's streets. An attempted assassination was carried out on PAD leader and media tycoon Sondhi Limthongkul. It failed, but the attempt sent further shockwaves throughout Thailand as more rumours quickly circulated of disturbing army plots and shady involvement of sinister 'third hands'.

As Thailand moves towards the end of 2009 it is still a country very much on the brink. A lot rests on PM Abhisit's young shoulders – the decisions he makes could have a massive bearing on Thailand for generations.

Culture & heritage

Detail from a Chinese temple at Surathani.

Non-Thai ethnic groups in the region

Sino-Thais (Chinese)

Anything between 9% and 15% of the population of Thailand is thought to be Sino-Thai. Immigrating to Thailand in the 19th and 20th centuries the Chinese were relatively quickly and easily assimilated into Thai society. They took Thai names, inter-married with Thais and converted to Buddhism. As elsewhere in the region, these Chinese immigrants proved to be remarkably adept at money-making and today control a disproportionate slice of businesses. Bangkok still supports a large Chinatown – you'll also find large Chinese communities in Ranong, Phuket and Trang. Here Chinese cultural and religious traits are clearly in evidence.

Malays

Of the various minority ethnic and religious groups in Thailand, the Thai Malays and Thai Muslims have often felt most alienated from the Thai nation. Not only do many in the southern four provinces of the country (Yala, Narathiwat, Pattani and Satun) speak Malay rather than Thai, but the great majority (about 80%) are also Muslim rather than Buddhist. Pattani was only incorporated into the Thai state at the beginning of the 20th century, and even then just loosely. At present a low-intensity guerrilla war is being waged in the Malay-dominated parts of Thailand and travel is not advised (see page for more details).

Moken or Chao Le

One of the smallest ethnic groups in Thailand the Moken – or in Thai the Chao Le or Chao Nam – are a nomadic people totalling roughly 2000-3000 who live on a number of islands along the Andaman Sea coast and particularly near Trang, Phuket, Krabi and Phang Nga. They speak their own distinctive language, are not particularly materialistic and have long relied on traditional methods of fishing and foraging to sustain themselves. The Thai government has made numerous attempts to resettle the Moken and there are now some permanent settlements. Often referred to by tourists as Sea Gypsies, a somewhat pejorative term, the Moken came to world press attention after the Asian Tsunami in 2004 when many escaped the ocean's onslaught due to their close relationship to the sea and their ability to read its actions. If you come across Moken villages please try to be respectful and not treat them as just another tourist attraction.

Art and architecture

Thailand's art and architecture, much like elsewhere, has been formulated over centuries with competing influences shaping the contemporary picture. The first recognised flourishing of Thailand-based arts was during the Dvaravati Kingdom (6th-11th centuries) which has since remained something of an enigma to art historians. There are only a few surviving Dvaravati Buddha images, mostly carved in stone, with smaller images cast in bronze.

The Srivijayan Empire (8th-13th centuries) was a powerful maritime empire that extended from Java northwards into Thailand. Srivijaya was a Mahayana Buddhist Empire and, unfortunately, there are few architectural remnants from the period, the two notable exceptions are Wat Phra Boromthat and Wat Kaeo, both at Chaiya.

What's wat?

Temples (or wats) are usually separated from the secular world by two walls. Between these outer and inner walls are found the monks' quarters or dormitories (*kutis*) and in larger complexes, schools and other administrative buildings. Traditionally, the *kutis* were placed on the south side of the wat. This section of the compound is known as the *sanghavasa*, or *sanghawat* (ie for the *Sangha* – the monkhood).

The inner wall, which in bigger *wats* often takes the form of a gallery or cloister (*phra rabieng*) lined with Buddha images, represents the division between the worldly and the holy, the sacred and the profane. Within the inner courtyard, the holiest building is the ordination hall, or *ubosoth*, often shortened to just *bot*. It is built on consecrated ground, is reserved for monks only and is characteristically a large, rectangular building with high walls and multiple sloping roofs, covered in glazed clay tiles. It will house a large Buddha image and numerous subsidiary images. The other main building is the assembly hall or *viharn*, but not all *wats* have one. Architecturally, this is often indistinguishable from the *bot*. It contains the *wat*'s principal Buddha images. The main difference between the *bot* and *viharn* is that the latter does not stand on consecrated ground. The *viharn* is for general use and, unlike the *bot*, is rarely locked.

Tip...

It is customary for pilgrims to remove their shoes on entering any Buddhist building.

About the region

Other major players in Thailand's cultural heritage are the Khmer and Lanna kingdoms though their influence didn't impact much on the Islands and Beaches region. However, that's not true of the Sukhothai style (late 13th to early 15th centuries) with the Sukhothai Buddha being one of the first representations of the Ceylonese Buddha in Siam. Sukhothai temples also incorporated Ceylonese bell-shaped stupas (see illustration, below).

Ayutthayan style (mid-14th to mid-18th centuries) is also very important, when scholarly work was undertaken to bring together the previous eras and create a unified style. The Bangkok or Rattanakosin period dates from the founding of the Chakri Dynasty in 1782. It is generally accepted that the Buddhas produced during the Bangkok era are, in the main, inferior compared with the images of earlier periods. In general, Rattanakosin wat buildings are airier and less ornate than those of Ayutthaya.

Buddha at Samet.

Religion

The Thai census records that 94% of the population is Buddhist. In Thailand's case, this means Theravada Buddhism, also known as Hinayana Buddhism. Of the rest of the population, 3.9% are Muslim (living predominantly in the south of the country), 1.7% Confucianist (mostly Sino-Thais living in Bangkok) and 0.6% Christian (mostly hill tribe people living in the north). Though the king is designated the protector of all religions, the constitution stipulates that he must be a Buddhist.

Buddhism

Theravada Buddhism was introduced into Southeast Asia in the 13th century, when monks trained in Ceylon (Sri Lanka) returned to spread the word, quickly gaining converts amongst the Tai. Theravada Buddhism, from the Pali word thera (elders), means the 'way of the elders' and is distinct from the dominant Buddhism practised in India, Mahayana Buddhism or the 'Greater Vehicle'. The sacred language of Theravada Buddhism is Pali rather than Sanskrit, Bodhisattvas (future Buddhas) are not given much attention, and emphasis is placed upon a precise and 'fundamental' interpretation of the Buddha's teachings, as they were originally recorded.

Buddhism, as it is practised in Thailand, is not the 'other-worldly' religion of Western conception. Ultimate salvation – enlightenment, or nirvana – is a distant goal for most people. Thai Buddhists pursue the Law of Karma, the reduction of suffering. Meritorious acts are undertaken and demeritorious ones avoided so that life, and more particularly future life, might be improved. Outside many wats it is common to see caged birds or turtles being sold: these are purchased and set free, and in this way the liberator gains merit. 'Karma' (act or deed, from Pali – kamma) is often thought in the West to mean 'fate'. It does not. It is true that previous karma determines a person's position in society, but there is still room for individual action, and a person is ultimately responsible for that action. It is the law of cause and effect.

The Muslim population in Thailand is not as radicalized in as it is in other countries.

In Thailand, Buddhism is a syncretic religion: it incorporates elements of Brahmanism, animism and ancestor worship. Amulets are worn to protect against harm and are often sold in temple compounds. Brahmanistic 'spirit' houses can be found outside most buildings. In the countryside, farmers have what they consider to be a healthy regard for the *phi* (spirits) and demons that inhabit the rivers, trees and forests. Astrologers are widely consulted by urban and rural dwellers alike.

Islam

While Thailand is often portrayed as a 'Buddhist Kingdom', the provinces of the far south are majority Muslim. This is because these provinces have, historically, come under the cultural influence of the former sultanates of the Malay peninsula. This Muslim population has not – in general, and despite a recent upsurge in violence – been radicalized to the extent it has in some other countries and regions. The veil, for example, is not widely worn while the consumption of alcohol is fairly widespread.

Regarding the faith, Islam is an Arabic word meaning 'submission to God'. The main Islamic scripture is the Koran or Quran. The practice of

Islam is based upon five central tenets, known as the Pillars of Islam. The first is the Shahada or the confession, and involves reciting, sincerely, two statements: 'There is no god, but God', and 'Mohammad is the Messenger [Prophet] of God'. A Muslim will do this at every Salat, the second important tenet of their faith. This is the daily prayer ritual which is performed five times a day. The third essential element of Islam is Zakat – charity or alms-giving and a Muslim is supposed to give up all of his/her 'surplus'. The fourth pillar of Islam is Saum or fasting during the daytime month-long fast of Ramadan – a time of worship and piety. The Haj or Pilgrimage to the holy city of Mecca in Saudi Arabia is the fifth tenet and is required by all Muslims once in their lifetime if they can afford to make the journey and are physically able to. The Koran also advises on a number of other practices and customs, in particular the prohibitions on usury, the eating of pork, the taking of alcohol, and gambling.

Thailand Islands & Beaches today

Preparing the beach at Choeng Mon Samui.

Red v Yellow

There's no doubt that in the last couple of years Thailand has been through its most turbulent period since the 1970s. Military coups, annulled elections, popular uprisings and occupations of key national assets have marked out the Thai political landscape. Yet, much of this – with the notable exception of the November 2008 seizure of Bangkok's airports – has had little impact on the traveller. In fact, almost the entirety of Thailand's Islands and Beaches have been largely unscathed by recent events.

While tanks and rioters roamed the streets of Bangkok, the tropical beaches of Phuket remained packed to the gunwales. There have even been reports that some tourists, when booking their Southeast Asian holidays against the backdrop of Thai political strife, weren't aware Phuket was even in Thailand. Furthermore, Phuket, with its own

Ousted Thai PM Thaksin Shinawatra at Red Shirt rally.

dominates the region covered in this book. Value is now the key word for visitors, and, thankfully, Thailand's Islands and Beaches still offer that in bucketfuls. As 2009 comes to an end and 2010 begins everything from the price of a flight through to the cost of a luxurious pool-villa is plummeting as the Thai tourist industry desperately tries to shore up business. For the traveller not put off by the dramatic newspaper headlines this is a perfect time to visit the region and genuine bargains and, sometimes, empty beaches can be had.

The present government is also using the downturn as an opportunity to promote the sectors of the tourism market that focus on sustainability and environmental awareness. In mid-2009 they even appointed a senior member of the award-winning Six Senses eco-resort company to a key government position. In addition to the top end of the eco-market, various homestay programmes are being actively encouraged and it is hoped that this sector gets the support from both government and travellers that it deserves.

That's not to say other problems, such as the low-intensity guerrilla war being waged in Thailand's most southerly reaches, don't persist, with successive governments failing to get to grips with the bloodshed. At present travel is not recommended to several of the provinces lined up along the Malaysian border (see page 232). So far this struggle has not extended into Thailand's key destinations such as Samui and Phuket but if it ever did the effect could be dramatic. The effects of the global downturn are still working their way through the economy and the likelihood is that many thousands of Thais who work in the travel and tourism industry will lose their jobs in the coming years.

However, if Thailand can keep relative domestic peace in the next few years there is no reason why the splendour of its Beaches and Islands won't carry on being a world class destination – and hopefully, at least in some places, set a global benchmark for sustainable travel.

international airport, has kept up a steady flow of tourist cash, even during the Bangkok airport occupation when Thailand was in almost complete lockdown.

Other parts of the region haven't fared as well as Phuket during the recent turmoil but have still held their own. Pattaya had a mini-boom when tourists stranded by the airport seizure were deposited in the resort town's hotels; thousands of Bangkok-bound tourists have also looked for easy routes out of the capital, opting for short hop flights to Samui and Koh Chang (Trat).

Against this backdrop – and the global recession – the Thai tourism industry has undoubtedly suffered. But it is still possible to have a wonderful and safe trip to the kingdom's fantastic beaches and islands without suffering too much from Thailand's travails.

Time for a change

Arguably, Thailand's recent upheavals have shifted the focus of a travel and tourism industry that

Nature & environment

Noppart Thara.

There are literally thousands of islands in Thailand, of which 250 could be able to sustain human life in some form. Most of these remained completely uninhabited (or had tiny populations) until Thailand's tourist boom of the last 30 years. In addition to these numerous islands there is more than 2600 km of coastline, comprising 1700 km along the entire Gulf coast and 950 km along the Andaman Sea. Thailand itself covers an area of 500,000 sq km (about the size of France) and, in 2001, had a population of 62.3 million, which is growing at 1.5% per year. It shares its borders with Burma, Laos, Cambodia and Malaysia.

Towards the southern extremity of the central plains of Thailand lies the Bangkok Metropolitan Region. With an official population of 8.16 million (2007), it is the country's economic and political hub. Indeed, it has outgrown its administrative borders and the population of the entire urban agglomeration is nearer to 10 million. Bangkok supports both the greatest density of businesses, as well as the key institutions of government.

Sandwiched between the sea and the Damrek Hills, is the Gulf's eastern coast. This has become an overspill area for Bangkok, with businesses moving to take advantage of cheaper land and less

Fig tree, Khao Sok National Park.

Bird life

With almost 1000 species of bird found in Thailand –
just under 1/10th of the planet's entire bird species
– the country is something of a birdwatchers
paradise. If twitching is your thing remember to pack
a pair of binoculars for your trip and a copy of *The
Birds of the Thai-Malay Peninsula* by David R. Wells
(2007). In short you should be able to spot various
kinds of grebes, cormorants, herons, egrets, ducks,
kites, sea eagles, gulls, terns, parrots, kingfishers,
hummingbirds, bee-eaters, owls, hornbills, swifts,
swallows, drongos, sunbirds and mynahs.

congested infrastructure. This stretch of coast
hosts the renowned seaside resorts of Pattaya, Koh
Samet and Koh Chang.

The south of Thailand, home to most of the
region covered in this book, stretches 1150 km
south from Bangkok to the border with Malaysia.
The climate is tropical, there are large Muslim and
Chinese population centres and the main cash
crops are coconuts and rubber. Most visitors go to
the beach resorts of Koh Samui, Phuket, Koh Phi
Phi, Hua Hin and Koh Phangan.

Flora

Thailand's dominant natural vegetation is tropical
forest. In the south and in pockets such as
Chantaburi province in the east, this means 'jungle'
or tropical rain forest. Tigers, elephants, *banteng*
(wild ox), *sambar* (deer) and tapirs still roam the
lowland forests, although not in great numbers.
Thailand's forests have been depleted to a greater
extent than in any other country in Southeast Asia
(with the one exception of Singapore, which
doesn't really count). In 1938, 70% of Thailand was

It's a fact...

It has been estimated that Thailand
supports 20,000 to 25,000 species
of plant, 6000 insect species, 1000
kinds of bird, and almost 300 species
of mammal.

Mammal species

There are reportedly 264 species of wild mammals in Thailand. You'll be incredibly lucky to see any of those listed even if you ventured deep into Thailand's jungles. Land mammals include elephant, tree shrew and various primates such as loris, macaque, langur and gibbon. There are flying and giant squirrels, several types of bat including fruit bats and also many different kinds of pangolins. The large felines include tigers, leopards, jungle cats and civets. Other carnivores can be found such as black bears, mongoose and jackals. While endangered there are still a few javan/sumatran rhinos, tapirs and various species of wild pig and antelope.

forested; by 1961 this had been reduced to 50% and today it accounts for roughly 10%. The tropical rainforests of Thailand, although not comparable with those of Malaysia and Indonesia, have a high diversity of species, exceeding 100 per hectare in some areas with the southern forests supporting the most. In many cases these are also highly degraded due to logging and farming.

Fauna

A century ago, wild elephants and tigers roamed the Bang Kapi area east of Bangkok – now it is overrun with shopping malls. It was only in 1960 that a law was enacted protecting wild animals, and even today it doesn't take an investigative journalist to find endangered – and protected – animals for sale, whether whole (and alive) or in bits. The effect is that Thailand's fauna is even more threatened than its forests. Many of the kingdom's bird and mammal species are endangered or critically endangered and the country's reptiles and amphibians don't fare much better either.

Thailand supports a rich and varied fauna, partly because it lies on the boundary between several zoogeographic regions: the Indochinese, Indian and Sundaic. It also lies on the crossroads between north and south, acting as a way station for animals dispersing north from the Sundaic islands, and south from the Asian mainland. The problem in trying to maintain the biodiversity is that most of the national parks and wildlife

National parks

Nearly 15% of Thailand's land mass is protected in some way. Though impressive on paper, this does not mean that there are some 70,000 sq km of protected forest, grassland, swamp and sea. Settled and shifting agriculturalists live in many parks, illegal logging is widespread (though better controlled today than in the 1980s), and poaching continues to be a problem.

The National Parks Division's management of the country's protected areas has been woefully inadequate. You may want to take into account when visiting that Koh Samet and Koh Phi Phi, both national parks, are – illegally – covered with accommodation developments. Koh Tarutao, in the far south is one of the few national park islands adequately protected in the region covered in this book.

sanctuaries are thought to be too small to be sustainable. A single male tiger, for example, needs about 50 sq km of forest to survive; some of Thailand's parks cover less than 100 sq km.

Marine life

Thailand's coastline abuts on to both the Indian Ocean (Andaman Sea) and the South China Sea (Gulf of Thailand), and therefore has marine flora and fauna characteristic of both regions. In the Gulf, 850 species of open-water fish have been identified while in the Andaman Sea, game fish such as blue and black marlin, barracuda, sailfish and various sharks are all present.

Among other sea animals, Thailand's shores provide nesting sites for four species of seaturtle: the leatherback, green, Ridley's and the hawksbill turtle. The latter is now very rare, while a fifth species, the loggerhead turtle, has disappeared from Thailand's shores and waters. Other marine animals include

several species of sea snake, the saltwater crocodile (which may now be extinct), three species of dolphin, and the dugong or sea cow.

Reefs

Coral reefs probably contain a richer profusion of life than any other ecosystem – even exceeding the tropical rainforest in terms of species diversity. Those in Thailand's Andaman Sea are among the finest in the region – and maritime parks like the Surin and Similan islands have been gazetted to help protect these delicate habitats. Although the country's reefs remain under-researched, 210 species of hard coral and 108 coral reef fish have so far been identified in the Andaman Sea. Literally tens of thousands of other marine organisms, including soft corals, crustacea, echinoderms and worms, would have to be added to this list to build up a true picture of the ecosystem's diversity.

Festivals & events

Songkran.

Thailand has a high number of public holidays – 16 in total – most of which are observed by both the private and public sectors. However, these are unlikely to affect the servicing of travel destinations. What they will affect is road traffic (both congestion and drunk driving are rife) and the price and availability of transport and accommodation. If you're planning to travel at the times listed here make sure you book in advance.

Many of the festivals below are predicated by the lunar calendar meaning that they can take place in different months.

A booklet of holidays and festivals is available from most TAT offices. For movable festivals (where only the month is listed), check the TAT's website, tourismthailand.org. Regional and local festivals are noted in appropriate sections.

January

New Year's Day (1st, public holiday)
No real celebrations but still a holiday that is more likely to be marked by public sector workers.

February/March

Old Phuket Town Festival
(1st weekend February)
The locals close off Thalang Rd, Krabi Rd and Soi Romanee to celebrate Old Phuket Town with foodstalls, music, plays and exhibitions.

Chinese New Year (late January/early February; movable)
Celebrated by Thailand's large Chinese population. The festival extends over 15 days; spirits are appeased, and offerings are made to the ancestors and to the spirits. Good wishes and lucky money are exchanged, and Chinese-run shops and businesses shut.

Magha Puja (movable, full moon; public holiday)
A Buddhist holy day that celebrates the occasion when the Buddha's disciples miraculously gathered together to hear him preach. Culminates in a candlelit procession around the temple *bot* (or ordination hall).

Thao Thep Kasattri and Thao Sisunthon Fair
(13 March)
Celebrates the two heroines who saved Phuket from the Burmese. Phuket only.

April

Chakri Day (6th; public holiday)
Commemorates the founding of the present Chakri Dynasty.

Songkran (movable; public holiday)
Marks the beginning of the Buddhist New Year. The festival is particularly big in the north, less so in the south and (understandably) the Muslim far south. It is a three- to five-day celebration with parades, dancing and folk entertainment. Traditionally, the first day represents the last chance for a 'spring clean'. Rubbish is burnt, in the belief that old and dirty things will cause misfortune in the coming year. The *wat* is the focal point of celebrations. Revered Buddha images are carried through the streets, accompanied by singers and dancers. The second day is the main water-throwing day. The water-throwing practice was originally an act of homage to ancestors and family elders. Young people pay respect by pouring scented water over the elders heads. The older generation sprinkle water over Buddha images. Gifts are given. This uninhibited water-throwing continues for all three days. On the third day birds, fish and turtles are all released, to gain merit and in remembrance of departed souls.

May/June

Labour Day (1 May; public holiday)

Coronation Day (5 May; public holiday)
Commemorates the present King Bhumibol's crowning in 1950.

Visakha Puja (full moon; public holiday)
This is the holiest of all Buddhist days, it marks the Buddha's birth, enlightenment and death. Candlelit processions are held at most temples.

Ploughing Ceremony (movable; public holiday)
Performed by the king at Sanaam Luang near the Grand Palace in Bangkok. Brahmanic in origin, it traditionally marks the auspicious date when farmers could begin preparing their rice land. Bulls decorated with flowers pull a sacred gold plough.

Hua Hin Jazz Festival
huahin jazzfestival.com.
Organized by the Hilton. Stages are set up in front of the Sofitel Central and railway station. Normally held in June.

Tongue 'n' cheek

Getting your ears pierced is a relatively straightforward and widely accepted practice in the West. It is also almost entirely painless – a quick spray of antiseptic and a stud is fired into your lobe in an instant.

But imagine several skewers pushed through your neck-skin or an ice cream parasol spiked through your cheek – that's going to take time and effort. Or how about a sword through your tongue and a giant chain through your lip? It's got to hurt.

For the devotees of the Chinese deity Mazu – the Taoist goddess of the sea and queen of heaven – spikes, swords, skewers and even ice cream parasols hold no fear. Once a year they gather for the festival of the Nine Emperor Gods to mark the gods' return from heaven to earth where they are embodied, as one, in Mazu. More commonly known in Thailand as Tesagan Gin Je, or the Vegetarian festival, the most famous site for celebration is Phuket, where thousands of devotees slash, pierce and undergo gruesome acts of endurance in one of the kingdom's most spectacular festivals.

This festival doesn't just take place in Phuket but is widespread throughout Thailand in varying degrees and formats. Where there is a Chinese community (which is pretty much everywhere in Thailand) you might find the Vegetarian festival.

An excellent and low-key place to experience Tesagan Gin Je is in the southern Thai town of Trang. A large Hainan Chinese community has resided here for over 100 years and the festival takes place at the same time of year as it does in Phuket.

Much like its better-known neighbours, the Trang festival involves large numbers of Mah Song – pure, unmarried devotees who invite the spirits of gods to possess their bodies and then perform acts of flagellation and self-mutilation – parading the streets in bright costumes and letting off extremely loud firecrackers.

During the entire festival all participants and the local community will abstain from eating meat, poultry, seafood and dairy products – hence the name Vegetarian Festival. In Trang you might find yourself invited by locals for a free vegetarian lunch in any one of a number of temporary kitchens set up for the event. Accepting the offer of lunch is a good way to get involved in festivities that, thankfully, involves no suffering.

Vegetarian festival.

July

Asalha Puja and Khao Phansa (movable; full moon; public holiday)
Commemorates the Buddha's first sermon to his disciples and marks the beginning of the Buddhist Lent. Monks reside in their monasteries for the three-month Buddhist Rains Retreat to study and meditate, and young men temporarily become monks. Ordination ceremonies take place and villagers give monks white cotton robes to wear during the Lent ritual bathing.

August

Queen's Birthday (12th; public holiday)

September/October

Chulalongkorn Day (23 October; public holiday)
Honours King Chulalongkorn (1868-1910), one of Thailand's most beloved and revered kings.

Ok Phansa (three lunar months after Asalha Puja)
Marks the end of the Buddhist Lent and the beginning of *Krathin*, when gifts (usually a new set of cotton robes) are offered to the monks. Particularly venerated monks are sometimes given silk robes as a sign of respect and esteem.
    Krathin itself is celebrated over two days. It marks the end of the monks' retreat and the re-entry of novices into secular society. Processions and fairs are held all over the country; villagers wear their best clothes, and food, money, pillows and bed linen are offered to the monks of the local *wat*.

Vegetarian Festival
Celebrated throughout Thailand by the Chinese community but predominantly in Phuket and Trang. It takes place from the eve of the ninth moon of the Chinese year, until the climax on the ninth day of the ninth moon, usually September or October. Visit phuketvegetarian.com for the confirmed dates.

November

Chak Phra Festival (movable)
Held in Surat Thani in Oct-Nov, the Chak Phra Festival (movable) marks the end of the 3-month Buddhist Rains Retreat and the return to earth of the Buddha. Processions of Buddha images and boat races on the Tapi River, in longboats manned by many oarsmen. Gifts are offered to monks as this is also *krathin*, celebrated across Buddhist Thailand.

Loi Krathong (full moon)
Comes at the end of the rainy season and honours the goddess of water. A *krathong* is a model boat made to contain a candle, incense and flowers. The little boats are pushed out on to canals, lakes and rivers. Sadly, few *krathongs* are now made of leaves: polystyrene has taken over and the morning after Loi Krathong lakes and river banks are littered with the wrecks of the previous night. The 'quaint' candles in pots sold in many shops at this time, are in fact large firecrackers.

December

King's Birthday (5th; public holiday)
Flags and portraits of the king are erected all over Bangkok, especially down Rachdamnern Av and around the Grand Palace.

Constitution Day (10th; public holiday)
Celebrates Thailand's constitution with processions etc in Bangkok.

New Year's Eve (31st; public holiday)
Likely to be some activities in Bangkok – normally referred to as 'countdown' – but not a particularly important festival.

Sleeping

Riverview at Khao Sok.

top ranked hotels and resorts in the region – yet, even in high season compared to other parts of the world prices are relatively low. Plan your trip carefully and combine the quieter off-peak months with some decent weather and you could get an absolute bargain.

City & town hotels

The cream of Bangkok's city hotels are consistently ranked as the best in the world. All will come with swimming pools, spa areas, several excellent restaurants and faultless service. Rooms are all air con, normally with giant tubs, massive beds and huge flatscreens complete with full satellite TV packages. The four and three star hotels will offer much of the same but obviously at lower standards. You can also expect to find a number of boutique hotels in Bangkok – and Phuket City – offering designer, exclusive and stylish environments but not normally all the luxuries you'd find in an established hotel chain. Around the rest of the region most medium-sized towns away from the beach areas will havea couple of three or four-star hotels usually aimed at travelling Thai businessmen – they can often provide decent accommodation at very reasonable rates.

The breadth of accommodation available in Bangkok and the Islands and Beaches is simply staggering. Everything from ฿100 a night rustic bungalows all the way through to ฿100,000 a night mega pool-villas, complete with butlers and hi-tech entertainment systems are available. As well as diversity the other big factor is value. The standards at the top end of the market are incredibly high – you'll find some of the planet's

Tip...

At more expensive resorts and hotels a service charge of 10% and government tax of 7% will be added to the bill for room, food, drinks and other services.

Beach hotels & resorts

The region's beach resorts are now a highly sophisticated mix of villas, bungalows and family orientated hotels. For this kind of accommodation you should expect, at the very least, en suite facilities, air con and TV. Some of the more expensive resorts have private pools, personalised service and in-villa spa treatments. The lower end of the market still has pretty high standards, though some can be lacking in friendliness and rooms can be dirty or rundown.

The mid-range often represents excellent value with good food, decent service, beachside location and neatly designed bungalows or rooms. Prices will fluctuate massively according to season.

Guesthouses

The best of the region's guesthouses are run efficiently, often by friendly families or couples. The more sophisticated ones tend to offer a mix of rooms, with the budget options being fan only and shared facilities while the expensive choice probably has air con and private bathroom. These better-run guesthouses are also likely to offer some kind of tour agent service, will often serve at least breakfast and can be excellent places to meet other travellers and to pick up local information. You'll normally find guesthouses in towns like Krabi rather than in beach areas.

Budget bungalows

This sector of the region's accommodation market is often the most generic and usually the worst value – particularly during high season. Expect a simple hut, with only a single lightbulb, mosquito net and a fan. Toilets and bathrooms are likely to be dirty and shared. The service is usually lamentable, the food poor and the management can be surly Thai teenagers. Having said that some of the budget places really stand out but the simple fact is that these are now thin on the ground.

Tip...

Security can be a problem particularly in budget beach resort areas. Keep valuables with the office for safekeeping.

Homestays

Expect to stay as part of the family, eating with them and sleeping in what is usually very basic accommodation – a mattress, fan and mosquito net inside a wooden house is typical. There might only be well-drawn water and toilets will be of the squat variety. The quality of the food and the friendliness of the people is often unforgettable. Your hosts may also offer you a choice of excursions and activities – everything from rubber tapping to fishing for crabs – which you will pay for separately. For more information of the region's homestays visit cbt-i.org.

National park accommodation

Some of the more popular national parks will offer bungalows; standards vary tremendously but locations can often be stunning. Usually you can expect a very average level of accommodation without TV or air con. For reservations at any of the national parks visit dnp.go.th/parkreserve or call T02-5614 2923.

Camping

It is possible to camp in Thailand particularly in the national parks most of which now provide pretty decent facilities. Some have tents (often smelly and badly kept) for rental, public toilets and shower blocks. Beaches are considered public property – anybody can camp on them for free though pick your spot carefully as you might attract unwarranted attention if you infringe on a guesthouse or resort. Decent enough camping equipment is available in most Thai towns – check in department stores.

Home from home

The idea of spending your hard-earned holiday in the home of an accountant is, at first glance, not the most inspiring idea. Locate that home on a tropical island, mix with beaches, bewitching sunsets, platefuls of mouth-watering seafood and some of the friendliest people in a country famed for its friendliness and it sounds more appealing. Then factor in that the accountant is a trained volunteer, working on the books of an award-winning community based tourist initiative. Doesn't sound so bad, does it?

To reach this accountant's home is easy enough. Take the small public ferry an hour east from the popular tourist destination of Phuket and you'll reach Koh Yao Noi – an island found in the middle of sparkling Phangnga Bay which, jutted with spectacular limestone karsts, is one of the most beautiful stretches of ocean in Thailand.

"Our guests can't decide which house they will stay in," says Bang Bao, the co-ordinator of the Koh Yao Noi Homestay Club as I get off the boat. "We have 25 families which are part of the programme and we operate a strict rotation policy," he says. "That way the money we receive gets as widely distributed as possible."

Koh Yao Noi's Homestay Club began life 13 years ago. It was set up by CBT-I (Community Based Tourism Initiative), a Thai NGO that trains communities to create tourism facilities that are directly controlled by the local population. The one on Koh Yao Noi – a largely Muslim island that depends on local crab and prawn fisheries – has helped fund a successful campaign for conservation in the local seas, forcing big factory ships to go elsewhere. "Part of your package fee is a direct donation for this campaign," says Bang Bao. Just as importantly, in a community where the average wage is probably US$6 a day, income derived from homestay guests goes straight into the hands of the local population. "About 80% of your money is given directly to the host family. It can really make a lot of difference over a whole year," adds Bao as we set off on a tour of the island.

We pass fishing villages extending into the sea on elaborate networks of stilts beset with the pungent briney aromas of crab and prawn. There are rice fields, excited waving children, buffaloes and small copses of tangled jungle. Compared to the acres of roasting flesh and troops of girlie bars found on nearby Phuket, tourism on the island is almost absent – there are a couple of high-end resorts hidden behind concrete walls and few bars but that's it. The east side of Yao Noi is also home to a smattering of average beaches. "Most visitors prefer the beaches on the islands nearby," says Bang Bao. "You'll be visiting one tomorrow."

I soon discover that my 'home' is in the small village of Lam Sai with a famed carpenter, Bang Sar ('Bang' means brother in the local Islamic dialect) and his wife Jah Bat ('Jah' means sister), the homestay programme's accountant. The cute, airy wooden house, surrounded by neatly tended lawns and tropical flowers has been hand-built by Bang Sar.

"This your room," says Bang Sar, in broken English, as he leads me through his home. What doesn't need translating are the huge smiles of my hosts, both eager to help me with my bags and proffering cooling glasses of icy water. The room itself is decidedly 'one star' but is completely spotless – a soft mattress, small electric fan and mosquito net make it comfy enough. Other facilities in the house are provided by a bucket-style shower where you sluice yourself with cool water – incredibly refreshing in the heat – and a squat-toilet.

What is 100% 'five-star' is the incredible dinner that follows my arrival. A mountain of succulent, fresh crab and prawn served with dishes of spicy lime dipping-sauce and bowls of thick beef curries. "I show you how to eat crab," says Bang Sar, expertly breaking open the shells, nimbly rescuing all the meat and decanting it onto my plate. That night I have the kind of sleep only a contented diner can enjoy.

The next few hours are spent in splendid isolation, lazing on the sands and jumping in the warming ocean – it's a perfect moment of relaxation.

Morning brings the loud calls of cockerels and prayer time at the mosque. Jah Bat scurries into the kitchen and brings hot tea and small banana leaf-wrapped goodies – slabs of sticky rice topped off with sweet jackfruit and flaked coconut. I share my breakfast with Karem, Jah Bat's younger brother, who speaks almost flawless English. "This morning we'll be heading over to an uninhabited island," he says.

A long, thin fishing-boat is our mode of travel. "The fisherman needs to get his crab-nets first," says Karem above the din of the engine. We make two stops – dozens of abalone and crabs pulled in by hand – but it's not long before we arrive at a tiny, tropical island, complete with gorgeous beach and small shaded grove.

The next few hours are spent in splendid isolation, lazing on the sands and jumping in the warming ocean. Jah Bat's massive picnic requires some effort but our energies are spent doing very little – it's a perfect moment of relaxation.

That evening we sit with cousins, nieces and nephews on the family balcony devouring another feast. Despite the humble surroundings – the usual

five-star boutique trimmings so beloved by the Thai tourist office's 'chic' PR campaigns are nowhere to be seen – there's a genuine and infectious warmth that the luxury end of the travel market could only dream of. This is the friendly, gracious Thailand that first bewitched travellers such as myself twenty-odd years ago but which is now almost completely lost to the advance of glam resorts and package tours. I've certainly found a gem on Yao Noi and a community seemingly strong enough to fend off the worst excesses of tourism while taking some of the best bits – our money – directly into their pockets.

As I sit restfully, semi-comatose from another divine dinner-time spread, I notice Jah Bat heading to her desk. She sits down and begins to work, by hand, on the Koh Yao Noi Homestay Club's accounts. It's a quietly inspiring moment that speaks volumes. And it dawns on me that the idea of holidaying with an accountant will never create the same image again.

Hosts at a Muslim homestay, Koh Yao Noi.

Eating & drinking

Lang Tuen Restaurant, Si Racha.

Thai food is an intermingling of Tai, Chinese, Malay, Laos/Isaan and, to a lesser extent, Indian cuisines. This helps to explain why restaurants produce dishes that must be some of the (spicy) hottest in the world, as well as others that are rather bland. *Larb*, traditionally raw – but now more frequently cooked – minced beef/chicken/pork mixed with rice, herbs and spices, is a traditional Laos/Isaan dish as is *som tam* (spicy papaya salad); *pla priaw waan* (whole fish with soy and ginger) is Chinese in origin; while *gaeng mussaman* (beef 'Muslim' curry) was brought to Thailand by Malay Muslim immigrants. Even satay, paraded by most restaurants as a Thai dish, was introduced from Malaysia and Indonesia.

A Thai meal is based around rice. When a Thai asks another Thai whether they have eaten they will ask, literally, whether they have 'eaten rice' (*kin khao*). Similarly, the accompanying dishes are referred to as food 'with the rice'. There are two main types of rice – 'sticky' or glutinous (*khao niaw*) and non-glutinous (*khao jao*). Sticky rice is usually used to make sweets (desserts) although it is the staple in the northeastern region and parts of the north. *Khao jao* is standard white rice.

In addition to rice, a meal usually consists of a soup like *tom yam kung* (prawn soup), *kaeng* (a curry) and *krueng kieng* (a number of side dishes). Thai food is spicy, and aromatic herbs and grasses (like lemongrass, coriander, tamarind and ginger) are used to give a distinctive flavour. *Nam pla* (fish sauce made from fermented fish and used as a condiment) and *nam prik* (*nam pla*, chillies, garlic, sugar, shrimps and lime juice) are two condiments that are taken with almost all meals. *Nam pla* is made from steeping fish, usually anchovies, in

Southern Thai Food

Lashings of coconut, heaps of seafood and oodles of vegetables play starring roles at meal times in southern Thailand where everything from spicy curries to mild soups make an appearance.

The food in southern Thailand usually packs a punch, full of intense flavours and aromas. Dishes are often laden with local herbs, while the *sataw* (stinky) bean is used to give meals a bitter taste.

Popular for breakfast, although great any time of the day, is *kanom jeen*, rice noodles served with your pick of curry sauce and veggies. You can spot places selling *kanom jeen* as they have simmering pots waiting to be inspected by hungry passers-by.

Southerners love to pack their dishes with chillies, so if you go for something like *kao yum* (rice salad), be prepared for your mouth to be dazzled. The Muslim curries offer a gentler alternative. *Gaeng* massaman is beef, chicken or duck smothered in mild curry sauce with potatoes. Eat it with *roti* (pan-fried bread).

Most street restaurants have dishes set out in vats so you can have a look and pick out what you'd like. In other places, you can order off a menu. Wherever you are, choose a few dishes, some steamed rice and get stuck in.

You'll often find a little platter of veggies and herbs at restaurants. They're there for the taking at no extra charge so mix them up with your dishes. When you order, you may be asked whether you want your dish *nam* (wet, like a soup) or *haeng* (dry). *By Matt Crook*

Fried fish at Plern Samut Prachuap, Kiri Khan.

It's a fact...

Remarkably, considering how ubiquitous it is in Thai cooking, the chilli pepper was only introduced into Thailand from the Americas in the late 16th century.

Snacks.

brine for long periods and then bottling the peatish-coloured liquor produced. Chillies deserve a special mention because most Thais like their food hot. Some chillies are fairly mild; others – like the tiny, red *prik khii nuu* ('mouse-shit pepper') – are fiendish. Also the further south you travel the spicier dishes will become – even northern-dwelling Thais will baulk at the chilli content in southern food.

Isaan food – from the northeast of Thailand – is also distinctive and very popular. Many of Thailand's most hardworking people hail from Isaan, and they have spread throughout the country. Even in the deep south you won't have to go far to find a rickety street stall selling sticky rice, aromatic *kaiyang* (grilled chicken) and fiery *som tam* (papaya salad).

Due to Thailand's large Chinese population (or at least Thais with Chinese roots), there are also many Chinese-style restaurants whose cuisine is variously 'Thai-ified'. Many of the snacks available on the streets show this mixture of Thai and Chinese, not to mention Arab and Malay. *Bah jang*, for example, are small pyramids of leaves stuffed with sticky rice, Chinese sausage, salted eggs, pork and dried shrimp.

To sample Thai food it is best to go in a group to a restaurant and order a range of dishes. To eat

alone is regarded as slightly strange. However, there are a number of 'one-dish' meals like fried rice and *phat thai* (fried noodles) and southern restaurants will also usually provide *raat khao* ('over rice'), which is a dish like a curry served on a bed of rice for a single person.

Strict non-fish-eating vegetarians and vegans are in for a tough time. Nearly every cooked meal you will eat in Thailand will be liberally doused in *nam pla* or cooked with shrimp paste. At more expensive and upmarket international restaurants you'll probably be able to find something suitable – in the rural areas, you'll be eating fruit, fried eggs and rice. There is a network of Taoist restaurants offering more strict veggie fare throughout the country – look out for yellow flags with red Chinese lettering. Also asking for *'mai sai nam pla khrup/ka'* (no *nam pla* please)– when ordering what should be veggie food might keep the fish sauce out of harm's reach.

It is possible to get a tasty and nutritious meal almost anywhere – and at any time – in Thailand. Thais eat out a great deal so that most towns have a range of places. The more sophisticated restaurants are usually air- conditioned, and sometimes attached to a hotel. In addition to these more upmarket restaurants are a whole range of places from noodle shops to curry houses and

The etiquette of eating

Eating is a relaxed, communal affair. Dishes are placed in the middle of the table where diners can help themselves. While food is eaten with a spoon and fork, the fork is only used to manoeuvre food onto the spoon. In the northeast most people – at least at home – use their fingers. Sticky rice is compressed into a ball using the ends of the fingers and then dipped in the other dishes. Thais will not pile their plates with food but take several small portions from the dishes arranged on a table.

seafood restaurants. Many small restaurants have no menus. But often the speciality of the house will be clear – roasted, honeyed ducks hanging in the window, crab and fish laid out on crushed ice outside. Away from the main tourist spots, 'Western' breakfasts are commonly unavailable, so be prepared to eat Thai-style (noodle or rice soup or fried rice).

Towards the bottom of the scale are stalls and food carts. These tend to congregate at particular places in town – often in the evening, from dusk. Stall holders will tend to specialize in easily prepared noodles, rice dishes, fruit drinks, sweets and so on. While stall food may be cheap – a meal costs only around ฿20-35 – they are frequented by people from all walks of life.

A popular innovation over the last 10 years or so has been the *suan a-haan* or garden restaurant. These are often on the edge of towns, with tables set in gardens, sometimes with bamboo furniture and ponds.

Tourist centres also provide good European, American and Japanese food at reasonable prices. Bangkok, Phuket, Samui and Hua Hin now boast some superb restaurants. Less expensive Western fast-food restaurants can also be found, including McDonald's and Kentucky Fried Chicken.

Drink

Water in smaller restaurants can be risky, so many people recommend that visitors drink bottled water or hot tea.

Coffee is available throughout Thailand, with some excellent beans being grown in the north of the country. The usual array of soft drinks is widely available as are good fresh fruit juices and coconut water – make sure no sugar is added by asking for *"mai sai nam taan khrup/ka"* – no sugar please. The most popular spirit among Thais is Mekhong – local cane whisky – which can be drunk straight or with mixers such as Coca-Cola. However, due to its hangover-inducing properties, more sophisticated Thais prefer Johnny Walker or an equivalent brand.

Beer drinking is spreading fast. The most popular local beer is Singha beer brewed by Boon Rawd. Singha, Chang and Heineken are the three most popular beers in Thailand. Beer is relatively expensive in Thai terms as it is heavily taxed by the government. It is considered a high status drink. Some pubs and bars also sell beer on tap – which is known as *bier sot*, 'fresh' beer.

Drink powder stall, Samet.

Menu reader

It is impossible to provide a comprehensive list of Thai dishes. However (and at the risk of offending connoisseurs by omitting their favourites), popular dishes include:

Soups (gaeng chud)
Kaeng juut bean curd and vegetable soup, non-spicy
Khao tom rice soup with egg and pork (a breakfast dish) or chicken, fish or prawn. It is said that it can cure fevers and other illnesses. Probably best for a hangover.
Kwaytio Chinese noodle soup served with a variety of additional ingredients, often available from roadside stalls and from smaller restaurants – mostly served up until lunchtime.
Tom ka kai chicken in coconut milk with laos (loas, or ka, is an exotic spice)
Tom yam kung hot and sour prawn soup spiced with lemon grass, coriander and chillies

Rice-based dishes
Single-dish meals served at roadside stalls and in many restaurants (especially cheaper ones).
Khao gaeng curry and rice
Khao man kai rice with chicken
Khao moo daeng rice with red pork
Khao naa pet rice with duck
Khao phat kai/moo/kung fried rice with chicken/pork/prawn

Noodle-based dishes
Ba-mii haeng wheat noodles served with pork and vegetables
Khao soi a form of Kwaytio with egg noodles in a curry broth
Kwaytio haeng wide noodles served with pork and vegetables
Mee krop Thai crisp-fried noodles
Phak sii-u noodles fried with egg, vegetables and meat/prawns
Phat thai Thai fried noodles

Curries (gaeng)
Gaeng khiaw waan kai/nua/phet/pla green chicken/beef/duck/fish curry (the colour is due to the large number of whole green chillies pounded to make the paste that forms the base of this very hot curry)
Gaeng mussaman Muslim beef curry served with potatoes
Gaeng phanaeng chicken/beef curry
Gaeng phet kai/nua hot chicken/beef curry
Gaeng plaa duk catfish curry

Meat dishes
Phat krapow moo/kai/nua fried meat with basil and chillies
Kai/nua phat prik fried chicken/beef with chillies
Kai tort Thai fried chicken
Kai tua chicken in peanut sauce
Kai yang garlic chicken
Larb moo/kai chopped (once raw, now frequently cooked) meat with herbs and spices
Moo waan sweet pork
Nua priaw waan sweet and sour beef
Priao wan sweet and sour pork with vegetables

Seafood
Haw mok steamed fish curry
Luuk ciin plaa fishballs
Plaa nerng steamed fish
Plaa pao grilled fish
Plaa priaw waan whole fried fish with ginger sauce
Plaa too tort Thai fried fish
Thotman plaa fried curried fish cakes

Salads (yam)
Som tam green papaya salad. The Thai version is watered down from the original Laos/Isaan dish which is less sweet and is served with pungent fermented fish sauce. Tomatoes, chillies, garlic, chopped dried shrimps and lime (can be extremely spicy).
Yam nua Thai beef salad

Vegetables
Phak phat ruam mit mixed fried vegetables

Sweets (kanom)
Kanom mo kaeng baked custard squares
Khao niaw mamuang sticky rice and mango (a seasonal favourite)
Khao niaw sankhayaa sticky rice and custard
Kluay buat chee bananas in coconut milk
Kluay tort Thai fried bananas
Leenchee loi mek chilled lychees in custard

Fruits

Chomphu rose apple
Khanun jackfruit (January-June)
Kluay banana (year round)
Lamyai longan; thin brown shell with translucent fruit similar to lychee (June-August)
Lamut sapodilla
Linchi lychee (April-June)
Majeung star apple
Makham wan tamarind (December-February)
Malakho papaya (year round)
Mamuang mango (March-June)
Manao lime (year round)
Mang khud mangosteen (April-September)
Maprao coconut (year round)
Ngo rambutan (May-September)
Noi na custard (or sugar) apple (June-September)
Sapparot pineapple (April-June, December-January)
Som orange (year round)
Som o pomelo (August-November)
Taeng mo watermelon (October-March)
Thurian durian (May-August)

Southern Thai specialities

Kanom jeen rice noodles with curry
Kao yum spicy rice salad
Gaeng ped spicy curry with pork or beef
Kao moek gai yellow rice and chicken
Gaeng som sour soup with vegetables
Pad ped sataw spicy red curry and sataw beans
Goong pad sataw stir-fried sataw beans with shrimp
Pla neung manao fish with garlic, lime juice and chillies
Gaeng massaman mild curry with potatoes, peanuts and meat
Penang gai dry chicken curry with coconut flavouring
Tom kha gai creamy coconut-milk-based chicken curry
Mee suo noodle soup with minced pork, bean sprouts and egg
Yam pla duk fu fluffy catfish with green mango salad
Gaeng tai pla spicy fish curry
Mee pad hokkien stir-fried noodles

Tip...

The Thai words for banana and penis are very similar – kluay and kruay. Get it wrong and you could send the street vendor into a fit of giggles particular if you are asking for "tort" – fried – or "yang" – grilled – bananas.

Entertainment

Fireshow at Ibiza Bar, Phi Phi.

Bars

Everything from sophisticated cocktail lounges through to the seediest drinking hole is available in the region. Bangkok encompasses the widest range of bars while places like Phuket and parts of Koh Samui also offer a good choice. Of course many bars in Thailand are associated with sex tourism and prostitution – they are pretty easy to spot so easy to avoid. In some areas, like Pattaya, it might mean finding a place to have a friendly drink gets a bit difficult – heading to an upmarket hotel can often provide more relaxed surroundings. Sports bars are also popular and will often show live football from around the world. Many small hotels, guesthouses and even budget beachside bungalow operations will have some form of bar attached to them. The backpackers' favourite, Krabi, has a good range of bars that focus on younger travellers – though the authenticity of the local Thai 'rastas' might be in doubt.

Beach parties

An important part of the region's nightlife scene are the beach parties. The Full Moon Parties on the beaches of Koh Phangan are the most famous, with thousands of intoxicated people dancing into the small hours and beyond. You can also find a smattering of lower-key beach parties at places such as Koh Samet, Koh Samui and Koh Chang. The Thais are also prone to show up on more 'local' beaches, like those north of Chumphon, with massive car stereos and crates of beer to hold impromptu gatherings.

Children

While the Thais are incredibly fond of children kid-orientated entertainment can be thin on the ground. Some resorts, such as the Le Méridien, Khao Lak, have exceptional facilities to keep the kids busy. There are a number of theme parks around the major destinations such as Bangkok, Phuket and Pattaya but the safety standards at some are dubious.

Cinema

Bangkok has an excellent range of cinemas that show films in their original languages with Thai subtitles – you need to check beforehand as some are also dubbed into Thai. Outside the capital cinemas showing original language films are a little harder to come by though Phuket and Pattaya are your best bet. Many budget guesthouses etc also show DVDs on TVs or other screens during the evening, making up for the lack of cinemas.

Clubs

The biggest club scene is in Bangkok though in recent months it has gained a poor reputation due to the devastating fire at the Santika nightclub on January 1 2009 that left 66 people dead. Many of Bangkok's more interesting clubs also appear and then disappear with great frequency – the best locations are along Royal College Avenue (known locally as RCA) or the lower *soi* numbers on Sukhumvit Road. Some of the better hotels will also host club lounges. Phuket has a burgeoning scene aimed at both Thais and foreigners – you'll get some top DJs coming through.

Gay, lesbian & transexual

Thailand is famed for its tolerance of the differing shades of sexuality and gender. Both Bangkok and Pattaya have large gay night-life areas. You'll find this to a lesser extent on Phuket and Samui. The transexual (*katoey*) community in Thailand is also

Thai boxing.

famed for being linked to the nightlife – some bars/clubs in Pattaya, Phuket and Bangkok are staffed almost entirely with *katoeys* and you can also find *katoey* cabaret shows.

Music

Many bars and clubs will host live acts usually playing appalling cover versions of pop and rock songs. Sometimes this can provide an hysterical level of kitsch entertainment – watching a local band murdering Deep Purple's *Smoke on the Water* at full volume is likely to be seared onto your memory. The Thais also love karaoke with drunken renditions of nasal Thai love songs often the favourite. Local Thai bars will often have in-house singers – usually heavily made-up females with big hair-dos and tight-fitting dresses. You might also be lucky enough to find hordes of backpackers on a beach playing bongos and didgeridoos.

Traditional arts & sports

You can witness *muay Thai* – Thai kickboxing – at stadiums and boxing rings all over the region. It can be quite a bloody and excruciating spectacle – some people may find this entertaining, others may find it off-putting. In Bangkok there are various places to witness performing arts. Sepak Takraw – a three-a-side game of volley ball – is a very popular and skilful game that Thai men play anywhere they string up a net. The shadow plays in Nakhon Si Thammarat are renowned throughout the country.

Shopping

Beachbum necklaces, Samet.

Bangkok and Phuket are the main shopping 'centres' in this region. Bangkok still offers the greatest variety and choice but it is difficult to find bargains any longer; ubiquitous department stores and shopping malls contain high-price, high-quality merchandise (at a fixed price), much of which is imported. Phuket City is home to an array of several upmarket designer shops and you can find various antique stores and giant shopping centres scattered across Phuket island.

Competition between the smaller shopkeepers is fierce. Do not be cajoled into buying something before having a chance to price it elsewhere – Thais can be very persuasive. Also, watch out for guarantees of authenticity – fake antiques abound, and even professionals find it difficult to know a 1990 Khmer sculpture from a 10th-century one.

In the main beach tourist destinations you will find the usual parade of flipflops, sarongs, cheap sunglasses, axe pillows, generic Buddha figurines and towels. As many of the beach towns have only sprung up with the influx of tourism do not expect to find much in the way of traditional Thai goods. You should still be able to find a market servicing locals but they tend to be filled with working implements and other non-aesthetic items. Giant

Tip...

You'll seldom see any decent handicrafts in any of the tourist beach areas – the best tend be available in other parts of Thailand, particularly in the north and northeast.

Tesco-Lotus superstores are slowly replacing the traditional Thai market and are very popular due to their rock-bottom prices.

Thailand has had a reputation as being a mecca for pirated goods: CDs and DVDs, Lacoste shirts, Gucci leather goods, Rolex watches, computer software and so on. These items are still available, but pressure from the US to protect intellectual copyright is leading to more enthusiastic crackdowns by the police. In Bangkok, genuine CDs can be bought at what are still bargain prices compared with the West; buying pirated DVDs often requires a retreat to some back room. Strangely though, most DVD sellers are quite honest and if your fake doesn't work they will replace it. When buying DVDs ask for 'master' copies – this way you should avoid purchasing a film shot from the back of a cinema. There have been a number of raids in Bangkok in places like Patpong in 2009 with huge stocks of DVDs and other goods seized – whether such police actions will have a long-term effect is still to be evaluated.

The widest selection of Thai silk is available in Bangkok; the traditional centre of silk weaving is in the northeast of Thailand. Tailor-made clothing is available although designs are sometimes outdated; it might be better for the tailor to copy an article of your own clothing. There are dozens of tailors – usually of Indian origin – in the tourist destinations and you can even find them on the beach in some locations. There are now some top designers in Bangkok. Leather goods include custom-made crocodile skin shoes and boots (for those who aren't squeamish).

Bangkok is also a good place to buy jewellery – gold, sapphires and rubies – as well as antiques, bronzeware and celadon. If you're brave you might even want to take on the gem dealers in Chantaburi to secure a bargain – we don't fancy your chances (see page 96).

Tip...

Most of the major department stores have a VAT refund desk. Go to them on your day of purchase with receipts and ask them to complete a VAT refund form, which you then present, with the purchased goods, at the appropriate desk in any international airport in Thailand. They'll give you another form that you exchange for cash in the departure lounge. You'll need to spend at least ฿4000 to qualify for a refund.

Bargaining

Bargaining is common, except in the large department stores (although they may give a discount on expensive items of jewellery or furniture) and on items like soap, books and most necessities. Expect to pay anything from 25-75% less than the asking price, depending on the bargainer's skill and the shopkeeper's mood.

Tricksters

Tricksters, rip-off artists, fraudsters, less than honest salespersons – call them what you will – are likely to be far more of a problem than simple theft. People may well approach you in the street offering incredible one-off bargains, and giving what might seem to be very plausible reasons for your sudden good fortune. Be wary in all such cases and do not be pressed into making a hasty decision. Unfortunately, more often than not, the salesperson is trying to pull a fast one. Favourite 'bargains' are precious stones, whose authenticity is 'demonstrated' before your very eyes. Although many Thais genuinely do like to talk to *farangs* and practise their English, in tourist areas there are also those who offer their friendship for financial rather than linguistic reasons. Sad as it is to say, it is probably a good idea to be suspicious.

Tip...

For up-to-date information on all scams visitbangkokscams.com.

Activities & tours

Diving

Thailand, with some fantastically rich and diverse reefs, can it make hard to choose where and when to dive, especially when you consider that diving in Thailand is seasonal. At its simplest, half the year you dive on the west, the other half on the east. The western Andaman Sea is where the best and most varied diving is found – the Similans are one of the highlights (see page 196). Corals are lush and marine life prolific. From November to late April, seas are mostly calm and visibility varies from good to outstanding and currents are acceptable to most divers. The east coast is a good choice for those months when the monsoon is blowing in across the Andaman Sea. The shallower waters of the Gulf of Thailand are calm from May to October – there are some particularly good dive sites here and the chance to see whalesharks (see page 148). The water in Thailand is invariably warm, with temperatures between 25-28°C (23°C at the lowest). There are more than enough operators and in general, dive businesses are extremely professional. Many work closely with one of the international governing bodies (PADI, NAUI, CMAS, BSAC), however, some facilities in far-flung areas may be limited. Koh Tao reputedly produces more Open Water PADI certified divers – the basic 'licence' for scuba diving – than anywhere else on the planet.

Fishing

Sea fishing as a tourist activity is still a developing market and at present resources to do this are limited. The main beach resorts – Pattaya, Phuket, Koh Phi Phi, Koh Samui and others – offer game fishing in both the Andaman Sea and Gulf of Thailand. The seas here are filled with barracuda, sail and swordfish, marlin, sea bass and a variety of sharks. Several species are protected and certain areas are in marine national parks so be very careful. Instead of fishing you might want to also consider diving – then you can see the fish in a living state in their natural habitat, rather than flopping around on the top of a boat. Visit phuket.com/fishing to get a full picture of what is available in the region.

Fishing boat, Koh Yao Noi.

Parasailing

Along with banana boating, parasailing is found at the more commercial beaches in Thailand like Pattaya Bay and Jomtien in Pattaya and Patong in Phuket. Perhaps one of the best places to enjoy this sport is Koh Lan, near Pattaya, where floating 'take-off and landing' platforms mean that the flight occurs exclusively above the sea and you don't even have to get wet.

Rock climbing

Rock climbing is emerging as a growing and very popular activity in southern Thailand. The two main centres are in Ao Nang, just outside Krabi (see page 223) and on Koh Phi Phi (see page 225). You can find courses for beginners while more experienced climbers will doubtlessly be engaged by the thousands of the limestone karsts that pepper the seas here. One of the big attractions of these sea-bound rock-faces is, with a watery cushion to land in, they provided a perfect site to practise 'free climbing' without ropes or other equipment.

Sea kayaking

This has become popular over the last decade or so. Limestone areas of the south such as Phangnga Bay provide a pock-marked coast of cliffs, sea caverns and rocky islets. Specialist companies, see below, have now been joined by many other companies based in Phuket, Krabi, Ao Nang, Koh Tao and Phi Phi. Kayaks can be hired on many commercial beaches by the hour but for a comprehensive tour including a guide and organized itinerary, the following tour operators offer trips for all. **Discover Asia**, 19/9 Soi Suk Chai, Sukhumvit 42, Prakhanong, Klongtoey, Bangkok, T02-381 7742, asiantraveladventures.com, runs day trips from Oct-Jun and longer tours around south Thailand's marine parks and islands. **Paddle Asia**, 9/71 Moo 3, Thanon, Rasdanusorn, Ban Kuku, Phuket, T076-216 145, seakayaking-thailand.com, offers traditional kayak tours around the marine parks, specifically for bird- and nature-lovers. **Sea Canoe Thailand**, 367/4 Yaowarat Rd, Phuket, T076-212172, seacanoe.net, is an established watersports company offering day trips and longer tours from Phuket.

Wakeboarding & kitesurfing

Offered as an option in a few watersports centres, wakeboarding has its own specialist school in Thailand: **Air Time**, 99/9 Tambon Mae Nam Khu, Amphur Pluak Daeng, Dok Krai, Rayong, T08-6838 7841, air-time. net. It runs wakeboard camps near Pattaya with dedicated English-, French-, German-, Dutch- and Thai-speaking coaches and the chance to try out monoboards, kneeboards, skyski and tubes. **Thailand Kitesurfing School**, Rawai, Muang, Phuket, T076-288258, kitethailand.com, also runs courses and there is a kitesurfing school in Hua Hin that offers one- to three-day courses and instructor training. The long beaches and laid-back atmosphere north of Chumphon are turning that spot into a kitesurfing mecca, particularly during November when the winds are at their strongest.

Wildlife watching

Thailand has an extensive network of national parks and protected areas. The most popular in the south is Khao Sok (see page 190) which has trails, camping grounds, hides, accommodation, visitor centres and more. Other good sites are the interior of Koh Chang and the southern tip of Koh Lanta. However, compared with other countries with a rich natural heritage, it is difficult not to feel that Thailand has not made the most of its potential. Trails are, generally, not well laid out and true nature lovers may find themselves disappointed rather than enthralled. But for those from temperate regions the sheer luxuriance and abundance of the tropical forest, and the unusual birds, insects and more, will probably make up for this. See also Nature and environment, page 40.

Kids' activities

In Bangkok older children may want to mingle with trendy Thai teens in Siam Square, a shopping district crammed with shops and stalls selling cheap 'designer' clothing and just about everything else. For somewhere green and clean, Lumphini Park has lawns to run about on, a lake to boat on and even a kite-flying season from February to April. For cooling down, slide over to Central World Ice Skating in the World Trade Centre. There's a Children's Discovery Museum at Chatuchak Park and, about 33 km outside the city, Muang Boran (ancientcity.com), an open-air museum with scaled replicas of Thailand's famous monuments. Heading south the beachside resort of Hua Hin has calm waters and pony rides on the beach. In the ancient tropical rainforest of Khao Sok National Park discover the jungle's strange nocturnal wildlife during a night safari. Learn to snorkel or scuba-dive on Koh Tao, see psychedelic coral reefs and paddle a kayak into the sea caves of Phangnga Bay. On Phuket head to the gibbon sanctuary and listen out for the haunting cry of a gibbon during a dawn walk in the rainforest.

Gibbon at play.

Wellbeing and spas

While lying around being massaged could hardly be considered an activity, the popularity of Thailand's spa industry should not be dismissed.

The roots of this industry lie mainly in traditional Thai massage, most of which springs from temples around the country, the most famous being Wat Po in Bangkok. The Wat Po School of Thai Massage, set in the grounds of the temple, offers authentic and affordable massage in communal, fan-cooled rooms by practitioners who are trained on site. And, if you want to master the fine art yourself, you can also learn massage here – for full details visit watpomassage.com. You can also get a pretty good temple massage in Nakhon Si Thammarat at the Thai Traditional Medicine Centre in Wat Sa-la Mechai (see page 122). Many local government run health centres – even in remote areas – will even have a massage therapist attached to them and they will treat foreigners for a small fee. If you want your wellbeing to extend inwards, Thai temples are also centres for Buddhist meditation – Wat Suan Mok near Surat Thani (see page 118) runs a famous 10-day course.

Beyond the temples, the massive array of therapies, massages, holistic treatments and general pampering is bewildering. You are guaranteed to find either a foot massage or Thai massage everywhere you find tourists, from shacks on a beach through to purpose built mega-complexes. However, much of what is on offer is watered down or badly delivered and a manipulative Thai massage could even result in injury – a good suggestion is to just settle for a foot-massage until you are completely sure of the masseuse's experience/qualifications

At the top end of the market sit the expensive health resorts such as Chiva Som in Hua Hin or the Banyan Tree in Phuket and Bangkok. If you do want to splurge, the Six Senses resort chain offer, some of the best holistic spa experiences on the planet – their Earth Spa in Hua Hin is set in pixie-like conical mud-huts from where they prepare an individually tailored detox and massage programme.

Chiva Som Thai Pavilions.

Contents

Bangkok

The Bangkok skyline by night.

Introduction

Dirty, dynamic and wild, Bangkok is a heaving scrum of humanity blended with ancient beauty, booming youth culture and the rituals of a bygone age. Don't arrive expecting an exotic, languid, dreamy place trapped in some imagined, traditional past. What will hit you is the size, pace, endless cacophony, friendliness of the locals and interminable gridlocked traffic. The whole place resembles a giant, out-of- control car-boot sale set in a sauna whose pavements are humming with open-air kitchens, clothes stalls, hawkers and touts.

Yet, some of the old *King and I* romanticism still persists. There are *khlongs* (canals), palaces and temples but, ultimately, what marks Bangkok out from the imaginings of its visitors, is its thrusting modernity in open struggle with ancient, rural traditions. Neon, steel, glass and futuristic transport rub shoulders with lumbering elephants, alms-collecting monks and crumbling teak villas. It's all here: poverty and wealth, smog-filled thoroughfares and backstreets smothered in alluring exotic aromas, cybercafés and barrows laden with fried bugs.

With your senses fully overloaded don't forget the sheer luxury that's on offer. Bangkok is home to some of the best, and most affordable, hotels in the world. Factor in the numerous spas, futuristic super-hip nightlife and the incredibly diverse range of markets and shops selling everything from amulets and sarongs to Prada and hi-tech gadgets and your head will be spinning.

What to see in...

...a weekend
If you're in the Thai capital for a short layover head to the **Grand Palace**, the staggering Royal splurge at the centre of the city – don't forget to take in an authentic Thai temple massage at nearby **Wat Pho**. A longer visit would give you a chance to delve into the culinary delights of **Chinatown**, take in a river tour and the silks of **Jim Thompson's House**.

...a week or more
With an extended visit longer than a week, try out the famous **Chatuchak weekend markets** or choose from a myriad of mega shopping centres in the hunt for elusive bargains. Lose yourself in the tastes of Bangkok streetfood and take in **Sukhumvit**'s wild nightlife.

The Demon Guardian at the Grand Palace, Wat Phra Kaeo.

Essentials

Getting around

From the airport Most international visitors to both Bangkok and Thailand will arrive at the capital's **Suvarnabhumi Airport** (suvarnabhumiairport.com), 25 km southeast of the city. Some domestic flights still arrive at the old airport at **Don Muang**, about 25 km north of the city centre. It can take over an hour to get to central Bangkok from either airport – outside of rush-hour the transit time should be 35-45 mins.

Airport **buses** operate every 15 mins (0500-2400), ฿150 to Silom Road (AE1), Khaosan Road (AE2), Wireless/Sukhumvit Road (AE3) and Hualamphong train station (AE4). The official taxi booking service is in the arrivals hall. A public **taxi** to downtown should cost roughly ฿300 including a ฿55 expressway toll and ฿50 airport surcharge on top of the meter cost. Make sure your driver puts the meter on before you start your journey. Construction of a 28-km overhead city **rail link** is underway (planned opening is late 2009 but could be delayed).

By public transport The **Metro** (bangkokmetro. co.th) loops through 18 stations across the city and fares range from ฿15 to ฿39. The **Skytrain** (T02-617 7300, bts.co.th) runs on an elevated track through the most developed parts of the city and costs between ฿15 for one stop ฿40 for the whole route. The extension over the river to Thonburi is now open.

There is a massive **bus** network (operated by the Bangkok Mass Transit Authority, bmta.co.th) including air-conditioned, micro and expressway vehicles. Buses run from 0500-2300 and there is a limited night bus service running from 2300-0500. Fares are in the region of ฿8.50 to ฿30.

You can also use the river-based Chao Phraya Express **boat service** which runs between Nonthaburi in the north and Rajburana in the south, passing near Khaosan Road, Wat Arun, Grand Palace, Chinatown and Saphan Taksin Skytrain station. Fares fall within the ฿10-฿32 range. A good map, *Rivers and Khlongs*, is available from the Tourism Authority of Thailand office (see tourist information, opposite). Be careful of pickpockets on all public transport in Bangkok.

By taxi There are three main 'taxi' vehicles in Bangkok: the usual metered car, the unmetered motorcycle taxi and three-wheeled tuk-tuk. When using **taxi cars** check that the meter is 'zeroed' before setting off. Fares are ฿35 for the first 2 km, ฿4.50 per km up to 12 km, and ฿5 per km thereafter. A typical city trip will cost ฿40-100 and it is usual to round fares up to the nearest ฿5. Reputable taxi firms include Siam Taxis (T1661) and Radio Taxi (T1681). **Motorcycle taxi** riders wear numbered vests and congregate at the end of the busier *sois*. Short-hop fares are around ฿10-20, though some drivers will agree to take longer journeys across town, costing between ฿25-100. **Tuk-tuks** are fine for shorter journeys, but the fare should be agreed before boarding. Many tuk-tuk drivers rip off tourists and taking a taxi will usually be less hassle and cheaper.

Bus station There are 3 main bus stations in Bangkok: The Northern bus terminal (also known as Mo Chit Mai, New Mo Chit or Mo Chit 2), is at the western side of Chatuchak Park on Kamphaeng Phet 2 Rd, T02-936 3659. It serves all destinations in the north and northeast as well as towns in the central plains that lie north of Bangkok. The Southern bus terminal is on Phra Pinklao Rd, T02-434 7192, near the intersection with Route 338. Buses for the west for places places like Kanchanaburi and the south leave from here. A/c town bus No 7 travels to the terminal. A/c buses to the south and west leave from the terminal on Charan Santiwong Rd, near Bangkok Noi Train Station in Thonburi, T02-435 1199.

The Eastern bus terminal, Sukhumvit Rd (Soi Ekamai), between Soi 40 and Soi 42, T02-391 2504, serves Pattaya and other destinations in the eastern region. To travel into Bangkok from this bus terminal by local bus, walk out of the terminal, turn left and enter the local bus terminal. Bus Nos 77 and 159 will travel down to the Siam Sq area.

Train station Bangkok has 2 main railway stations. Hualamphong, Rama IV Rd, T02-223 7010/20, is the primary station, catering for most destinations; condensed railway timetables in English can be picked up from the information counter on the main concourse. Bangkok Noi (Thonburi station), on the other side of the Chao Phraya River, is where trains to Nakhon Pathom and Kanchanaburi depart/arrive.

ATMs There are thousands of ATMs all over Bangkok that accept all major international bank cards. In April 2009 Thai banks started charging ฿150 per transaction on foreign cards.

Hospital Bangkok Adventist Hospital, 430 Phitsanulok Rd, Dusit, T02-281 1422/ 282 1100.

Bangkok General Hospital, New Phetburi Soi 47, T02-318 0066.

Post office Central General Post Office (Praysani Klang for taxi drivers) is located at 1160 Charoen Krung, Mon-Fri 0800-2000, Sat, Sun and holidays 0800-1300. There are many small post offices in most districts and many shopping centres.

Tourist information Tourism Authority of Thailand (TAT). Main office: 1600 New Phetburi Rd, Makkasan, Ratchathewi, T02-250 5500, tourismthailand.org; also at 4 Rachdamnern Nok Av (intersection with Chakrapatdipong Rd), daily 0830-1630; two counters at Suvarnabhumi Airport. T1672 between 0800-2000 for the English-speaking TAT call centre.

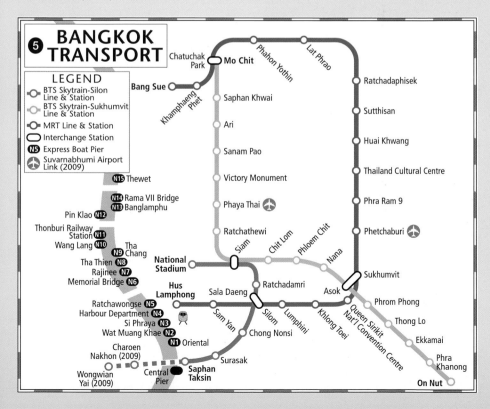

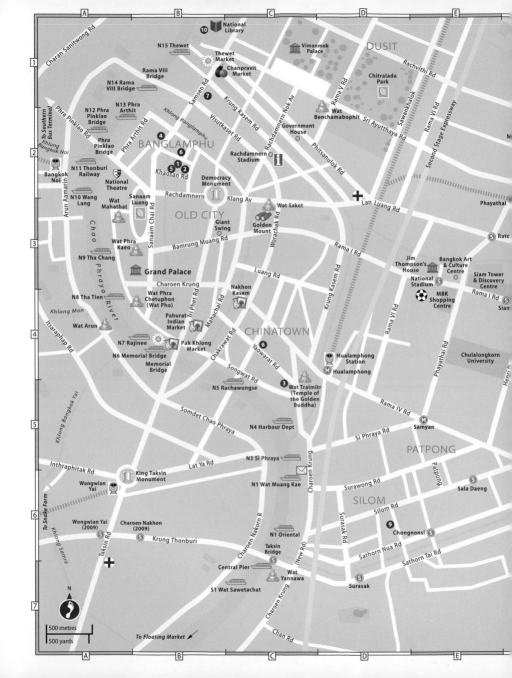

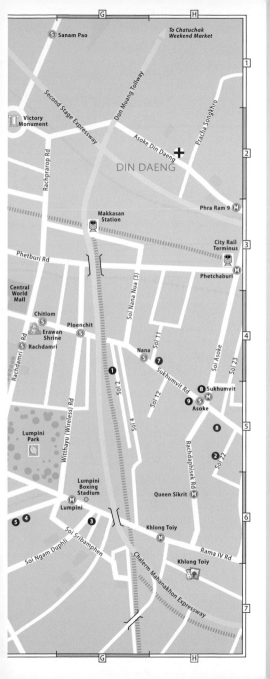

Bangkok listings

❶ Sleeping
1 Atlanta *78 Sukhumvit Soi 2*, G4
2 Buddy Lodge *265 Khaosan Rd*, B2
3 Charlie's House *Soi Saphan Khu*, G6
4 Lamphu House *75 Soi Rambutri*, B2
5 Metropolitan *27 South Sathorn Rd*, F6
6 Orchid House *Rambutri St*, B2
7 Phranakorn Nornlen *46 Thewet soi 1*, B1
8 Sam's Lodge *2nd floor, Sukhumvit 19*, H5
9 Sheraton Grande Sukhumvit *250 Sukhumvit*, H5
10 Tavee *83 Sri Ayutthaya Rd, Soi 14*, B1

❶ Eating
1 Bai Bau *146 Rambutri St*, B2
2 Ban Mai *121 Sukhumvit Soi 22, Sub-Soi 2*, H5
3 Canton House *530 Yaowarat Rd*, C5
4 Cy'an *Metropolitan Hotel, 27 South Sathorn Rd*, F6
5 D'Rus *Khaosan Rd*, B2
6 Hua Seng Hong *371-372 Yaowarat Rd*, C4
7 Nasir al-Masri *4-6 Sukhumvit Soi Nana Nua*, H4
8 Rang Mahal *Rembrandt Hotel, Sukhumvit Soi 18*, H5
9 Taling Pling *60 Pan Rd*, D6

Around the city

The official name for Thailand's capital city is Krungthepmahanakhon Amornratt-anakosin Mahintharayutthaya Mahadilokphop Noppharat Ratchathaniburirom Udom-ratchaniwetmahasathan Amonphiman Awatansathit Sakkathattiyawitsanukamprasit. It is not hard to see why Thais prefer the shortened version, Krungthep, or the 'City of Angels'. The name used by the rest of the world – Bangkok – is derived from 17th-century Western maps, which referred to the city as Bancok, the 'village of the wild plum'. Founded in 1767 when Ayutthaya, then the capital of Siam, fell to the marauding Burmese for the second time, the remnants of the court moved to a more defensible position on the western banks of the Chao Phraya, far from the Burmese. These days Bangkok is one of Asia's most dynamic, vibrant cities that is not only a hub for travel to Thailand's famed beaches, but also a destination in its own right.

Reclining Buddha at Wat Pho.

Filled with palaces and temples, the Old City is the ancient heart of Bangkok. These days it is the premier tourist destination although controversial plans are afoot to change it into a 'tourist zone'. This would strip the area of the usual chaotic charm that typifies Bangkok, moving out the remaining poor people who live in the area and creating an ersatz, gentrified feel.

Wat Phra Chetuphon (Wat Pho)

Entrance on south side of the monastery, watpho.com.
Daily 0800-1700, ฿50.
Map: Bangkok, B4, p72.

Wat Phra Chetuphon, or Wat Pho, is the largest and most famous temple in Bangkok. The 'Temple of the Reclining Buddha' was built in 1781 and houses one of the largest reclining Buddhas in the country. The bustling grounds of the *wat* contain more than 1,000 bronze images, mostly rescued from the ruins of Ayutthaya and Sukhothai, while the *bot* (ordination hall) houses the ashes of Rama I. One of Wat Pho's biggest attractions is its role as a respected centre of traditional Thai massage – visitors are welcome to try this out in a sub-building in the temple complex (same opening times, from ฿400 an hour, see page 85).

Wat Arun

Water-taxi from Tha Tien pier (at the end of Thai Wang Rd near Wat Pho) or from Tha Chang (at the end of Na Phralan near Wat Phra Kaeo).
Daily 0730-1730, ฿30.
Map: Bangkok, A4, p72.

Facing Wat Pho across the Chao Phraya River is the famous Wat Arun (Temple of the Dawn). Standing 81 m high, making it the highest *prang* (tower) in Thailand, Arun was built in the early 19th century on the site of Wat Chaeng, the Royal Palace complex when Thonburi was briefly the capital of Thailand. The *prang* is completely covered with

Wat Arun.

fragments of Chinese porcelain and is really meant to be viewed from across the river; its scale and beauty can only be appreciated from a distance. The best view of Wat Arun is during sunset from the Bangkok side of the river.

Wat Phra Kaeo & Grand Palace

Entrance is via the Viseschaisri Gate, Na Phralan Rd, T02-222 0094, palaces.thai.net.
Ticket office open daily 0830-1130, 1300-1530 except Buddhist holidays when Wat Phra Kaeo is free but the rest of the palace is closed. Admission to the Grand Palace complex ฿350. Map: Bangkok, B3, p72.

The Grand Palace is situated on the banks of the Chao Phraya River and is the most spectacular – some say 'gaudy' – collection of buildings in Bangkok. The complex, which began life in 1782, covers an area of over 1.5 sq km and the architectural plan is almost identical to that of the Royal Palace in the former capital of Ayutthaya.

The buildings of greatest interest are clustered around **Wat Phra Kaeo**, or the **Temple of the Emerald Buddha**. Inside the temple, the Emerald Buddha peers down on the gathered throng from a lofty position above a golden altar. Facing the Buddha on three sides are other gilded Buddha images, depicting the enlightenment of the Buddha when he subdues the evil demon Mara, the final temptation of the Buddha and the subjugation of evil spirits. Around the walls of the shaded **cloister** that encompasses Wat Phra Kaeo, is a continuous mural depicting the *Ramakien*. To the west of the *mondop* is the large Golden Stupa or *chedi*, with its circular base, in Ceylonese style. To the north of the *mondop* is a model of Angkor Wat constructed during the reign of King Mongkut (1851-1868) when Cambodia was under Thai suzerainty.

To the south of Wat Phra Kaeo are the buildings of the **Grand Palace**. These are interesting for the contrast that they make with those of Wat Phra Kaeo. Walking out through the cloisters, on your left is the French-style **Boromabiman Hall**, which was completed during the reign of Rama VI. The **Amarinda Hall** has an impressive, airy interior, with chunky pillars and gilded thrones. The **Chakri Mahaprasart** (Palace Reception Hall) stands in front of a carefully manicured garden with topiary. The Grand Palace is now only used for state occasions.

Around the city

Sanaam Luang & Banglamphu

*To the north of the Grand Palace,
across Na Phralan Rd.*
Map: Bangkok, B3, p72.

The large open space of the Pramane Ground (the
Royal Cremation Ground) is better known as
Sanaam Luang. This area was originally used for
the cremation of kings, queens and important
princes. Sanaam Luang has also been a regular site
for political demonstrations – if Bangkok is going
through any kind of political upheaval it might be
best to avoid this area.

A short walk north and east from Sanaam
Luang is the district of **Banglamphu** and the
legendary Khaosan Road, backpacker haunt and
epicentre of Bangkok's travellers' culture.

Wat Mahathat

*North along Na Phrathat Rd, on the river side of
Sanaam Luang.*
Daily 0900-1700.
Map: Bangkok, A3, p72.

Wat Mahathat (the Temple of the Great Relic), is a
temple famous as a meditation centre; walk under
the archway marked 'Naradhip Centre for Research
in Social Sciences' to reach the *wat*. At No 24
Maharaj Road a narrow *soi* (lane) leads down
towards the river and a large daily market selling
exotic herbal cures, amulets, clothes and food.

Wat Mahathat.

Chinatown
Map: Bangkok, C4, p72.

South of the Old City, Chinatown covers the area
from Charoen Krung (or New Road) down to the
river. Few other places in Bangkok match
Chinatown for atmosphere. The warren of alleys,
lanes and tiny streets are cut through with an
industrious hive of shops, temples and restaurants.
Weird food, mountains of mechanical parts, gaudy
temple architecture, gold, flowers and a constant
frenetic bustle will lead to many hours of happy
wandering. This is an area to explore on foot,
getting lost in the many nooks and crannies.

Woeng Nakhon Kasem (Thieves' Market),
between Charoen Krung and Yaowarat Road, sits in
the heart of Chinatown and its boundaries are
marked by archways. This market used to be the
centre for the fencing of stolen goods. It is not quite
as colourful today but there remain a number of
second-hand and antique shops.

Vimanmek Palace

*Just off Rachvithi Rd, to the north of the National
Assembly, T02-628 6300 ext 5119-5121,
vimanmek.com.*
Daily 0830-1600 (last tickets at 1500), ฿100, ฿20
for children, admission by guided tour only (1 hr).
Tickets to the Grand Palace include entrance to
Vimanmek Palace. Dance shows 1030, 1400. No
shorts or short skirts; sarongs available for hire
(฿100, refundable).
Map: Bangkok, C1, p72.

The present home of the Thai royal family and the
administration is located north of Banglamphu in
an area called Dusit. The wide boulevards are more
in keeping with a European city. The Vimanmek
Palace is the largest golden teakwood mansion in
the world, but don't expect to see huge expanses
of polished wood – the building is almost entirely
painted. It was built by Rama V in 1901 who was
clearly taken with Western style. It looks like a large
Victorian hunting lodge and is filled with china,
silver and paintings from all over the world.

Chinatown.

Siam Square & Ratchaprasong
Map: Bangkok, E3/4, p72.

A 10-minute walk east along Rama I Road is the biggest and busiest modern shopping area in the city, centred on a maze of tiny boutiques and a covered market known as **Siam Square**. Head to this area if you want to be at the apex of Thai youth culture and the biggest spread of shopping opportunities in the city. Strolling along the skywalk to Ratchaprasong Intersection, you will find another large mall, **Central World**. On the corner of Rama I and Phayathai Road is **MBK**, Bangkok's largest indoor shopping area, crammed with bargains and outlets of every description. Opposite MBK is the newly opened **Bangkok Art and Culture Centre** (T02-214 6630-1, bacc.or.th, Tues-Sun 1000-2100) worth a visit for contemporary arts and cultural activities.

Jim Thompson's House
Soi Kasemsan Song 2, opposite the National Stadium, jim thompson.com.
Mon-Sat 0900-1700, ฿100, children ฿50.
Map: Bangkok, E3, p72.

Jim Thompson's House is an assemblage of traditional teak northern Thai houses, some more than 200 years old, transported here and reassembled. Jim Thompson arrived in Bangkok as an intelligence officer attached to the United States' OSS (Office of Strategic Services) and then made his name by reinvigorating the Thai silk industry after the Second World War. He disappeared mysteriously in the Malaysian jungle on 27 March 1967. Jim Thompson chose this site for his house partly because a collection of silk weavers lived nearby on Khlong Saensep. The house contains an eclectic collection of antiques from Thailand and China.

Silom and Patpong
Hi-tech, high-rise and clad in concrete and glass, **Silom**, south of Siam Square, is at the centre of booming Bangkok. Banks, international business and many media companies are based in this area, as is the heart of Bangkok's gay community. Stylish, tacky and sweaty, head down the length of Silom for a full slice of contemporary Bangkok life.

Many people flock to the red-light district of **Patpong**, which runs along two lanes (Patpong 1 and 2) linking Silom to Surawong. These streets were transformed from a row of 'tea houses' (brothels serving local clients) into a high-tech lane of go-go bars in 1969 when an American entrepreneur made a major investment.

Sukhumvit Road
With the Skytrain running its length, Sukhumvit Road, east of Siam Square and Silom, has developed into Bangkok's most vibrant strip. Shopping centres, girly bars, some of the city's best hotels and awesome places to eat have been joined by futuristic nightclubs. The grid of *sois* that run off the main drag are home to a variety of different communities including Arab, African and Korean, as well as throngs of Westerners.

Sleeping

From humble backstreet digs to opulent extravagance, Bangkok has an incredibly diverse range of hotels, guesthouses and serviced apartments. The best bargains are often to be had in the luxury sector – many offer their rooms at knock-down prices.

Old City and around

Buddy Lodge $$$
265 Khaosan Rd, T02-629 4477, buddylodge.com.
Map: Bangkok, B2, p72.
One of the more upmarket options around the Khaosan Rd area and one of the first to use the now ubiquitous term 'boutique', Buddy Lodge deserves the title with rooms featuring modern interiors and chic fittings as well as a fridge and TV. There is also a restaurant, a coffee shop and a pool.

Phranakorn Nornlen Hotel $$$
46 Thewet soi 1, T02-628 8188, phranakorn-nornlen.com.
Map: Bangkok, B1, p72.
Airy Thai-style rooms with artistic design are as homely as an artfully crafted doll's house. Wooden shutters, a garden café, beautiful rooftop views and an intimate, relaxed atmosphere. The small team of amicable staff include an informative 'City Guide' who can help with bookings, etc. Cookery classes and other creative pursuits.

Lamphu House $$
75 Soi Rambutri, T02-629 5861, lamphuhouse.com.
Map: Bangkok, B2, p72.
Undoubtedly one of the best budget options on offer. Situated down a very quiet *soi*. Clean, modern, very pleasantly decorated rooms with a/c and very comfy beds, the superior rooms have a large balcony and are the best value. Great restaurant downstairs and an extremely professional spa on the roof terrace.

Tavee $$-$
83 Sri Ayutthaya Rd, Soi 14, T02-282 5983.
Map: Bangkok, B1, p72.
A quiet, relaxed, and respectable place with a small garden, restaurant and a number of fish tanks. Friendly management – a world away from the chaos of Khaosan Rd. The Tavee family keep the rooms and shared bathrooms immaculately clean and are a good source of information for travellers. Dorms are also available for ฿80 per night. This place has been operating since 1985 and has managed to maintain a very high standard.

Orchid House $
Rambutri St, T02-280 2619.
Map: Bangkok, B2, p72.
Orchid House is cosy, clean and safe with pretty interior touches in the rooms and communal areas. Both fan and a/c rooms with showers are available. The ground-floor terrace restaurant is a nice quiet spot for reading or people watching. Other services include internet café and travel agent.

East of the Old City

Metropolitan $$$$
27 South Sathorn Rd, T02- 625 3333, metropolitan.como.bz.
Map: Bangkok, F6, p72.
From its funky members/guest-only bar through to the beautiful, contemporary designer rooms and the awesome restaurants (**Glow** and **Cy'an**) this is one of Bangkok's hippest hotels.

Sheraton Grande Sukhumvit $$$$
250 Sukhumvit, T02-649 8888, luxurycollection.com/bangkok.
Map: Bangkok, H5, p72.
A superbly managed business and leisure hotel, the service, food and facilities are impeccable. The rooftop garden is an exotic delight and the spa offers some of the best massage in town. The **Rossini** and **Basil** restaurants are also top class. Great location and, if you can afford it, the best place to stay on Sukhumvit.

Atlanta $$$-$$
78 Sukhumvit Soi 2, T02-252 1650, theatlantahotel.bizland.com.
Map: Bangkok, G4, p72.
Basic a/c or fan-cooled rooms are available in this hotel, which appears to be the cheapest and

is certainly the most appealing hotel in the area at this price. It prides itself on its literary, peaceful atmosphere and is particularly suited for families, writers and dreamers. Large pool and children's pool, restaurant and 24-hour email available.

Charlie's House $$$-$$
Soi Saphan Khu, T02-679 8330, charlieshousethailand.com.
Map: Bangkok, G6, p72.
Helpful owners create a friendly atmosphere and the rooms are carpeted and very clean. This is probably the best of the budget bunch. There is a restaurant and coffee corner with good food at reasonable prices.

Sam's Lodge $$-$
28-28/1, 2nd floor, Sukhumvit 19, T02-253 2993, samslodge.com.
Map: Bangkok, H5, p72.
Budget accommodation with modern facilities and roof terrace, close to the Skytrain.

Smart Suites
Sukhumvit Soi 11,Bangkok 10110, T +662 254 6544, martsuites11.com
Suitable for short and long stay.

The hip option.

Eating

Bangkok is one of the greatest food cities on earth. You could spend a lifetime finding the best places to eat. Many restaurants, especially Thai ones, close early (2200-2230). Street food can be found across the city and a rice or noodle dish will cost ฿25-40 instead of a minimum of ฿50 in the restaurants.

The street food in **Chinatown** is some of the best in Thailand. You'll find everything from fresh lobster through to what can only be described as grilled pig's face. It's very cheap; look for the more popular places and dive in.

Old City & around

Travellers' food such as banana pancakes and muesli is available in the guesthouse/travellers' hotel areas. However, the Thai food sold along Khaosan Rd is some of the worst and least authentic in town, watered down to suit the tastebuds of unadventurous backpackers.

D'Rus $$
Khaosan Rd.
Open 0700-2400.
Map: Bangkok, B2, p72.
A typical big-screen sports and sofas Khaosan place, but the Thai/Western food is decent and cheap and the coffee is freshly brewed.

Bai Bau $
146 Rambutri St.
Map: Bangkok, B2, p72.
Tasty Thai food in a quiet corner; your best bet for a relaxed, authentic meal in a friendly environment. Good value.

Hua Seng Hong Restaurant $$
371-372 Yaowarat Rd, T02-222635.
Map: Bangkok, C4, p72.
The grimy exterior belies the fantastic restaurant within. Dim sum, noodles, duck and grilled pork are awesome.

The Canton House $
530 Yaowarat Rd, T02-221 3335.
Map: Bangkok, C5, p72.

This popular dim sum canteen is set on the main drag. The prices – ฿15 – for a plate of dim sum are legendary. the food is OK but nothing exceptional. The friendly atmosphere is however 100% authentic Chinatown.

East of the Old City

Cy'an $$$
In the Metropolitan Hotel, 27 South Sathorn Rd, T02-625 3333, metropolitan.como.bz.
Map: Bangkok, F6, p72.
With a menu concocted by one of Asia's leading chefs, Amanda Gale, Cy'an is a scintillating dining experience the like of which is not matched in the entire Thai capital. This is international cuisine of the highest order.

Rang Mahal $$$
In the Rembrandt Hotel, Sukhumvit Soi 18, T02-261 7107.
Map: Bangkok, H5, p72.
Some of the finest Indian food in town, award-winning and popular with the Indian

What the locals say

Escape the tourist trap of Khaosarn Road and head to Thanon Dinsor towards the City Hall for some real local food. Charming and lively, this street food paradise houses Mitr Go Yuan, the fantastic, friendly Chinese/Thai restaurant opened over 50 years ago, and Mon Nom Sod, the legendary milk and bread café guaranteed to send those with a sweet tooth into sweet, buttery dreams. With this food in your stomach you'll be the coolest kid on the block.

Warisara Sornpet, Bangkok resident

community. Spectacular views from the rooftop position, elegant and expensive.

Taling Pling $$$
60 Pan Rd, T02-236 4830.
Daily 1100-2200.
Map: Bangkok, D6, p72.
A favourite of locals, attracting a good mix of foreigners. Set in a comfortable converted house, serving up simple yet authentic dishes, decent desserts and offering a reasonable wine list.

Nasir al-Masri $$
4-6 Sukhumvit Soi Nana Nua, T02-253 5582.
Map: Bangkok, H4, p72.
Reputedly the best Arabic food in Bangkok, serving falafel, tabouleh, hummus. Frequented by lots of Arabs who come for a taste of home.

Anotai $
676/17 Soi Rama IX Hospital, T02-641 5366.
Vegetarian restaurant and bakery. Ingredients are sourced from its own organic farm. A creative menu with healthy Thai dishes and comfort food. Not in the most convenient location, but the food justifies the journey.

Ban Mai $
121 Sukhumvit Soi 22, Sub-Soi 2.
Map: Bangkok, H5, p72.
Thai food served amongst Thai-style decorations in an attractive house with a friendly atmosphere. Good value.

Bars & clubs
Bangkok has a fantastic nightlife. You can listen to decent jazz and blues or get into the latest overseas DJs. Check the listing magazines for information.

Old City & around

Brick Bar at Buddy Lodge
365 Khaosan Rd, T02-629 4477.
An upmarket and pleasant venue overlooking Khaosan Rd. Great live bands at night, open all day.

Gazebo
44 Chakrapong Rd, T02-629 0705.
Popular with both Thais and *farangs*. The open-air terrace is home to live bands, the indoor area plays dance music.

East of the Old City

Many bars can be found in the 'red-light' districts of Patpong and back *sois* off Sukhumvit Rd.

Bamboo Bar
In the Oriental Hotel, 48 Oriental Av, T02-236 0400.
Sun-Thu 1100-0100, Fri-Sat 1100-0200.
One of the best jazz venues in Bangkok, classy and cosy with good food and pricey drinks.

Bed Supper Club
26 Sukhumvit Soi 11, T02-651 3537, bedsupperclub.com.
Daily 2000-0200.
A futuristic white pod, filled with funky beats, awesome cocktails,

superb food, designer furniture and hordes of beautiful people.

Cheap Charlie's
1 Sukhumvit Soi 11.
Open 1500 until very late.
Very popular with expats, backpackers and locals. Lively, cheap and unpretentious open-air bar.

Q Bar
34 Sukhumvit Soi 11, T02-252 3274, qbarbangkok.com.
Housed in a modern building, it is the reincarnation of photographer David Jacobson's bar of the same name in Ho Chi Minh City.

Gay & lesbian
DJ Station
Silom Soi 2, dj-station.com.
Daily 2200-0200, ฿100.
The busiest and largest club on an already busy *soi*. Three floors of pumping beats and disco.

Freeman
Silom Soi 2.
Worth seeking out to find one of Bangkok's funniest *katoey* (ladyboy) cabarets. There's a dance floor on the top level.

Tip...

The hub of Bangkok's gay scene can be found among the clubs, bars and restaurants on Silom, Sois 2 and 4. Utopia Tours (utopia- tours.com) are specialists in organizing gay travel.

Shopping

Cinema

Bangkok cinemas are a great escape from the heat of the city. Prices can range from ฿100 to ฿500. Details of showings can be found in English-language newspapers and at movieseer.com. There are two international film festivals every year. Easily accessible cinemas with English soundtracks include **Siam Paragon Cine-plex** (Rama I Rd, T02-515555), **EGV** (6th floor, Siam Discovery Centre, Rama I Rd, T02-812 9999), **SFX Emporium** (Sukhumvit Soi 24, T02-260 9333) and **SFX Mahboonkrong** (MBK shopping centre, T02-260 9333). Bangkok's only independent art house cinema is **House** (houserama.com, T02-641 5177).

Muay Thai (Thai Boxing)

Thai boxing (muaythaionline.org) is both a sport and a means of self-defence. There are two main boxing stadiums in Bangkok.

Theatre

College Siam Thai Classical Dance and Restaurant Theatre
496 Sukhumvit Road, between Soi 22 and 24, T02-259 5128.
1930 and 2100 each evening.

Joe Louis Puppet Theatre
1875 Rama IV Rd, T02-252 9683.
Office open Mon-Fri 0930-2130, Sat and Sun 0100-2100. Shows daily at 1900-2045. Book before 1400. Tickets ฿900, ฿300 for children and free for under 7s.

Classical stage productions with puppets based on Thai masked dancers. Arrive by 1800 to take the tour of the puppet gallery.

National Theatre
Na Phrathat Rd, T02-221 4885, for programme.
Thai classical dramas, dancing and music on the last Friday of each month at 1730.

Patravadi Theatre
Soi Wat Rakhang, Thonburi, patravaditheatre.com, T02-412 7287.
An open-air theatre with classical and contemporary dance and innovative theatre.

The Thailand Cultural Centre
Thiam Ruam Mit Road, thaiculturalcenter.com, T02-247 0028 (ext 8 for English).
Performances from ballet and theatre groups as well as Bangkok Symphony Orchestra.

Lumpini
Rama IV Rd, near Lumpini Park, T02-251 4303.
Tue and Fri 1830, Sat 1700, 2030. Tickets cost up to and over ฿1500 for a ringside seat; cheaper seats cost about ฿500-800.

Rachdamnern Stadium
Rachdamnern Rd (near TAT office), T02-281 4205.
Monday, Wednesday and Thursday 1800-2230, 1830 and Saturday 1600 and 2000. Seats from ฿500-1500.

From flowers and fruit sold at energetic all-night markets through to original and fake Louis Vuitton, Bangkok has the lot.

Antiques

Jim Thompson's
Surawong Rd, jimthompson.com.
A range of antiques, wooden artefacts, furnishings and carpets.

L'Arcadia
12/2 Sukhumvit Soi 23.
Burmese antiques, beds, ceramics, doors, good quality and prices are fair.

Clothes & tailoring

Bangkok's tailors are skilled at copying anything. Always request two fittings, ask to see a finished garment, inspect it for stitching quality, ask for a price in writing and pay as small a deposit as possible.

Ambassador & Smart Fashion
28-28/1 Sukhumvit 19, T02-253 2993, ambassadorfashion.com.
Bespoke tailors. Free pick-up available from your hotel (call 02 255 4516).

Kai Boutique
187/1 Bangkok Cable Building, Thanon Rachdamri, kaiboutique.com.
This building is worth visiting for those interested in what the best designers in Thailand are doing. One of Bangkok's longest-standing high-fashion outlets.

Jewellery

Thailand has become the world's largest gem-cutting centre and Bangkok is an excellent place to buy both gems and jewellery. Always insist on a certificate of authenticity and a receipt. Avoid any taxi or tuk-tuk drivers who try to take you to a jewellery outlet.

Ban Mo, on Pahurat Rd, north of Memorial Bridge, is the centre of the gem business although there are shops in all the tourist areas particularly on Silom Rd near the intersection with Surasak Rd, eg **Rama Gems** (987 Silom Rd). **Uthai Gems** (28/7 Soi Ruam Rudi, off Ploenchit Rd, just east of Witthayu Rd) and **PJewellery** (9/292 Ramindra Rd, Anusawaree Bangkhan, T02-5221857) are recommended.

Markets

The markets in Bangkok are an excellent place to browse, take photos and pick up bargains.

Nakhon Kasem, known as the Thieves' Market, in the heart of Chinatown (see page 76) houses a number of 'antique' shops selling brassware, old electric fans and woodcarvings (bargaining is needed and don't expect everything to be genuine).

Pahurat Indian Market, a small slice of India in Thailand, with mounds of sarongs, batiks, buttons and bows.

Pak Khlong Market is a wholesale market selling fresh produce, orchids and cut flowers and is situated near the Memorial Bridge on Tri Phet Rd. An exciting place to visit at night.

Chatuchak Weekend Market

Just off Phahonyothin Rd.
Sat-Sun 0800-1800 (although some shops open at about 0700, some at about 0900), it's best to go early in the day or after 1500.
Skytrain to Mo Chit station or Chatuchak Park and Kampaeng Phet Metro stations.
Chatuchak is a huge conglomeration of 15,000 stallholders spread over an area of 14 ha selling virtually everything under the sun. There are antique stalls, basket stalls, textile sellers, carvers and

Activities & tours

Exploring the *khlongs*

One of the most enjoyable ways to see Bangkok is by boat – and particularly by the fast and noisy *hang yaaws*, or 'longtails', powerful, lean machines that roar around the river and the *khlongs* (canals) at breakneck speed. There are innumerable tours around the *khlongs* of Thonburi taking in a number of sights, which include the floating market, snake farm and Wat Arun. Boats launch from the various piers located along the east bank of the Chao Phraya River. The route skirts past laden rice barges, squatter communities on public land and houses overhanging the canals. On private tours the first stop is usually the Floating Market.

painters along with the usual array of fishmongers, vegetable hawkers, butchers and candlestick makers. Beware of pickpockets. The head office and information centre can be found opposite Gate 1 off Kampaengphet Rd. The clock tower serves as a good reference point should visitors become disoriented.

Shopping malls
Central World
Ratchaprasong intersection.
The latest addition to the mega shopping mall experience, with eating outlets and a cineplex.

Mah Boonkhrong Centre (MBK)
Corner of Phayathai and Rama I Rd.
A long established and downmarket mall packed full with bargains with countless small shops/stalls.

Siam Paragon
Rama I Rd, next to Siam Centre, siamparagon.co.th.
The undisputed holder of the title of most ostentatious shopping experience in town and home to genuine luxury brands.

Silk
Silk varies greatly in quality. Generally, the heavier the weight the more expensive the fabric. There are a number of specialist silk shops at the top of Surawong Rd (near Rama IV) and shops along the bottom half of Silom Rd (towards Charoen Krung) and in the Siam Centre on Rama I Rd.

Anita Thai Silk
294/4-5 Silom Rd.
Slightly more expensive than some, but the extensive range makes it worth a visit.

Jim Thompson's
Top of Surawong Rd, jimthompson.com.
Daily 0900-2100.
Famous-but-expensive silk shop with the best selection.

Boat tours
Either book a tour at your hotel or go to one of the piers and organize your own trip. The most frequented piers are located between the Oriental Hotel and the Grand Palace, or under Taksin Bridge (which marks the end of the Skytrain line). Organizing your own trip gives greater freedom to stop and start when the mood takes you. It is best to go in the morning (0700).

Cookery courses
Blue Elephant
233 Thanon Sathorn Tai, Bangrak, T02-673 9353. blueelephant.com.
One of the most famous cooking schools with an innovative menu. A 1-day course is ฿2800.

May Kaidee
111 Tanao Rd, T02-281 7137. may kaidee.com.
A vegetarian restaurant with its own veggie cooking school. At ฿1200 for 10 dishes it's also one of the best budget options.

asian trails

Journey through lost kingdoms and let Asian Trails be your guide.

Massage

Wat Pho

The centre is located at the back of the wat, on the opposite side from the entrance (see main listing, page 74), T02-221 2974, watpho.com.

The school offers body massage with or without herbs and foot massage. The service is available from 0800-1700 and costs from ฿250 for a 30-minute body massage to ฿400 for a 1-hour body massage with herbal compress. A foot massage is ฿250 for 45 minutes. For Westerners wishing to learn the art of traditional Thai massage, special 30-hour courses can be taken for ฿8500.

Tour operators

Asian Trails Ltd

9th floor, SG Tower, 161/1 Soi Mahadlek , Luang 3, Rajdamri Rd, Bangkok, T66-2626 2000, asiantrails.info.
Southeast Asia specialist.

Bangkok Tourist Bureau

17/1 Phra Arthit Rd, under Phra Pinklao Bridge, T02-225 7612, bangkoktourist.com.
Daily 0900-1900.
Offers every imaginable tour of Bangkok by river, bike and even bus. Their white booths are found in popular tourist areas and are easy to spot. Knowledgeable and reliable.

Real Asia

T02-712 9301, realasia.net.
Cycling and walking tours around the city's 'greenbelt' including the less-explored rural riverside areas of Bang Kra Jao and Phra Padaeng.

Contents

Eastern Coast

Detail from the dragon-head sculpture in the Chinese temple, Pattaya.

Introduction

Head east from Bangkok into a region that blends trashy gaudiness and gorgeous beaches. Add to the mix some remote forested islands and oddball idiosyncrasy and you won't look back.

On the enigmatic island of Koh Si Chang there are weird abandoned palaces, sacred Chinese temples and platoons of monkeys. Next stop is Pattaya. Even a mere utterance of this name sends anti-tourism activists apoplectic. Polluted waters and bad planning have done little to endear Pattaya to the more discerning traveller but amid the neon and fleshpots, it has some of the best hotels in the country and there is no better place in Southeast Asia to dig ironic kitsch.

A little further east is Koh Samet, a national marine park. Samet used to be a sleepy island surrounded by azure seas and crested with crystalline beaches. These days it has been transformed into the weekend destination of choice for Bangkok's younger, trendier and wealthier crowd. As for Koh Chang: the traveller's idyll of isolated, white-sand beaches secreted away from the machinations of contemporary consumer society is quickly disappearing. Yet, if you look hard enough, there are still some wonderful spots to lounge about, losing yourself in the alluring sunsets, swimming in the calm, clear waters. Koh Chang's interior is also largely untouched, filled with waterfalls, jungle tracks and a colourful, noisy population of tropical birds and forest beasties.

What to see in...

...a weekend
You'll probably need at least a weekend to appreciate any of the Eastern Coast's charms with **Koh Si Chang** and **Koh Samet** both making for a perfect short break. **Jomtien Beach** near **Pattaya** provides some relief from the latter's more raucous charms and is popular with Thai families.

...a week or more
Koh Chang is the Eastern Coast's quintessential beach hammock hangout and is now geared to providing one or two week long holidays. Spend longer and you'll get a chance to explore the even remoter islands of **Kohs Kood** and **Mak**.

Around the region

Eastern Coast to Pattaya

Head down the coast east from Bangkok and you'll find trashy gaudiness, some decent beaches and oddball idiosyncrasy. Enigmatic Koh Si Chang is home to weird abandoned palaces, sacred Chinese temples and platoons of monkeys. The notorious fleshpots of Pattaya may recommend little to travellers eager to experience local culture, but this place is still distinctively Thai – right the way down to the *katoey* (transexual or 'ladyboy') cabarets.

Koh Si Chang

Si Chang's famous oversized tuk-tuks will greet you on arrival – it costs ฿50-100 to get around the island though most accommodation is within walking distance. For further information on Si Chang see also ko-sichang.com.

The nearest island getaway to Bangkok, Koh Si Chang has thankfully never made it on to most people's travel itineraries and is one of those places that had a moment in the spotlight – King Rama V built a palace here – and then history moved on. It does make for an entertaining, idiosyncratic short break and is a popular spot for weekenders from the capital. At the northern edge of the town, set up on a hill overlooking the town, the **Chaw Por Khaw Yai** Chinese temple is an odd assortment of decorated shrines and caves. From here there are great views of the island and this is a very important temple for Thailand's Chinese community. On the east coast – you might see monkeys here – are the ruins of Rama V's palace. Abandoned in 1893 when the French took control of the island during a confrontation with the Thais, not much remains though what does has a peculiarly eerie quality. The island also has a number of beaches with reasonable swimming and snorkelling. The quietest beach with the best coral and swimming is **Tham Phang** on the western side of the island.

Pattaya by night.

Pattaya

Brash, brazen and completely over the top, whatever you feel about Pattaya, it will certainly leave an impression. These days it is almost impossible to imagine its origins as a sleepy fishing village before the US Navy set up at nearby Sattahip (40 km further down the coast) during the Vietnam War and turned it into an R & R centre for US forces. As the war in Vietnam escalated, so the influx of GIs grew and Pattaya responded enthusiastically. Given these roots, it is hardly surprising that Pattaya's stock in trade is sex tourism and at any one time, about 4,000 girls are touting for work around the many bars and restaurants.

The official line on Pattaya is that it is going out of its way to promote itself as a 'family' resort. To be fair some of this has paid off and there are some excellent hotels and resorts here and plenty of top-notch food. Yet this emphasis on wholesome family fun is still hard to reconcile with reality. The busiest and noisiest area is at the southern end of town along what is now known as '**Walking Street**'. It's here that you'll find the highest concentration of bars, brothels, pole-dancers, ladyboys and drunken sexpats. Many people find this aspect of Pattaya repugnant.

Jomtien beach.

Surprisingly there's still a reasonable beach stretching along Pattaya Bay and the huge efforts to reduce water pollution have been largely successful. Pattaya is also justifiably popular with water sports lovers: there is sailing, parasailing, windsurfing, ski-boating, snorkelling, deep-sea fishing and some excellent scuba-diving.

Jomtien Beach

Set on a bay a little south of the main centre, Jomtien Beach offers a different face of Pattaya. Some gaudier elements still hold sway closer to Pattaya Bay but the further south you head the more presentable it becomes. Cute, mid-range, boutique hotels appear, each with their own laid-back bar and restaurant. At the far end – the beach here is about 4 km long – it becomes decidedly tranquil. If you have time, take a trip up the 240-m **Pattaya Park Tower** (Jomtien headland, T038-251201, ฿200) as it provides spectacular views.

Around Pattaya

Day trips can be taken to some of the sights that have sprung up around Pattaya. **Siriporn Orchid Farm** (235/14 Moo 5, Tambon Nong Prue,

T038-429013, daily 0800-1700) displays an array of the specimens, some of which are for sale. **Mini Siam** (T038-421628, daily 0700-2200) is a cultural and historical park where 80 of Thailand's most famous 'sights' – including Wat Phra Kaeo and the Bridge over the River Kwai – are recreated at a scale of 1:25. Mini Siam lies 3 km north of Pattaya Beach, on the Sukhumvit highway (Route 3) at the km 143 marker. The **Nong Nooch Tropical Garden** (T038-429321, daily 0900-1800, ฿20) is a 200-ha park containing immaculate gardens with lakes (and boating), an orchid farm, family zoo, Thai handicraft demonstrations and a thrice-daily (1015, 1500 and 1545) 'cultural spectacular' with Thai dancing, Thai boxing and an elephant show. The garden is 15 minutes from Pattaya town, 3 km off the main road, at the km 163 marker.

The island of **Koh Larn**, a short hop from the main Pattaya pier (boats depart at 0930 and 1130, returning at 1600, 45 mins, ฿250), offers a decent respite from the intense pace of Pattaya. There is a place to stay here (see page 99) and there's some decent snorkelling and scuba-diving.

Koh Samet.

Koh Samet

A 6-km-long, lozenge-shaped island sited in a national park, rimmed with stunning beaches and lapped by azure seas, Koh Samet is just a short boat trip from the mainland. Over the years it has transformed from the perfect Bangkok getaway into a noisy spot for weekending Thai students. It can still be a charming place and the beaches are gorgeous but if you desire quiet moments to absorb the stunning sunrises and sunsets then arrive mid-week – at that time accommodation is cheaper as well. The island is also one of the driest places in Thailand (1350 mm rain per year) and a good place to pitch up during the rainy season.

Around the island

There has been a settlement on Koh Samet for many years; junks from China used to anchor here to be checked before the authorities would allow them to sail over the sandbar at the mouth of the Chao Phraya River and north to Bangkok. It is possible to explore Koh Samet on foot though take plenty of water – the beach walk from end to end is a good adventure.

A fishy tale

The famous 19th-century Thai romantic poet Sunthorn Phu retired to Koh Samet and, suitably inspired, proceeded to write his finest work, the epic *Phra Aphaimani*. The poem recounts the story of a prince, banished by his father to live with a sea-dwelling, broken-hearted giantess. Escaping to Koh Samet with the help of a mermaid, the prince kills the pursuing giant with his magic flute and marries the mermaid.

The beaches

The northernmost is **Ao Klong**, a stretch of sand that runs to the west of the Na Dan Pier – there are a few 'floating' guesthouses and seafood restaurants built on wooden stilts in the bay. **Hat Sai Kaew** (Diamond or White-Sand Beach) is a 10-minute walk southeast from Na Dan Pier, and remains the most popular place to stay. This is still a beautiful spot, even if it has been disfigured by uncontrolled development. Despite the crowded, bustling atmosphere, the beach remains clean and is sandy at the bottom. Just south along the coast from Hat Sai Kaew is **Ao Hin Khok** while a short distance further south still is **Ao Phai**, which is less developed and more peaceful. Ao Phai is home to where Koh Samet's one and only sight is to be found: a rather tatty statue depicting the tale of Phra Aphaimani (see box, opposite). About 2 km from Ao Phai, past the smaller Ao Tubtim, Ao Nuan and Ao Cho, is **Ao Vong Duen**. This crescent-shaped bay has a number of more upmarket resort developments and a good range of facilities: water-skiing, diving, boat trips, and windsurfing. Continuing south is **Ao Thian**, **Ao Wai** and **Ao Kiu NaNok**. These are the most peaceful locations on Koh Samet and the island's finest coral is also found off the southern tip of the island. **Ao Phrao** (Paradise Beach), 2 km from Sai Kaew, is the only beach on the west side of the island.

Koh Chang & around

Koh Chang, Thailand's second-largest island, is part of a national marine park that includes 50-odd islands and islets covering 650 sq km. Despite the 'protection' that its national park status should offer, Koh Chang is developing rapidly, with resorts and bungalows springing up along its shores. Yet it is still one of Thailand's last tropical island idylls – at least of any size – to be developed and it supports excellent beaches, sea, coral and diving. There are treks, waterfalls, rivers and pools, villages, mangroves, three peaks of over 700 m, and a rich variety of wildlife. Koh Chang also forms the fulcrum of the Koh Chang National Park – an archipelago of dozens of smaller islands that stretch to the south. These outlying islands have developed at a much slower rate than Koh Chang, though the likes of Koh Kood are now figuring in the plans of travellers. If you do visit the smaller islands be very aware of your impact on them – some are becoming overwhelmed.

As you set sail from the mainland across the glittering seas, Koh Chang (Elephant Island), covered in thick, verdant forest and with a vivid, sweeping skyline, rises up to meet you. This 40-km-long and 16-km-wide island is teeming with wildlife, rustic appeal and wonderful beaches that have long attracted the more adventurous traveller.

Koh Chang.

Tip...

While the waters around Koh Chang are clear, there have been some reports of deterioration in water quality connected with coastal gem mining on the mainland. Nonetheless, hard and especially soft corals are abundant. Fish are less numerous and varied than on the other side of the Gulf of Thailand or in the Andaman Sea. During the wet season visibility is very poor, due to high seas, which also makes diving dangerous. The months between November and March are best for diving. Diving is better in the waters to the south of the island.

Things, however, are changing. Koh Chang has now been earmarked as Thailand's next big destination. Hotel chains and tour operators are moving in and the beaches are now almost entirely colonized by Thai and European package tourists. It's not all upmarket; odious 'monkey schools' (where monkeys are forced to perform degrading tricks) and that definitive marker of tourist saturation, the 'girly bar', have now made their home on Koh Chang. Any recent visitor has to work harder to find the most rewarding parts of the island.

For walkers, there is a path crossing the middle of the island from Ban Khlong Phrao to Than Ma Yom but it is a strenuous day-long hike and locals recommend taking a guide. Khlong Son, near the northern tip, is the island's largest settlement. Even so, there's not much here: a health clinic, a few small noodle shops, a monastery, post office and school. There are several places claiming to be official tourist information offices – all are agents trying to get you to buy day trips.

Ship near the pier at Bang Bao village.

Tip…

Best time to visit is November to May. Koh Chang is a wet island with an annual rainfall of over 3000 mm (the wettest month is August). Mosquitoes (carrying malaria) and sandflies are a problem on Koh Chang and surrounding islands, so repellent and anti-malarials are essential. Take a net if camping.

Trat

The best route to Koh Chang is via Trat, a pleasant enough-town that is worth a day or two if only to plan your next move. The closest mainland town of any size to both Koh Chang and the nearby Cambodian border, Trat is a gem centre that has flourished as a host to cross-border commerce. Most people visit Trat en route to Koh Chang, not staying any longer than they need to catch a bus or boat out. If you decide to stay longer you'll have the chance to sample some excellent guesthouses, a bustling covered market and **Wat Buppharam** (Wat Plai Klong), located 2 km west of town, which dates from the late Ayutthaya period and is notable for its wooden *viharn* (assembly hall).

A great source of local information is the Tratosphere bookshop (23 Rimklong Soi) where the French- and English-speaking owner is exceptionally helpful and knowledgeable about everything to do with Trat, Koh Chang and the surrounding islands. Stopping off here is advisable to get up to the minute info before heading on to the islands.

The beaches

Koh Chang's best beaches are on the western side of the island – **Hat Sai Kaew** (White Sand) and **Hat Khlong Phrao** – and, on the southern coast – **Hat Bang Bao**. Hat Khlong Phrao, 5 km south of Hat Sai Kaew, and 2 km long, is spread out each side of the mouth of the Khlong Phrao canal and is a beautiful beach but the water tends to be very shallow. At **Ao Khlong Makok** there is almost no beach at high tide and just a couple of bungalow operations that are virtually deserted in the low season. **Ao Kai Bae** is the southernmost beach on the west coast. It is beautiful but swimming is tricky as the water is very shallow and covered with rocks and dead coral.

Haad Tha Nam (Lonely Beach) is an attractive stretch of coastline and much quieter and more relaxed than the more accessible northern stretches. However, most of the well-run, cheap operations have been pushed out to be replaced with awful bungalows or dull generic resorts.

Ao Bang Bao and **Ao Bai Bin** are lovely beaches on the south coast of the island. The bay dries out at low tide and is virtually inaccessible in the low season when accommodation tends to shut down.

Although there is a scattering of bungalows on the east coast, few people choose to stay here. The only beach is at **Sai Thong**.

Inland

Than Ma Yom Waterfall is on the east side of the island. King Chulalongkorn (Rama V) visited this waterfall on no fewer than six occasions at the end of the 19th century, so it counts as an impressive one (in fact there are three falls). To prove the point, the king carved his initials (or had them carved) on a stone to mark one of his visits. Rama VI and VII also visited the falls, although it seems that they didn't get quite so far – they left their initials inscribed on stones at the nearest of the falls. The falls are accessible from either Ban Dan Mai or Thaan Ma Yom, both on the east coast. Getting to the first of the cascades involves a walk of an hour; it is around 4 km to the furthest of the three falls.

Khlong Phu Falls, at **Ao Khlong Phrao**, are perhaps even more beautiful than Than Ma Yom. There is a good pool here for swimming as well as a restaurant and some bungalows. Because this is a national park it is also possible to camp. To get here, it's a 10-minute taxi or motorbike ride from Hat Sai Kaew; you can also travel to it from the road by elephant for ฿200 or for free by walking just 3 km.

Koh Chang's **forest** is one of the most species-rich in the country and while the island's coast may be undergoing development, the rugged, mountainous interior is still largely inaccessible and covered with virgin rainforest (around 70% of the island is said to be forested). There is a good population of birds, including parrots, sunbirds, hornbills and trogons, as well as Koh Chang's well-known population of wild boar, although the chances of seeing any are slim. It is advisable, however, to take a guide for exploring – Jungle Way bungalows (see page 101) organizes guided hikes for ฿450 including lunch.

Outlying islands

Koh Kood Speedboats leave daily 0800, 0830 and 0900 (90 mins, ฿550) from Dankao pier near Trat. Slow boats also depart from the pier, daily 1000 (5 hrs, ฿300). There are also some speedboat connections with Chang though these vary annually.

Koh Mak Boats leave daily 0930, 1000, 1400, 1600 (฿450) from Klom Long Chumporn pier in Laem Ngop. Times are all for high season (Nov-Mar) – expect a reduced schedule at other times.

The next largest island after Koh Chang, **Koh Kood** has lovely beaches, especially on the west side, and a number of small fishing villages linked by dirt roads. So far it has managed to escape the ravages of development; there aren't any 7-Elevens, banks or girly bars, making this an ideal place to escape and relax. There is an impressive waterfall and the coral is also said to be good.

Koh Mak is the third largest island in the archipelago, is privately owned by a few wealthy local families and a little over half of the island has been cleared for coconut plantations. But there is still a reasonable area of forest and the coral is also good. The best beach is on the northwest shore. It is said that many of the prime pieces of shorefront have been sold to Bangkok-based developers, so it remains to be seen what happens to Koh Mak.

The remaining islands in the national park are tiny, with most home to one or two resorts that are only open for a few months a year. Koh Kham is a tiny island that is well known for its swallows' nests and turtle eggs, as well as good coral and rock formations for divers. Boats leave from Laem Ngop (3½ hrs, ฿150). Koh Ngam, two hours from Laem Ngop by the resort boat, is a very small island with lush vegetation and beautiful beaches. It has two upmarket resorts. Koh Whai has two resorts but these are better value than those at Koh Ngam. There's a daily ferry from Laem Ngop at 0800, returning at 1500 (฿130). During high season, when the seas are calmer and visibility greater, many of the more sophisticated bungalow operations on Koh Chang also organize day trips to the mostly uninhabited islands of Koh Lao Ya, Koh Phrao, Koh Khlum, Koh Kra Dad (which has exceptionally beautiful beaches and lush vegetation) and Koh Rayang Nok.

Chantaburi

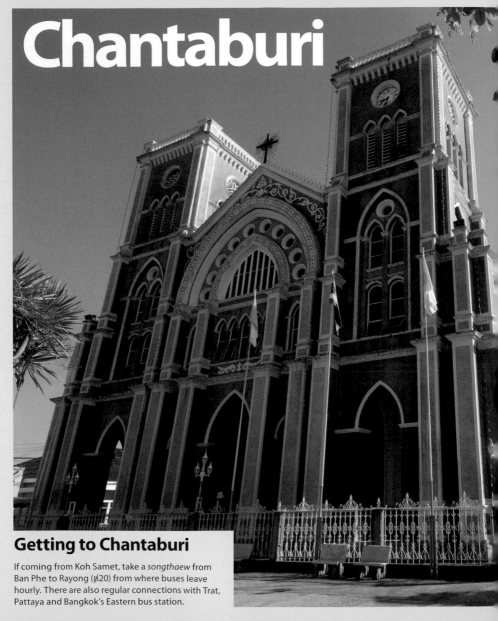

Getting to Chantaburi

If coming from Koh Samet, take a *songthaew* from Ban Phe to Rayong (฿20) from where buses leave hourly. There are also regular connections with Trat, Pattaya and Bangkok's Eastern bus station.

Head east towards Koh Chang from either Bangkok or Pattaya and you'll have to pass through one of Thailand's most famous towns, Chantaburi. Renowned for its trade in precious stones – Chantaburi's gem traders are known for being particularly hardnosed – and superb durian, a strong smelling and tasting, giant, prickly fruit that is considered a delicacy by many Thais, Chantaburi is also famed for its large population of ethnic Vietnamese, a strong Catholic presence, well-preserved traditional shophouses and excellent restaurants. It is easily possible to stop off in Chantaburi for a few hours en route down the coast but an overnight stay makes for a nice short break.

Muang Chan – as it is locally known – has a large Chinese and Vietnamese population, lending the town an atmospheric run of narrower streets, shuttered wooden shophouses, Chinese temples and an industrious air. This atmosphere is most palpable along **Rim Nam** or **Sukhaphiban Road**. The French-style **Catholic Cathedral of the Immaculate Conception** was built in 1880 and is the largest church in Thailand. Architecturally uninspiring, it is significant for its very presence. The cathedral was built to serve the many Vietnamese Catholics who fled their homeland and settled here. The Vietnamese part of town is north of the cathedral, on the opposite side of the river.

The **gem market** can be found on Si Chan and Thetsaban roads all day on Fridays and Saturdays, and on Sunday mornings. Chantaburi has built its wealth on rubies and sapphires with many of the gem mines being developed during the 19th century by Shan people from Burma, who are thought to be among the best miners in the world. Be very careful if you're thinking of buying gems or precious stones (see box, page 61).

Left: The Catholic Cathedral of the Immaculate Conception.
Right: Saan Chao Pho Laem Sing Chinese temple.

Sleeping & eating

Maneechan River Resort and Sport Club $$$
110 Moo 11 Plubpla Rd, T039-343777, maneechanresort.com.
Good value, leafy resort-style hotel with an excellent range of amenities including pool and decent sports facilities. Comfy rooms come with a/c, en suite and cable TV. Excellent pool, tasty Thai food and free Wi-Fi. Slightly outside the town centre.

Meun-ban ('Homely' restaurant) $$
Saritdet Rd, next to the bus terminal.
Probably the best mid-range restaurant in town offering a multitude of Thai dishes (including a huge vegetarian selection). The owners speak good English and are a helpful source of local information. It is also in an ideal location if you arrive tired and hungry after a long bus journey and need some refreshment.

Sleeping

There's a huge range of sleeping options along the Eastern Coast with everything from luxurious 5-star hotels through to simple thatched huts. What does mark it out is the cost: Koh Samet is expensive throughout the year – try to come mid-week – Koh Chang is pricey in high season while there are few budget options available in Pattaya.

Eastern Coast to Pattaya

Koh Si Chang
Rim Talay $$$-$$
250 m north of entrance to Rama V Palace, T038-216116.
A mix of rooms and eccentric bungalow/barge affairs (for up to seven people) that come complete with sea views. All rooms have TV, a/c and are en suite – the cheapest ones have cold water only. Book ahead.

Sichang View Resort $$
West coast of island, T038-216210.
Great location set along the Khao Khaad cliffs in a remote corner of the island. Nice gardens make this a great spot for sundowners – huge rooms are well kept with en suite facilities, a/c and TVs. Good food too.

Sripitsanu Bungalows $$-$
Hat Tham, T038-216024.
A range of rooms and bungalows built into the cliff-face overlooking the sea, not far from Hat Tham. The new

management, who speak little English, are settling into this bungalow operation. You'll often see troops of monkeys passing by here and the location has a remote feel.

Pattaya
Dusit Thani Pattaya $$$$-$$$
240/2 Beach Rd (north end), T038-425611, dusit.com.
An excellent hotel with good service and comprehensive facilities including: health club, tennis, children's pools, table tennis, water sports and shopping arcade.

Diana Inn $$-$
216/6-9 Pattaya 2 Rd, between Sois 11 and 12, Naklua, T038-429675, dianapattaya.co.th.
Set on a busy road but the rooms have good facilities for the price. This modern, well-run, friendly and popular hotel has a/c, restaurant and pool.

Jomtien Beach
Sheraton Pattaya Resort $$$$
437 Phra Tamnak Rd, T038-259888, sheraton.com/pattaya.
Superb luxury resort in a great location perched up on the cliffs, which adds fantastic views to the stunning rooms and bungalows. Possibly the best luxury resort in town, there is an outstanding spa and great views, restaurants, and huge pool area. All the trimmings you'd expect in such a top-end establishment.

Birds and Bees Resort $$$$-$$$
366/11 Moo 12 Phra Tamnak Rd, T038-250556, cabbagesandcondoms.co.th.
Run by **Cabbages and Condoms**, Thailand's famous AIDs awareness organization, this is a charming and wonderful resort with pool, gardens, children's play area and awesome cliff-top location – a path leads to a secluded beach. It

The Lagoon pool at the Dusit Thani Pattaya hotel.

is irreverent with subversive flourishes (check the paths to Communism and Capitalism that both end up in the same place – by a pond filled with frantic, hungry fish that are called 'Greedy Politicians'). It is slightly pricey, though cheaper in low season. The suites offer best value with balcony jacuzzis and sea views.

Sarita Chalet and Spa $$$$-$$$
279/373 Jomtien Beach Rd, T038-233952, saritachalet.com.
Relaxed hotel in nice part of Jomtien. Stylish rooms, all en suite, with a/c, TV and breakfast included. There's a small pool and spa. Some rooms face the beach. Often booked out.

Jomtien Twelve $$$-$$
240/13 Moo 12, Jomtien Beach Rd, T038-756865, jomtientwelve.com.
Great little hotel right on the beach road in a very quiet part of Jomtien – perfect for a short weekend break. All rooms are well designed with nice touches and an eye for the aesthetic. All have en suite facilities, full cable TV and a/c, and the ones at the front have decent-sized beach-facing balconies. Breakfast included. The best deal on this stretch of beach.

Koh Larn Resort $
Office at 183 Soi Post Office, Pattaya, T08-1996 3942 (mob).
Decent bungalows set alongside a nice beach. Price includes the boat fare and transfer to the accommodation. Watch out for annoying jet-skiers.

Ao Phrao Resort and Le Vimarn $$$$
Ao Phrao, T02-438 9771, kohsametaoprao.com and kohsametlevimarn.com.
Run by the same company, both offer excellent luxurious and expensive accommodation. Ao Phrao has a family atmosphere while Le Vimarn is more stylish and comes complete with an excellent spa. Both resorts run their own boat service from Ban Phe, where they have an office. The beach here is much quieter than on the other side of the island but isn't as pretty.

Sai Kaew Beach Resort $$$$
kohsametsaikaew.com, Hat Sai Kaew.
A wide range of neat, airy, cabins, some facing on to the beach. It also has a set of beautiful, de luxe bungalows in a tranquil spot just over the headland. All have a/c and cable TV. Well-appointed with nice designer flourishes and bright interiors.

Vongduern Villa $$$$-$$
Ao Vong Duen, T038-644260, vongduernvilla.com.
One of the better run places on the island. Cabins are spread out through the trees and face on to the quieter end of this busy beach. The more expensive ones come with DVD players, all have hot water, TVs and a/c.

Jep's Bungalow and Restaurant $$$$-$
Ao Hin Khok , T038-644112, jepbungalow.com.
Good value rooms that come in a wide range of prices and options (a/c, fan etc), some set directly on the beach. All are clean and well-tended. The restaurant has a large range of tasty dishes. Booking ahead is essential.

Samet Villa Resort $$$-$
Ao Wai, bookable through the boat Phra Aphai at Ban Phe T08-1321 1284 (mob).
The only accommodation on this beach – good bungalows but quite expensive. The location is peaceful and attractive, but lacks places to sit with sea views.

Lost Resort $$-$
Ao Hin Khok, T038-644041, thelostresort.net.
Set by the road just behind the beach, this is one of Samet's only proper guesthouses. Friendly English owner but the rooms – some with a/c and hot water – look a bit tired. One of the best budget options on the island.

Samet Villa $$-$
Ao Phai, T038-644094,
F038-644093.
This clean and friendly Swiss-run establishment offers some of the best-value accommodation on Samet, all rooms with fans and attached bathrooms. It organizes a number of trips and excursions to neighbouring islands and rents out snorkelling equipment.

Lung Dam Hut $
Ao Thian, T038-651810.
There are basic huts with grass roofs, or you try their treehouse just a few feet from the sea. Only some huts have fans, some have own bath. Friendly - the beach here can be quiet and relaxed.

Koh Chang & around

Trat
Basar $
87 Thana Charoen Rd,
T039-523247.
Beautifully restored teak house with a modern, funky touch. All rooms have bathroom and mosquito net. There's a small restaurant on the ground floor.

Ban Jai Dee $
Chaimongkon Rd, T039-520678.
The best of the bunch, with very friendly English-speaking owners. The cute rooms, complete with a few pleasing touches of contemporary Thai design, have fans and shared bathrooms. This is an excellent budget guesthouse.

Koh Chang
Rapid development means the list below may date quickly. The best source of information is at the Tratosphere bookshop in Trat. Prices rise in December and January. Some accommodation closes during low season.

Aana Resort & Spa $$$$
Hat Khlong Phrao, 19/2 Moo 4,
T09-551539, aanaresort.com.
Set back quite a distance from the beach. The most interesting style of accommodation at this luxury resort and spa are the villa rooms. Built on stilts, the individual huts are connected by elevated wooden walkways. All rooms have a/c, TV, DVD player and fridge. There are two pools and a restaurant that overlooks the river. A boat transfers guests to the beach.

Aiyapura Resort & Spa $$$$
Ao Khlong Son, T039-555111,
aiyapura.com.
Luxurious and very expensive development of huge villas built into a hillside that offers great views. Nicely shaded with trees, the villas are well furnished but not particularly elegant. Pool and all the other facilities you'd expect for the price.

Amari Emerald Cove $$$$
T039-552000, T02-255 2588
(reservations), amari.com.
The island's first 5-star resort has wonderful rooms, great restaurants (the best veggie selection on the island) and all the amenities you'd expect.

Nirvana $$$$
Ao Bai Bin, 12/4 Moo 1, T039-558
0614, nirvanakohchang.com.
On a secluded part of the beach, this hotel is recommended for its peaceful location. There are large, well-appointed rooms with somewhat chunky furniture. Both fresh-water and salt-water swimming pools available.

Koh Chang Kacha Resort $$$$-$$$
88-89 Moo 4, Hat Sai Kaew,
T039-551223,
kohchangkacha.com.
Exceptionally well designed villas and bungalows set in a luscious garden with a beautiful pool. De luxe villas have huge baths. The friendly management makes a stay here recommended.

Mac Bungalow $$$$-$$$
T081-864 6463 (mob).
A very popular centrally located resort with some hotel rooms available in addition to the bungalows. Possibly overpriced. The restaurant is probably the best on the beach and has fantastic barbecues and breakfasts.

Bang Bao Sea Hut $$$
28 Moo 1, Ao Bang Bao,
T081-285 0570.
Stunning location at the end of
the pier, these spacious wooden
huts are on stilts on the water.
A/c, TV, fridge and balcony. Prices
include breakfast.

Siam Bay Resort $$$
Southern end of beach,
Ao Kai Bae, T081-859 5529,
siambayresort.in.th.
Spacious modern bungalows
with TV, a/c and sea view.
Located in a secluded spot at the
foot of jungle-covered cliffs,
there is a swimming pool and
restaurant.

Boutique Resort
and Spa $$$-$$
T02-325 0927,
boutiqueresortandhealthspa.com.
Brilliant pixie-like huts with
beautiful interiors, a/c, TV and en
suite facilities. A health spa is
attached where you can
fine-tune your yoga. A short walk
takes you to the beach.

Warapura Resort $$$-$
T081-824 4177.
Swish and modern, the sea-view
bungalows have a lounge area,
equipped with a flatscreen TV
and a huge balcony right on the
water's edge. New cheaper
cottages with fans have been
built a little way back from the
sea. There's no sandy beach here;
that's a 10-minute walk away.

Kachapura $$-$
40/20 Moo 1, T086-050 0754,
kachapura.com.
These bungalows, set in a
landscaped garden, are
incredible value. A/c or fan, they
come with roofless bathrooms.
The beach is a 5-minute walk.

Rock Inn $$-$
4/7 Moo 1, Bai Lan Bay,
T039-558126, gerhard@
rockinn-kohchang.com.
These huts, with bathroom and
fan, are set in a nice garden
about 5 minutes' walk from a
sandy beach. They are all
individually designed and have
lots of character. There is a
restaurant serving good quality
Thai and Western food.

Jungle Way $
2 km from the coastal road into
the interior (there's a big sign in
Khlong Son pointing the way),
T089-247 3161, jungleway.com.
Closed Jun-Sep.
Simple bungalows in pretty
jungle location, next to stream.
Run by an English/Thai couple.
Yoga and reiki courses available.

Paradise Cottage $
104/1 Moo 1, T039-558121,
y_yinggg@hotmail.com.
Laid-back vibe, with plenty of
chill-out areas. There is internet, a
bar and a restaurant. The
bungalows (fan only) are basic
but well designed and have been
built using natural materials. On a
rocky part of the beach.

Tonsai Home $
T089-895 7229 (mob).
Tastefully designed wooden
bungalows with fan, mosquito
net and bathroom. Set back from
the road in a small garden, a
2-minute walk from the beach.
Best of the cheap options. Also
has a great restaurant.

Koh Kood
Koh Kood Resort & Spa $$$
45 Moo 5, Ao Bang Bao,
T01-829 7751,
kohkoodresortandspa.com.
Spacious wooden bungalows in
a tropical garden that leads to a
secluded beach. All the
bungalows have mosquito nets,
a/c and a huge bathroom.

Mangrove Bungalows $$
Further along the road from
Mark House Bungalows (see
below), Ao Klong Chao.
About a 5-minute walk behind
the beach, these clean a/c and
fan bungalows overlook the
mangroves of the Klong Jao
River. The restaurant serves good
Thai and Western food and the
price includes breakfast. There
are kayaks for rent so you can
explore the river.

Mark House Bungalows $$
43/4 Moo 2, Ao Klong Chao,
T086-133 0402,
markhousebungalow.com.
These comfortable and clean
wooden bungalows, fan and a/c,
are a 5-minute walk from the
beach. Set in a small garden.

Eating

Happy Days Guesthouse & Restaurant $$-$
Next to the post office, Ao Klong Chao, 1-min walk from beach, T087-144 5945, kaikohkood@ yahoo.com.
Spotlessly clean rooms, all with bathroom, fan and a/c. There are two family bungalows. The extremely helpful and knowledgeable owners speak English, Thai and German. Motorbikes available for hire (฿300).

Baan Klong Jao Homestay $$-$
Next to Mark House Bungalows, Ao Klong Chao, T087-075 0943.
Clean and homely a/c and fan rooms, with shared bathroom. This is a traditional Thai teak house on stilts overlooking the river. The Thai food in the restaurant is recommended.

Ngamkho Resort $
Next to Hindard Resort, Ao Ngam Kho, T08-1825 7076, kohkood-ngamkho.com.
Beautiful huts made of natural materials on a gentle slope leading to the beach. All bungalows have a mosquito net, hammock, bathroom and fan. Exceptional value.

Koh Mak
Ban Laem Chan $$$$-$$$
T08-1914 2593 (mob).
Consisting of seven wooden cottages with sea views, attached bathrooms and 'club house', this resort is aimed mainly at Thai weekenders on package deals. Walk-in rates are certainly overpriced.

TK Hut Bungalow $$-$
T087-134 8435.
Affordable, simple and clean, these bungalows have a decent location near the beach. A great place to get away from it all, though everything is pretty basic. Free Wi-Fi and pick-up from the pier.

Koh Ngam
Royal Paradise Koh-Ngam Resort $$$-$$
Simple bungalows on stilts arranged in a row. Pricey; you're paying for the location, which admittedly is pretty gorgeous (a secluded beach with private feel). Restaurant.

As with most of Thailand's tourist destinations the food is not as authentic as most would like. Also, in the more popular beach locations, restaurants tend to blur into one, serving the same mix of barbecue, seafood, watered down Thai and badly-made Western dishes. Si Chang is famed for seafood, Pattaya is home to some excellent high-end eateries while Samet and Chang tend to serve up purely backpacker/ mass-market tourist fare. That's not to say you can't eat well – the more adventurous should aim for the places popular with Thais and locals.

Eastern coast to Pattaya

Koh Si Chang
Pan and David $$-$
167 Asdang Rd (200 m before Rama V Palace, next to Marine Police) T038-216075.
Mon-Fri 1100-2130, Sat and holidays 0830-2000, Sun 0830-2030.
Fantastic place to eat run by long-term Si Chang residents. Pan cooks up superb steaks, Isaan grub and fresh seafood. David is an American expat who can tell you pretty much anything you need to know about Si Chang. They also run the very informative ko-sichang. com website. Make reservations for weekend bookings.

Lek Naa Wang and Noi A
Set in a basic hut beside the road to the palace, a 10-min walk out of town.
Famed for serving up the island's best seafood. The prawn, crab and steamed fish are stunning. Often busy and rightly so.

Pattaya
Head to the far southern end of Jomtien beach for a run of basic seafood places.

La Gritta $$$
Beach Rd.
Some people maintain this restaurant serves the best Italian in town. Pizzas, pasta dishes and seafood specialities.

Mex $$$
In the Sheraton Pattaya Resort, 437 Phra Tamnak Rd, T038-259888, sheraton.com/pattaya. Mon-Sat 1830-2230.
This is an excellent restaurant and quite possibly one of the best hotel restaurants in the country. Playful blends of tastes, textures and aromas – from Asia and beyond – are accompanied by an eye for the finest and freshest ingredients available. Pricey but this is somewhere really worth the splurge.

Ruen Thai $$$
Pattaya 2 Rd, opposite Soi Post Office.
One of the best Thai restaurants in town, in nice surroundings and with good service.

Snacks on offer at Pattaya beach.

Jomtien Twelve $$$-$$
In the Jomtien Twelve Hotel 240/13 Moo 12, Jomtien Beach Rd, T038-756865, jomtientwelve.com.
Good stylish spot to stop for fresh coffee and Western-style breakfast on Jomtien beach. Also serves some decent Thai food making it a nice choice for dinner or lunch. Cocktails and beer also available.

Kiss $$
Pattaya 2 Rd, between Sois 11 and 12, next to Diana Inn.
Good range of Western and Thai food at low prices. An excellent place to watch the world go by.

Koh Samet

Just about all the resorts and guesthouses on Koh Samet provide the usual Thai dishes and travellers' food. Most also set up axe-cushions and lights on the beach in the evening, along with barbecues of fresh seafood.

There's not much difference in quality though the increased number of Thai visitors to Samet has improved the food on offer.

Hoi Pim $$
Opposite the main pier.
A/c restaurant providing a good pitstop if you've just arrived. Serves good, reasonably priced Thai and Western food.

Naga $$
Ao Hin Khok.
Home-baked cakes, bread and pastries, and a popular nightspot, set under some trees just back from the beach. Nice dreamy location in the quieter hours. There is also a hotel and bar here.

Vonguern Villa $$
Ao Vong Duen.
A vast range of Thai and Western dishes. Some of the Thai food here is excellent making it very popular with Thai families. Also a hotel, see page 99.

Foodstall (no name) $
Between Le Vimarn and Ao Phrao Resort.
There is an excellent foodstall set up by the resort owners mainly to feed their own staff – which sells a variety of authentic Thai and Isaan dishes in a breezy beach-side location.

Koh Chang & around

Trat
The municipal market has a good range of stalls to choose from.

Isaan Shophouse Restaurant $
Than Charoen Rd.
If your tastebuds are crying out for the authentic flavours of *som tam* (papaya salad), *larb moo* (mince pork salad) and sticky rice this is an excellent choice. Basic but awesome.

Pier 112 $
132 Thanachareon Road.
Laid-back restaurant and bar set in a garden. Good range of Western and Thai food, including vegetarian. Serves cocktails.

Koh Chang
For an island that, 15 years ago, was almost completely uninhabited the eating options on Koh Chang are aimed almost entirely at tourists. Much like Koh Samet expect the usual run of beach-side barbecues with almost every guesthouse and hotel serving up roughly the same menu at every location.

Texas Steak House $$$-$$
Hat Sai Kaew
Tasty steaks in pleasant surroundings, sea views from the balcony, just!

India Hut $$
Next to the post office on the main road, Hat Sai Kaew.
One of the best places on the island to eat a range of fairly authentic Indian food.

Thor's Palace $$
Hat Sai Kaew
Excellent restaurant where you sit on the floor at low, lamp-lit tables, good Thai curries, very friendly management and popular library.

Crust Bakery $$-$
19/5 Moo 4, Hat Khlong Prao.
Bakery, deli, restaurant and bar. Fantastic range of gourmet food: truffles, Bavarian beer, Bavarian bread, salami … the list goes on.

Tapas Bar $$-$
Close to Mac Bungalow, Hat Sai Kaew.
Funky and friendly beach-front bar serving pizza and baguettes. Nice place for sundowners.

Tonsai Restaurant $$-$
Hat Sai Kaew.
This 2nd-floor restaurant is built around a 'Tonsai' tree and is a magical place to enjoy food or cocktails. Friendly staff, delicious Thai food.

A Biento Coffee $
Hat Sai Kaew, Main road, opposite Kacha Spa and Resort.
Fresh coffee and sandwiches in pleasant a/c café, offering respite from the heat.

Koh Kood
Away Restaurant $$
43/8 Moo 2.
Delicious Thai and Western food. Cocktails and fresh coffee are also available. Restaurant overlooks the bay.

Baan Klong Jao Homestay $
Baan Klong Jao.
Serves tasty and highly authentic Thai food. Remember to order your food not spicy if you can't handle the chillies!

Siam beach.

Entertainment

Pattaya is famed for its nightlife – but this mostly takes the form of go-go bars. There will be generic beach hangouts on Koh Samet and Koh Chang, serving up cocktails and beers in fairly relaxed surroundings. Some of the hipper bars in these locations tend to appear and disappear with astonishing speed, many only lasting one season, so you may need to ask the locals when you arrive. Also, do expect some form of reggae bar – a ubiquitous part of any backpacker holiday – where dreadlocked youth pay homage to Marley et al.

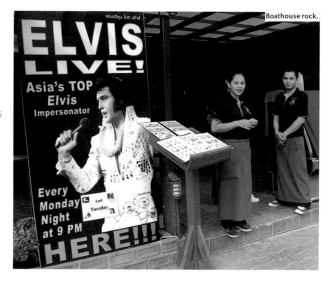
Boathouse rock.

Pattaya

Latitude Lounge

In the Sheraton Pattaya Resort, 437 Phra Tamnak Rd, T038-259888, sheraton.com/pattaya. Get away from the flotsam and jetsam of Beach Rd and head to this very relaxed, cool, bar-cum-lounge. Beautiful design and breezy location mean you can spend all evening here supping cocktails while the contemporary sounds add to the ambience.

Jomtien Boathouse

380/5-6 Jomtien Beach Rd, T038-756143, jomtienboathouse.com. You'll find a highly entertaining Elvis impersonator performing twice a week (call for details) at this well run Jomtien bar. Also have a giant screen for sports.

Ladyboy Cabaret

Mostly performed by members of Pattaya's legendary *katoey* (transexual) population, a night at the cabaret is a quintessential cultural experience in these parts. The biggest and best are **Alcazar** and **Tiffany's**, both found on the northern end of Pattaya 2 Rd. Shows at Tiffany's are daily at 1900, 2030 and 2200, T038-429642 for reservations – prices start at ฿255-400. Tiffany's is housed in an easily spotted gaudy neoclassical, gold trimmed pile. Bizarrely there's also a gun range in Tiffany's basement – from ฿600 – should you want to let off some steam after the show.

Koh Chang

Dolphin Divers Bar

Open bamboo huts serve drinks at bargain prices. Happy Hour 1800-2000 – buy 1 get 1 free.

Sabay Bar

Night-time location where you can either relax on cushions on the beach or dance the night away inside.

White Sands Cat Bar

A friendly little well-stocked bar and an excellent source of information as well as a good place to hire motorbikes.

Shopping

Apart from a few shopping centres in Pattaya, which tend to sell imported goods that are more expensive than in the West, the shopping possibilities are fairly limited along the Eastern coast. Once again, most of the places on Koh Samet and Koh Chang are aimed at tourists and sell the usual mix of cheap sunglasses, flipflops, beach towels and souvenirs.

Activities & tours

Diving & snorkelling

A lot of work has been done to revitalize Pattaya's diving – dynamite fishing has been outlawed and coral beds are now protected. Marine life, after years of degrading, is slowly

Jet ski at the beach at Pattaya.

returning to normal with stunning coral, sea turtles, rays and angelfish all making an appearance. There are even a couple of wrecks within easy reach as well as some great dive schools. This makes Pattaya an excellent place to learn to dive.

Seafari

Soi 12, opposite Lek Hotel, T038-429060, seafari.co.th.
A 5-star PADI resort. A PADI Open Water course costs ฿14,000, including all equipment (except course manuals), dives and boat fees. Certified divers can do a day's diving (all equipment, 2 dives, boat fees, lunch and soft drinks) to the nearby islands and wrecks for ฿3,200.

Other operators include **Aquanauts**, 437/17 Soi Yodsak, T038-361724, aquanautsdive.com; **Dave's Divers Den**, Pattaya-Naklua Rd, T038-420411 (NAUI); and **Mermaid's Dive School**, Soi Mermaid, Jomtien Beach, T038-232219.

Game fishing

There are several game-fishing operators in Pattaya. Commonly caught fish include shark, king mackerel, garoupa and marlin. **The Fisherman's Club** (Soi Yodsak/Soi 6) takes groups of 4-10 anglers and offers 3 different packages (including an overnight trip).

Tours

There are countless tours organized by travel agents in town: the standard long-distance trips are to Koh Samet, the sapphire mines near Chantaburi, Ayutthaya, Bangkok, the floating market, Kanchanaburi and the River Kwai Bridge (2 days). Prices for day tours (meal included) range from ฿600-1200.

The major beaches offer sailing, windsurfing, snorkelling, waterskiing and jet-skiing – many of the bungalows display notices requesting visitors not to hire jet skis because they are dangerous to swimmers, damage the coral and disrupt the peace. Some of the jet-ski operators are notorious rip-off artists and the whole activity is best avoided.

You can scuba dive here but the diving isn't great and you'd be better saving your money to dive in other parts of the country. Ao Vong Duen has the best watersports. The best snorkelling is to be found at Ao Wai, Ao Kiu Na Nok and Ao Phrao. Samet Villa, at Ao Phai (see page 107), runs an adventure tour to Koh Mun Nok, Koh Mun Klang and Koh Mun Nai for ฿500 per person, trips to Thalu and Kuti for ฿300, and trips around the island for ฿200 per person.

Transport

Buses leave every 30 minutes from Bangkok's Eastern Terminal for a 70-minute journey to the town of Si Racha, where hourly boats run to Si Chang (daily 0700-1900).

Koh Chang

Regular buses leave Bangkok's eastern bus terminal for the 5-hour journey to Trat. From Trat, *songthaews* (pick-up trucks) leave for Laem Ngop and several other ferry piers. During the high season (Nov-May) boats leave every hour from Laem Ngop for Koh Chang. Bangkok Airways have daily flights to Trat from Bangkok. Koh Chang is also firmly on backpacker mini-bus routes with direct services from Samet, Khao San Rd and other popular spots. These services, while convenient, can be over-priced, unsafe and often lack comfort.

Koh Chang

Adventure activities
Ban Kwan Chang Elephant Camp
Near Khlong Son.
Set up to look after elephants that were no longer working in northern Thailand. To fund the project it runs elephant treks ranging from ฿900. The price includes transport, food and drink, and a trek.

Tree Top Adventure Park
Ao Bai Lan, T084-310 7600.
Obstacle course in the jungle, test your skill and daring by walking along platforms suspended from trees. Costs ฿700 (฿100 cheaper for Thais).

Diving & snorkelling
Diving Dolphin Divers
T087-028 1627,
dolphinkohchang.com.
This Swiss-owned outfit has its main office on Khlong Phrao and offers all PADI courses from Open Water through to Instructor. It runs dive trips (2 dives) around the Koh Chang archipelago.

Koh Kood

Diving & snorkelling
Away Resorts
T08-4466 5554.
The only place on the island with PADI-certified diving instructors.

The **Happy Days Info Centre** rents snorkelling equipment (฿150 per day), kayaks and motorbikes (฿300 per day).

Contents

Gulf Coast

Hua Hin.

Introduction

Great beaches, world class resorts, gorgeous national parks and cultured towns garland the length of the Gulf Coast. Head south from Bangkok and the first stop is the friendly down-to-earth beach town of Cha-am, popular with both locals and foreigners alike. A shorter hop further down the coast is Thailand's very own royal resort town of Hua Hin. Loved by Thai royalty for generations this was Siam's first ever beach destination of note – it is now one of the premier spots in the nation, the golf courses and luxurious accommodation pulling in wealthy Thais and foreigners. Remarkably, friendly Prachuap Khiri Khan fails to attract many foreign visitors – with its awesome seafood restaurants, the perfect sands at nearby Ao Manao, good transport links both north and south and excellent accommodation, it is well worth a stopover.

Chumphon provides both ferry links to Koh Tao and the other Gulf Islands but also has some pretty decent beaches nearby. More famous as the transport hub for visiting Samui and Phangan, Surat Thani is a proud town that has a relaxing river setting.

The furthest point south this guide will take you is the thriving town of Nakhon Si Thammarat, unmuddied by full-scale tourism, which offers an opportunity to see the unusual art of shadow puppetry and savour confectioners' delicate pastries. There are also some reasonable beaches nearby.

What to see in...

...a weekend
Hua Hin is the quintessential Thai weekend destination for wealthy Bangkokians. You can join them sampling the golf, spas and food available in the town. Nearby **Cha-am** is a more down-to-earth beach weekend destination favoured by blue collar Thais, as is **Prachuap Khiri Khan**.

...a week or more
A journey all the way down the Gulf Coast would be an engaging journey. After the luxury of **Hua Hin** take in the seafood at **Prachuap**, the diving and remote beaches near **Chumphon**, a river tour in friendly **Surat Thani** before reaching rootsy **Nakhon Si Thammarat** where ancient temples and traditions combine.

Cha-am beach.

Hua Hin & around

Hua Hin, Thailand's first beach resort, has had an almost continuous royal connection since the late 19th century. In 1868, King Mongkut journeyed to Hua Hin to observe a total eclipse of the sun. In 1910, Prince Chakrabongse, brother of Rama VI, visited Hua Hin on a hunting trip and was so enchanted by the area that he built himself a villa. These days Hua Hin is a thriving resort town that, in places, has managed to retain some of its charm – particularly the waterfront. The suburbs are filled with holiday villas, while most of the high-end hotels are several kilometres to the north of the town. These luxury places are some of the best in Thailand, if not the world, and are a big draw for many visitors.

North of Hua Hin, Cha-am is reputed to have been a stopping place for King Naresuan's troops when they were travelling south with the name possibly being derived from the Thai word cha-an, meaning to clean the saddle. Cha-am is a beach resort with some excellent hotels and a sizeable building programme of new hotels and condominiums for wealthy Bangkokians.

South of Hua Hin, Prachuap Khiri Khan is a small and peaceful resort with a long, crescent-shaped beach. At either end of the crescent, vegetation-draped limestone towers rear up from the sea creating beautiful symmetry and stunning views. The town is more popular with Thais than with *farangs* and has a reputation for good seafood.

Early guidebooks, nostalgic for English seaside towns, named the resort Hua Hin-on-Sea. Hua (head) Hin (rock) refers to a stone outcrop at the end of the fine white-sand beach. The resort used to promote itself as the 'Queen of Tranquillity'; until the 1980s, it was a forgotten backwater of an earlier, and less frenetic, tourist era. However, in the last few years the constant influx of tourists has livened up the atmosphere considerably; with massage parlours, tourist shops and numerous Western restaurants and bars lining the streets, it's hard to get a moment's peace. And just when you think the town is as chock-a-block as possible, the sound of drills and construction work reminds you otherwise. Condominiums are springing up all along the coast to cater for wealthy holidaymakers from Bangkok; high-rise buildings scar the horizon and vehicles clog the streets. New golf courses are being constructed to serve Thailand's growing army of golfers – as well as avid Japanese players – and the olde-worlde charm that was once Hua Hin's great selling point is being lost.

As Hua Hin is billed as a beach resort people come here expecting a beautiful tropical beach but that isn't quite the case. Many of the nicest stretches of sand are in front of hotels – the Hilton, Marriott and Sofitel in particular.

The famous **Railway Hotel** was built in 1923 by a Thai prince, Purachatra, who headed the State Railways of Thailand. It became Thailand's premier seaside hotel, but by the 1960s had fallen into rather glorious disrepair. It experienced a short burst of stardom when the building played the role of the **Phnom Penh Hotel** in the Oscar-winning film about the Khmer Rouge era in Cambodia, *The Killing Fields* but it still seemed destined to rot into oblivion. Saved by privatization, it was renovated and substantially expanded in 1986 and is now an excellent five-star hotel. Unfortunately, it has been

Essentials

● **Getting around** Hua Hin is compact and most places are within walking distance. There is a good network of *songthaews* which run along fixed routes and tuk tuks. Bicycles, motorbikes and cars are all available for hire.

● **ATM** There are dozens of banks, ATMs and currency exchange booths all over town.

● **Hospital** San Paulo Hospital, Phetkasem Rd, opposite the Marriott, T032-532581.

● **Pharmacy** Medihouse Pharmacy, Naresdamri Rd, daily 0930-2300.

● **Post office** 21 Damnoenkasem Rd.

● **Tourist information** Tourist office, 114 Phetkasem Rd, T032-532433, Mon-Fri 0830-1200, 1300-2000. Also useful is huahin.go.th.

Hua Hin station.

renamed, and goes under the unromantic name of the Sofitel Central Hua Hin Resort (see Sleeping, page 127). At the other end of Damnoenkasem Road from the hotel is the railway station itself. The station has a rather quaint Royal Waiting Room on the platform.

Throne out

The first of Hua Hin's royal palaces, Saen Samran House was built by Prince Naris, son of Rama V. In the early 1920s, King Vajiravudh (Rama VI) – no doubt influenced by his brother Chakrabongse – began work on a teakwood palace, 'Deer Park'. The final stamp of royal approval came in the late 1920s, when King Phrajadipok (Rama VII) built another palace, which he named Klai Kangwon, literally 'Far From Worries'. It was designed by one of Prince Naris' sons. The name could not have been more inappropriate: the king was staying at Klai Kangwon in 1932 when he was dislodged from the throne by a coup d'état.

Khao Takiab (Chopstick Hill), south of town, is a dirty, unremarkable hill with a large standing Buddha facing the sea. Nearby is **Khao Krilat**, a rock covered in assorted shrines, stupas, ponds, *salas* and Buddha images. To get there, take a local bus from Dechanuchit Road.

North of Hua Hin

Cha-am

The beach is a classic stretch of golden sand, filled with beach umbrellas and inner-tube renters. The northern end of the beach is much quieter, with a line of trees providing cooling shade. The town also has a good reputation for the quality of its seafood and grilled pork. It has become a popular weekend spot, so sizeable discounts are available during the week when most hotels are close to empty. At the weekend something of a transformation occurs and it buzzes with life for 48 hours before returning to its comatose state.

It is easy to walk everywhere in Cha-am. The tourist office 2 km from the beach on Phetkasem Rd, T032-471005, tat. or.th/central2, daily 0830-1630, is responsible for the areas of Cha-am and Prachuap Khiri Khan, Phetburi and Hua Hin. There are ATMs along the beach road. There are a number of pharmacies near the beach road. For medical care head to Bangkok or Hua Hin.

Between Cha-am and Hua Hin is the **Maruekkhathayawan Palace** (daily 0800-1600, entry by donation), which was designed by an Italian and built by Rama VI in 1924; the king is reputed to have had a major influence on its design. The palace is made of teak and the name means 'place of love and hope', which is rather charming. It consists of 16 pavilions in a very peaceful setting. To get there, take a *saamlor* or catch a bus heading for Hua Hin and walk 2 km from the turn-off.

Kaeng Krachan National Park & caves

Entrance ฿200 with another charge of ฿200 for the Pa La-U waterfalls.
To get to the park, take a minibus from the station on Srasong Rd to the village of Fa Prathan, 63 km (฿15). For the caves, take the same bus but get off at Nongphlab village (฿10) and ask at the police station for directions. The caves are a 45-min to 1-hr walk. Accommodation is available at the park HQ, see Sleeping, page 129.

The park, 63 km northwest of Hua Hin, is Thailand's largest protected area covering 2915 sq km. It was gazetted in 1981 and is said to support significant populations of large mammal species (elephant, tiger, leopard, gibbon, the Malayan pangolin) and birds (hornbills, minivets, pheasants and bee-eaters). Endangered species include the woolly-necked stork and the plain-pouched hornbill. Few visitors see many of these animals though. Extensive trails lead through undisturbed forest and past a succession of waterfalls (the best being Pa La-U, which has 11 tiers and is renowned for its butterflies) to hot springs and a Karen village. Guides are advisable and charge ฿500 per day, but many of them don't speak English, so make sure you meet the guide before paying your money. The Tenasserim mountain range cuts through the park; the highest peak stands at 1207 m. **Phanoen Thung Mountain** offers superb views of the surrounding countryside. It's a six-hour hike to the summit; warm clothes are needed for chilly mornings.

En route to Pa La-U, 27 km from Hua Hin and close to Nongphlab village, are three caves: Dao, Lablae and Kailon, which contain the usual array of stalactites and stalagmites. Guides with lanterns will take visitors through the caves for ฿30 and boat trips can be made on the reservoir.

South of Hua Hin

Khao Sam Roi Yod National Park Park HQ

T032-619078, ฿200, children ฿100.
Take a bus from Hua Hin to Pranburi from where you can charter a *songthaew* (฿250) or take a motorcycle taxi (฿150) to the park HQ. Be sure you are taken to Khao Sam Roi Yod National Park, and not Khao Sam Roi Yod village. For Laem Sala Beach (located within the park), there are regular *songthaews* from Pranburi market to Bang Pu village from 0800-1600, ฿20. Or take a tour with one of the many tour operators in town, ฿900. Accommodation is available at the park HQ, see Sleeping, page 129 .

Khao Sam Roi Yod National Park ('Mountain of Three Hundred Peaks') occupies an area of limestone hills surrounded by saltwater flats and borders the Gulf of Thailand. It lies about 45 km south of Hua Hin, east off Route 4. Its freshwater marshes provide 11 different categories of wetland habitat. The area is a haven for waterbirds and has been extensively developed (and exploited) as a centre for prawn and fish farming, limiting the marshland available to the water birds who breed here. The park has the advantage of being relatively small (98 sq km) with readily accessible sights: wildlife, forest walks and quiet beaches. The main beach is **Laem Sala** where a campsite, bungalows and a restaurant are located.

Prachuap Khiri Khan

Tuk tuks provide local transport – ฿30 pretty much anywhere in town and ฿50 to Ao Manao. Bob, who runs the internet office and tourist information in the Hadthong Hotel (see sleeping), speaks good English and is helpful. There is an ATM at the Hadthong Hotel with many more scattered around the town.

At the northern end of town, at the end of Salashiep/Sarathip Road, is **Khao Chong Krachok**. An exhausting 15-20-minute climb up the 'Mountain with the Mirror' – past armies of aggressive, preening monkeys – is rewarded with fine views of the surrounding countryside and bay. At the summit there is an unremarkable shrine built in 1922 containing a footprint of the Buddha.

There is a good **night market** at the corner of Phitakchat and Kong Kiat roads and a daily market with stacks of fruit along Maitri Ngam (the road south of the post office, opposite the Hadthong Hotel). The daily market which runs along Salashiep/Sarathip Road has stalls of orchids, fruit and metal

Prachuap Kiri Khan.

sculptures. South of the Hadthong Hotel on Susuek Road are a couple of Chinese shophouses.

Ao Manao, a gorgeous bay 5 km south of town, is one of best beaches on this stretch of coast. A gently sloping slice of sand is fringed by refreshing woodlands and framed by distant islands. At some points of the year the place can get infested with jellyfish, so bring a rash guard. Ao Manao was also the site of the Japanese invasion in the Second World War and is sited slap bang in the middle of a military base. This is no bad thing as development is strictly controlled – you'll find none of the usual trappings expected at other Thai resort towns, bar girls, booming music etc. There is also one military-run hotel, good, cheap Thai food, toilets, deckchairs and umbrellas to hire. Foreigners normally need to sign in at the gate – bring some ID, just in case.

South from Prachuap there are a number of beaches but most are infested with sandflies, difficult to reach and are set up to cater mainly for Thai tourists. Around **Bang Saphan**, 60 km south of Prachuap Khiri Khan, several small beach resorts are developing. It is a pretty area and if you are heading south under your own steam then driving through this area makes for a nice diversion.

Chumphon and around

Taxis/*songthaews* run to/from the bus station, Hat Thung Wua Laen, Hat Sai Ree and the piers. There are ATMs around the town and at the Thai Farmers' Bank, Saladaeng Rd.

Chumphon is considered the 'gateway to the south' and is where the southern highway divides, one route running west and then south on Route 4 to Ranong, Phuket and the Andaman Sea; the other, south on Route 41 to Surat Thani, Nakhon Si Thammarat and the waters of the Gulf of Thailand. You'll find some pretty beaches nearby which are also gaining a reputation for kitesurfing.

There isn't much to see in the town itself, although there are some good beaches and islands nearby; the town is an access point for Koh Tao. In his book *Surveying and Exploring in Siam* (1900),

James McCarthy writes of 'Champawn' marking the beginning of the Malay Peninsula. A group of French engineers had already visited the area with a view to digging a canal through the Kra Isthmus and it was clearly a little place at that time: the "harbour was full of rocks covered with oysters. The usual cocoa-nut palms and grass shanties marked the position of the village".

Around Chumphon

Pak Nam Chumphon, 11 km southeast of Chumphon on Route 4901 (take a *songthaew* from opposite the morning market on the southern side of town), lies on the coast at the mouth of the Chumphon River. It's a fishing village with boats for hire to the nearby islands where swiftlets build their nests. The swiftlets are used to make the Chinese speciality of bird's nest soup – *yanwo*, in Chinese. Many of the bird's nest islands have armed guards who can be trigger happy; visitors should seek permission before venturing to the nest sites. Islands include Koh Phrao, Koh Lanka Chiu and Koh Rang Nok. Other activities such as diving, jungle treks and boat trips to the caves can be organized through a guesthouse or travel agent (see Tour operators, page139).

Much of the coastline and islands off Chumphon form part of the **Chumphon Marine National Park (Mu Ko Chumphon)**. The park headquarters T077-558144 is 8 km from Hat Si Ree and can provide details of bungalows and campsites. The park contains mangrove forest, limestone mountain forest as well as marine life offshore.

Hat Thung Wua Laen, 18 km north of Chumphon, is a beautiful beach – a broad curving bay and a long stretch of white sand, which slopes gently towards the sea, though this also means it's a long walk out to the water at low tide. The beach is also filled with sandflies which makes sunbathing almost impossible. From November to January, when the winds are high and the sea unsuitable for bathing, this beach turns into something of a mecca for kitesurfers – some claim that you can find the best kitesurfing conditions in Southeast

Hat Thung Wua Laen.

Diving around Chumphon

The waters off the coast off Chumphon provide excellent diving opportunities. There are dive sites around the islands of Koh Ngam Noi (parcelled out to bird's nest concessionaires) and Koh Ngam Yai. Rock outcrops like Hin Lak Ngam and Hin Pae, are also becoming increasingly popular with dive companies for their coral gardens, caves and rock piles. Of particular note are the 500 varieties of rare black corals found in the vicinity of Hin Lak Ngam. The sea here is plankton-rich, which means an abundance of sea life including whaleshark, other species of shark, and sea turtles, as well as coral gardens.

Asia here. There are also a number of hotels and bungalows operating here but the beach is still mercifully free of tourist paraphernalia and even when most accommodation is fully occupied the area is large enough to maintain a sense of peace and seclusion. In March the waters become inundated with plankton, which locals harvest using nets. It is considered a delicacy and is known as *kuey*. To get to the beach, take a *songthaew* (฿20) from the market in Chumphon; you can also charter a tuk-tuk (฿250).

Another beach, **Hat Sai Ri**, is 3 km south of Hat Pharadon and close to Koh Thong Luang. There is good snorkelling in the area. There is also a shrine to His Royal Highness Prince Chumphon, the self-styled father of the Royal Thai Navy. To get to Hat Sai Ri take a *songthaew* (฿20) from opposite the New Infinity Travel Agency in Chumpon, or from the post office.

At **Amphoe Lang Suan**, 62 km south of Chumphon, there are two beautiful caves – Tham Khao Ngoen and Tham Khao Kriep. There are 370 steps leading to the latter which is studded with stalagmites and stalactites. The district is also locally renowned for the quality of its fruit. You can take a bus there from the bus station in Chumphon.

Surat Thani

The riverside town of Surat Thani – or 'City of the Good People' is a provincial capital and although the town has an interesting riverfront worth a visit and some fabulously stocked markets, its main role is as the launch pad for transport to the gulf islands of Samui, Phangan and Tao. North of the town is the ancient settlement of Chaiya, once an important outpost of the Sumatran-based Srivijayan Empire and Wat Suan Mok, a Buddhist retreat, known for its meditation courses. The pig-tailed macaque has been trained to collect the millions of coconuts that grow in the region and on the islands. There's a macaque training centre outside Surat Thani that can be visited.

There's not much of note in Surat Thani town with much of the more interesting sights being in the nearby towns. Boats can be hired for trips on the river (฿200 for up to six people) – the better journey is upstream. There is a big **Chinese temple** and an attractive old *viharn* in the compound of **Wat Sai**, both on Thi Lek Road. The town brightens up considerably during the Chak Phra Festival in September or October.

Chaiya temple at Surat Thani.

Essentials

❶ Getting around *Songthaews* run around town.

⑤ ATM Several banks with ATMs on Na Muang and Chonkasem roads.

⊕ Hospital Taksin Hospital, Talat Mai Rd, heading south towards Nakhon, T077-273239.

⌁ Post office Near the corner of Talat Mai and Chonkasem roads and on the corner of Na Muang and Chonkasem roads.

❶ Tourist information TAT, I5 Talat Mai Rd, T077-288817, tatsurat@tat.or.th, daily 0830-1200, 1300-1630.

Chaiya

Northbound trains from Surat Thani's Phun Phin station stop at Chaiya (40 mins). There are regular buses from Surat Thani to Chaiya from Talat Kaset Nung (I). Regular *songthaews* from close to Talat Kaset Song (II) (฿30).

Chaiya was an important outpost of the Sumatra-based Srivijayan Empire and dates from the late seventh century making it one of the most ancient settlements in Thailand. Given the quantity of antiquities found in the area, some scholars have suggested that Chaiya may have been the capital of Srivijaya, rather than Palembang (Sumatra) as is usually thought. Recent excavations in Sumatra, however, seem to have confirmed Palembang as the capital. Chaiya today is a pleasant, clean town with many old wooden houses.

About 2 km outside Chaiya, 1 km from the Chaiya railway station, stands **Wat Phra Boromthat Chaiya**, one of the most revered temples in Thailand. Within the *wat* compound, the central *chedi* is reminiscent of the eighth-century *candis* of central Java, square in plan with four porches and rising in tiers topped with miniature *chedis*. The *chedi* is constructed of brick and vegetable mortar and is thought to be 1200 years old. Even though it was restored in 1901 and again in 1930, its Srivijayan origins are still evident. A museum Wednesdy-Sunday, 0900-1600, ฿30, nearby, exhibits relics found in the vicinity which have not been 'acquired' by the National Museum in Bangkok.

Wat Suan Mok

Wat Suan Mok is 50 km north of Surat Thani on Route 41, T077-431597, suanmokkh.org.
Take a bus from Talat Kaset Nung (I); the road passes the *wat* (1 hr). The town of Chaiya is closer to the monastery, so if arriving by train direct from Bangkok alight here and catch a *songthaew* to Wat Suan Mok.

Wat Suan Mok is a popular forest *wat* (*wat pa*), which has become an international Buddhist retreat. Courses for Westerners are run with the aid of a number of foreign monks and novices. The monastery was founded by one of Thailand's most revered monks, the late Buddhadasa Bhikkhu, on a peaceful plot of land covering around 50 ha of fields and forest. Ten-day *anapanasati* meditation courses are held here, beginning on the first day of each month. Enrolment on to the course takes place on the last day of the previous month, on a first-come first-served basis. Courses are ฿1500, which covers the cost of the meals (rice and vegetable dishes at 0800 and 1300). For those considering taking the course, bear in mind that students sleep on straw mats, are woken by animal noises at 0400, bathe in a communal pool, and are expected to help with chores around the monastery. No alcohol, drugs or tobacco are permitted and the sexes tend to be segregated. If intending to visit the monastery or enrol on a course, it is worth bringing a torch and mosquito repellent (or buy these at the shop by the entrance).

The Kradaejae Monkey Training Centre

The monkey training centre is south of Surat Thani on Route 401, towards Nakhon Si Thammarat, 2 km off the main road.

Take a *songthaew* or bus from Surat Thani heading towards Nakhon Si Thammarat, on Talat Mai Rd, which becomes Route 401. The turning to the centre is on the right-hand side, just over the Thathong Bridge, past a *wat* and a school. (T08-9871 8017 call to make a reservation).

A unique and easily reached place to visit. The only monkey capable of being trained to pick coconuts is the pig-tailed macaque (*ling kung* in Thai). The female is not usually trained as it is smaller and not as strong as the male; strength is needed to break off the stem of the coconut. The training can start when the animals are eight months old. The course lasts three to five months, and when fully trained, the monkeys can pick as many as 800 coconuts in a day and will work for 12-to-15 years. "Working monkeys are very cheap – they cost no more than ฿10 a day but make millions of baht a year", according to Somphon Saekhow, founder of a coconut-collecting school.

A trained monkey picks a coconut.

Nakhon Si Thammarat & around

Nakhon Si Thammarat ('the Glorious city of the Dead') or Nagara Sri Dhammaraja ('the city of the Sacred Dharma Kings') has masqueraded under many different aliases: Marco Polo referred to it as Lo-Kag, the Portuguese called it Ligor – thought to have been its original name – while to the Chinese it was Tung Ma-ling. Today, it is the second biggest city in the south and most people know it simply as Nakhon or Nakhon Si. Nakhon was at its most powerful and important during King Thammasokarat's reign in the 13th century, when it was busily trading with south India and Ceylon. Buddhist monks from Nakhon are thought to have propagated religion throughout the country perhaps even influencing the development of Buddhism in Sukhothai, Thailand's former great kingdom.

Nakhon is probably best known today for its prawn farms and nielloware industry. It is friendly and manageable with a wide range of hotels, some excellent restaurants, a good museum and a fine monastery in Wat Phra Mahathat. It is also famed for its shadow puppetry.

Around Nakhon are the quiet beaches of Khanom and Nai Phlao. The Khao Luang and Khao Nan national parks offer waterfalls, caves and whitewater rafting.

Wat Phra Mahathat

T075-345172, 2 km south of town on Rachdamnern Road.
Cloisters open daily 0800-1630

This is the oldest temple in town and the biggest in South Thailand – as well as being one of the region's most important. The *wat* dates from AD 757 and was originally a Srivijayan Mahayana Buddhist shrine. The 77-m high stupa, Phra Boromathat – a copy of the Mahathupa in Ceylon – was built early in the 13th century to hold relics of the Buddha from Ceylon. The *wat* underwent extensive restoration in the Ayutthayan period and endured further alterations in 1990. The *chedi's* square base, its voluptuous body and towering spire are all Ceylonese-inspired. Below the spire is a small square platform decorated with bas-reliefs in gold of monks circumambulating (*pradaksina*) the monument. The spire itself is said to be topped with 962 kg of gold, while the base is surrounded by small stupas. The covered cloisters at its base contain many beautiful, recently restored Buddha images all in the image of subduing Mara. The base is dotted with attractive elephant heads. Also here is **Vihara Bodhi Langka** 0800-1600, entry by donation, a jumbled treasure trove of a museum. It contains a large collection of archaeological artefacts, donated jewellery, bodhi trees, Buddhas and a collection of sixth- to 13th-century Dvaravati sculpture – some of the latter are particularly fine. The mural at the bottom of the stairs tells the story of the early life of the Buddha, while the doorway at the top is decorated with figures of Vishnu and Phrom dating from the Sukhothai period.

Puppet workshop & museum

110/18 Si Thammasok, Soi 3, T075-346394.
Daily 0830-1700, 20-min performance, ฿100 for 2; 3 or more ฿50 each.

Not far from Wat Mahathat is the puppet workshop and museum of Nakhon's most famous *nang*

Essentials

❶ **Getting around** The centre is comparatively compact and navigable on foot. Otherwise take a public *songthaew, saamlor* or motorcycle taxi.

Ⓢ **ATM** Rachdamnern Rd and at numerous other spots in the centre.

❶ **Tourist information** TAT, Sanam Na Muang, Rachdamnern Rd, T075-346515-6, daily 0830-1630.

Wat Phra Mahathat.

thalung master – Khun Suchart Subsin. His workshop is signposted off the main road near the Chinese temple (hard to miss). As well as giving shows and selling examples of his work starting at ฿200 or so for a simple elephant, the compound itself is interesting and peaceful with craftsmen hammering out puppets under thatched awnings and dozens of buffalo skulls hung everywhere. There is also a small museum exhibiting puppet characters from as far back as the 18th century.

Statue of Vishnu at the Nakon Si Thammarat National Museum.

Some exhibits are labelled in English. The section on art in South Thailand explains and charts the development of the unusual local Phra Phutthasihing (or Buddha Sihing) style of Buddha image, which was popular locally in the 16th century. Also in this section is the oldest Vishnu statue in Southeast Asian art (holding a conch shell on his hip), which dates from the fifth century. The museum has sections on folk arts and crafts and local everyday implements. To the right of the entrance hall, in the prehistory section, stand two large Dongson bronze kettle drums – two of only 12 found in the country. The one decorated with four ornamental frogs is the biggest ever found in Thailand.

Chapel of Phra Buddha Sihing

The chapel is sandwiched between two large provincial office buildings just before Rachdamnern Road splits in two, and may contain one of Thailand's most important Buddha images. During the 13th century an image, magically created, was shipped to Thailand from Ceylon (hence the name – Sihing for the Sinhalese people). The Nakhon statue, like the other two images that claim to be the Phra Buddha Sihing (one in Bangkok and one in Chiang Mai), is not Ceylonese in style at all; it conforms with the Thai style of the peninsula.

The **Thai Traditional Medicine Centre** located just past Wat Mahathat is the small **Wat Sa-la Mechai**. Here, at one end of the temple grounds is a recently established centre for traditional medicine, including massage. If you want a traditional massage, it costs about ฿100 per hour – you pay before you begin. You can also take a course in massage, paying by the hour, and learn more about traditional herbal medicine (there is a small garden of medicinal plants at the front).

The Nakhon Si Thammarat National Museum

Rachdamnern Rd, about 700 m beyond Wat Mahathat.
Wed-Sun 0830-1630.

One of the town's most worthwhile sights. The impressive collection includes many interesting Indian-influenced pieces as well as rare pieces from the Dvaravati and later Ayutthaya periods.

Beach at Khanom.

Tip...

Regular buses from Nakhon (฿20), a/c micro buses (฿60) leave from Wat Kit Rd and also from Surat Thani. The beaches are about 8 km off the main road; turn at the Km 80 marker.

The Khao Luang National Park

To get to Karom Waterfall take a bus to Lan Saka (then walk 3 km to falls) or charter a minibus direct. To get to Phrom Lok Waterfall take a minibus from Nakhon then hire a motorbike taxi for the last very pleasant 8 km. The villagers at Khiriwong village can organize trips up Khao Luang mountain but do not speak English. See Activities and tours for further options, homestays and guides. *Songthaews* leave Nakhon for Khiriwong every 15 mins or so.

Around Nakhon

Eighty kilometres north of Nakhon, near Khanom district, there are some secluded stretches of shoreline: Khanom beach (2 km from town), Nai Phlao beach to the south, and a couple of other bays are opening up to development. This area is predominantly visited by Thai tourists. Newer operations seem to be targeting Western markets and while there are better beaches you're likely to have most of what you find to yourself – particularly if you come mid-week. Khanom beach is a long run of coconut-grove fringed sand that slopes steeply into the sea. Development is picking up here but it still has a remote feeling. Khanom town is a very lively rough and ready fishing port. There are few facilities aimed at *farang* in this town meaning that it offers a genuine slice of Thai rural life. Nai Phlao beach offers a much shorter run of beach and has a greater concentration of resorts. That's not saying much though as it still feels like a relatively untouched spot, despite the best efforts of the new development at the Chada Racha Resort to introduce an unhealthy dose of concrete to the coastline.

The Khao Luang National Park is named after Khao Luang, a peak of 1835 m – the highest in the south – which lies less than 10 km west of Nakhon. Within the boundaries of the mountainous, 570-sq-km national park are three waterfalls. **Karom Waterfall** lies 30 km from Nakhon, off Route 4015, and has a great location with views over the lowlands. Also here are cool forest trails and fast-flowing streams. The park is said to support small populations of tiger, leopard and elephant, although many naturalists believe they are on the verge of extinction here. **Phrom Lok Waterfall** is about 25 km from Nakhon, off Route 4132. However, the most spectacular of the waterfalls is **Krung Ching** – 'waterfall of a hundred thousand raindrops' – 70 km out of town, and a 4-km walk from the park's accommodation. The 1835-m climb up Khao Luang starts from Khiriwong village, 23 km from Nakhon, off Route 4015.

Phetburi

The historic town of Phetburi (or Phetchaburi), with perhaps the best-preserved Ayutthayan *wats* in Thailand, is about 80 km north of Hua Hin and 160 km south of Bangkok and can be visited as a day trip from both. It is a historic provincial capital on the banks of the Phetburi River and is one of the oldest cities in Thailand and, because it was never sacked by the Burmese, is unusually intact. Initially, Phetburi's wealth and influence was based upon the coastal salt pans found in the vicinity of the town. By the 16th century, Phetburi was supplying salt to most of Siam and the Malay Peninsula. Later, during the 19th century, Phetburi became a popular retreat for the Thai royal family who built a palace here. Today, Phetburi is famous for its paid assassins who usually carry out their work from the backs of motorcycles with large-calibre pistols. Each time there is a national election, 15 to 20 politicians and their canvassers (so-called *hua khanen*) are killed.

Sights

Situated in the centre of town on Damnoenkasem Road, Wat Phra Sri Ratana Mahathat is dominated by five restored, Khmer- style *prangs*. Inside the *bot* are three highly regarded Buddha images. The complex makes an attractive cluster of buildings.

Across Chomrut Bridge and east along Pongsuriya Road is Wat Yai Suwannaram. The *wat* was built during the Ayutthaya period and then restored during the reign of Rama V. The *bot* contains some particularly fine Ayutthayan murals - note the six-toed bronze Buddha image on the rear wall which is thought to be pre-Ayutthayan. Behind the *bot* is a teak pavilion (*sala kan parian*) with three doorways at the front and two at the back. The front door panels have fine coloured-glass insets, while the mark on the right-hand panel is said to have been made by a Burmese warrior en route to attack Ayutthaya. South down Phokarong Road and west a short distance along Phrasong

Tip...

A cable car Monday-Friday 0815-1700, Saturday-Sunday, 0815-1730, ฿30, children ฿10, takes visitors up the west side of Khao Wang.

Road, is Wat Kamphaeng Laeng. The five Khmer laterite *prangs* have been dated to the 12th century and are reminiscent of those in the northeast of the country.

West back towards the centre of town and south down Matayawong Road, are, in turn, Wat Phra Song, Wat Laat and Wat Chi Phra Keut, all on the left-hand side of the road. Just before reaching a bridge over Wat Ko Canal, is Wat Ko Kaeo Sutharam. The bot contains 18th-century murals showing scenes from the Buddha's life.

At the western edge of the city is Phra Nakhon Khiri, known as Khao Wang (Palace on the Mountain), built in 1858 during the reign of Rama IV. Perched on the top of a 95-m hill, is the museum Royal Palace (daily 0900-1600, ฿40). Also on this peak is the Hor Chatchavan Viangchai, an observatory tower. On the central rise of the hill is the Phra That Chomphet, a stupa erected by Rama IV. On the east rise sits Wat Maha Samanaram (also known as Wat Phra Kaeo), which dates from the Ayutthayan period.

Sleeping

$$$$ Royal Diamond Hotel
555 Phetka-sem Rd, T032-411061, royaldiamond hotel.com.
Luxurious hotel compared to most others in Phetburi. The 58 rooms have a/c and are adequately furnished. The restaurant does a range of international food. There's a beer garden and pleasant, peaceful atmosphere.

Eating

Phetburi is known for its desserts including *khanom mo kaeng* (a custard made of mung bean, egg, coconut and sugar, baked over an open fire), *khao kriap* (a pastry with sesame, coconut and sugar) and excellent *kluai khai* (sweet bananas). There are several restaurants along Phetkasem Rd selling Phetburi desserts. There is a night market at the southern end of Surinreuchai Rd underneath the clock tower.

Getting to Phetburi

Trains take 1½ hours/2½ hours from Hua Hin/ Bangkok. The main bus terminal is about 1.5 km west of town while a/c buses stop near the town centre. Buses take about one/two hours from Hua Hin/Bangkok. There are connections south to Cha-am, Hua Hin and onward. *Songthaews* meet the buses and take passengers into the town centre. The town is small enough to explore on foot.

Sleeping

There is a huge variety of accommodation along the Gulf Coast that will suit every budget. Hua Hin, the premier destination on the coast, is home to some of the best resorts in the country while the beaches around places like Chumphon offer great budget options.

Hua Hin

Many hotels reduce prices in the low season. Rack rates are extortionate. For better deals check the internet or tour operators. Prices quoted here are for high season.

Chiva Som International Health Resort $$$$
73/4 Phetkasem Rd, T032-536536, chivasom.com.
This is a luxury health resort (Chiva-Som means Haven of Life) set in 3 ha of luxury grounds which ooze calm and peace. It has a large spa building housing a spacious gym, Roman bath, enormous jacuzzi, circular steam room and dance studio. There is also an outdoor freshwater pool close to the sea. With health consultants, hydrotherapy and lots of herbal tea and healthy food, this is the place to come to lose weight or firm up those buttocks without feeling that life is too miserable. There are many treatment and accommodation packages on offer.

Evason Hua Hin Resort and Spa $$$$
9 Paknampran Beach, Prachuap Khiri Khan, T032-618200, six-senses.com.
About 20 km south of Hua Hin (not far from Pranburi) is this stylish resort, set in spacious grounds with a pool. The owners have created a unique environment, with light and airy rooms, furnished with contemporary, locally produced furniture. Some of the more expensive villas have private plunge pools. The Earth Spa provides the last word in pampering as well as health programmes for the more committed. There are plenty of other (complimentary) facilities including watersports (sailing, kayaking), tennis courts, a gym, archery. The kids' club has a separate pool and playground plus daily activities. Low-season prices are good value.

Hilton Hua Hin Resort and Spa $$$$
33 Naresdamri Rd, T032-512879, hilton.com.
This rather unappealing white tower block dominates the town centre. However, it is a pleasant and comfortable hotel offering a luscious spa, lovely pool, restaurants and a nice stretch of

The pool at Chiva Som.

Evason Resort.

you're not really meant to leave. The best and most unique feature is the giant, snaking swimming pool which can be reached straight off the balconies of most groundfloor rooms. Otherwise it's a bog-standard 5-star place with all the usual trimmings – the beachside bar is a nice spot for a drink.

Sofitel Central Hua Hin Resort $$$$
1 Damnoenkasem Rd,
T032-512021, sofitel.com.
Hua Hin's original premier hotel, formerly the Railway Hotel. A beautiful place set in luscious gardens. It maintains excellent levels of service and enjoys a good position on the beach, and while the new rooms are small they are well appointed. Rooms are beautifully decorated. Lovely grounds with pools near the beach. The seafood restaurant here is worth seeking out.

Araya $$$-$$
15/1 Chomsin Rd, T032-531130,
araya-residence.com.
Officially this is a small apartment block that offers monthly and annual rates on the rooms. They also offer rooms by the night and while it's not the cheapest Araya does represent excellent value. With enough contemporary design and art to add to the 'cool' factor, the rooms are comfy and spacious. The best (and most expensive) are the two rooftop 'villas', which come

beach. The 296 rooms are attractively decorated although the bathrooms are lacking in grandeur in comparison. Views from the rooms are superb.

Hua Hin Marriott Resort and Spa $$$$
107/1 Phetkasem Rd,
T032-511881,
marriotthotels.com.
A large resort with an attractive lobby. The Mandara Spa architecture and ambience is beautiful, with a blend of Thai and Balinese style and large stepping stones to cross ponds. The 216 rooms enjoy top facilities. The beach in front of the hotel is white, clean and pleasant. The pool gets busy and there are 4 restaurants and 2 bars. Good sports facilities,

including tennis, fitness centre, watersports and a kids' club.

Hyatt Regency Hua Hin $$$$
99 Hua Hin-Khao Takiap Rd,
T032-521234, huahin.regency.
hyatt.com.
All the facilities you'd expect from a top-class hotel, including an extensive range of water-sports and a cyber-games centre. It is a lovely low-rise resort of 204 rooms set in an expanse of well-maintained gardens.

Sheraton Hua Hin Resort and Spa $$$$
1573 Petchkasem Rd,
T032-708000,
sheraton.com/huahin.
With its entrance set on the main road between Hua Hin and Cha-am, this is the kind of resort

complete with huge, private roof terrace, flatscreen TV, DVD players, fridge and free Wi-Fi. All this and it's in a great location and friendly to boot.

Supasuda/Ananthara Guesthouse $$$-$$
1/8 Chomsin Rd, T032-516650, spg house.com.
Friendly guesthouse opposite the pier in the heart of old Hua Hin. Rooms are all a/c, with TV and en suite – some have balconies/sea-views and there's even a private terrace on the roof. There's also a relaxing lounge bar on the ground floor. At present seems to be trading under two names.

Fulay Guesthouse $$$-$
110/1 Naresdamri Rd, T032-513145, fulay-huahin.com.
A delightful little place with old world look, with teak frontage and white carved wooden railings and splashes of pastel green. Only a/c rooms have hot water. Fan rooms have shared bathrooms. Good restaurant. The Thai house is a little getaway on the top deck with ocean views.

Sunshine Guesthouse $$$-$
113/30 Soi Hua Hin, Phetkasem Rd, T032-515309, sunshine guesthouse@yahoo.com.
Super-friendly management at this guesthouse, which is slightly cheaper than the others. Rooms have minibars, a/c and TVs. Internet café in the lobby.

Chomsin Hua Hin Hotel $$
130/4 Chom-sin Rd, T032-515348, chomsinhuahin.com.
Smart, well-tended boutique joint on a nice quiet street in central Hua Hin. All rooms come with a/c, en suite and TV – some have balconies. Rooms are excellent value, plus there's a small café downstairs.

Bird Guesthouse $
31/2 Naret Damri Rd, T032-511630, birdguesthousehuahin@ hotmail.com.
10 rooms on a wooden platform on stilts above the beach. Atmospheric place with friendly management. There is no restaurant but you can get breakfast here, sitting area with sea views, more ambience and character than most.

Pattana Guesthouse $
52 Naresdamri Rd, T032-513393, huahinpattana@hotmail.com.
Attractive location down a small alley. 13 twin-bedded rooms with fans in 2 original Thai teakwood buildings set around a flower-filled compound, some rooms with own bathrooms. 50 m from the beach, breakfast.

Cha-am

A number of hotels on the seafront offer more bungalows and simple rooms in the $$$-$$ price range, with a few in the Drange. Unless you speak Thai, it will be difficult to make a phone booking, but it is highly likely that you'll find available rooms on arrival. Mid-week tends to be quieter and cheaper.

Bann Pantai $$$$-$$$
Ruamchit Rd, T032-433 111, bannpantai.com.
New in 2008, an upmarket mini-resort complex, complete with nice pool, contemporary-Thai styled bungalows and some cheaper rooms. Everything (a/c, en suite, cable TV) you'd expect from a place in this price range. Low-season, mid-week prices can be negotiated down.

Methavalai $$$$-$$
220 Ruamchit Rd, T032- 433250, methavalai.com.
A/c bungalows, some with several bedrooms – ideal for families – and a small area of private beach, pool, good seafood and Thai restaurant.

Dee-Lek $$-$
225/30-33, Ruamchit Rd, T032-470548.
Friendly guesthouse on the main beach road. The pricier rooms have nice balconies overlooking the beach and everything is clean, tidy – maybe a little dull –

and comes with hot water, TV and a/c. Also serves decent food.

Viwathana $$-$
263/21 Ruamchit Rd,
T032-471289.
One of the longer-established, with some simple, fan-cooled wooden bungalows as well as a new brick-built block. The more expensive bungalows have 2 or 3 rooms and a/c. Good value for families.

Jitravee $$-$
241/20 Ruamchit Rd,
T032-471382.
Clean rooms, friendly. More expensive rooms have a/c, TV, fridge, room service, bathroom. Cheaper rooms have clean, shared bathroom, some English spoken.

Pratarnchoke House $
240/3 Ruamchit Rd,
T032-471215.
Range of rooms available here from simple fan-cooled, through to some more luxurious a/c rooms with bathrooms. Some English spoken.

Kaeng Krachan National Park & caves

Bungalows $$ sleeping 5-6 are available at the park HQ but you must bring all necessities with you (eg blankets, food and water) as nothing is provided.

Khao Sam Roi Yod National Park

Bungalows $$ either for hire in their entirety or per couple. Camping ground, with tents for hire, ฿100. You can also pitch your own tent here for around ฿20. Bungalows are available at both the park HQ and at Laem Sala Beach. Remember to take mosquito repellent.

Prachuap Khiri Khan

With the influx of Thais at weekends, accommodation is hard to find. During the week, room rates can be negotiated.

Fah Chom Klun $$
Ao Manao beachfront,
T032-661088.
This military-run establishment is the only accommodation next to the Ao Manao beach and is often booked out. Rooms are basic and spotlessly clean – all en suite, some have sea views. Reservations are essential.

Sun Beach Guesthouse $$
60 Chaitalae Rd, T032-604770,
sunbeach-guest house.com.
Brand new property on the seafront. Has a pool and each en suite room is comfortably fitted complete with a/c and balcony, though the 'sea view' claim is a bit tenuous. Friendly.

Hadthong $$
21 Susuek Rd, T032-601050,
hadthong.com.
Comfortable rooms (but small bathrooms in the standard rooms) overlooking the sea with great views. The pool also enjoys views of the bay. It is good value and the best hotel in town. The restaurant serves good Thai food and a reasonable breakfast.

Feang Fa 5 Soi 4 Tam pramuk $
Susek Rd, T08-77928395.
Cute, very friendly guesthouse set in a nice wooden building in a leafy compound. Run by friendly Thai owner, Maggie, the simple fan-rooms are completed with some stylish touches. Shared bathrooms. Also rent bikes from ฿100 a day.

Chumphon

Chumphon Gardens $$$-$
66/1 Tha Tapao Rd,
T077-506888.
New hotel in central location, though set back a little from the road, so quiet. The cheaper rooms are excellent value – clean, with TV, en suite.

Paradorn Inn $$-$
180/12 Soi Paradorn, Saladaeng Rd, T077-511500, chum phon-paradorn.com.
A/c rooms with TV that are brighter, whiter and nicer than anything the competition offers. The restaurant has bamboo

furniture and offers a wide range of reasonably priced food (0800-2200).

New Chumphon Guesthouse $
27 Soi 1 Krom Luang Rd, T032-502900.
Clean, cosy rooms with wood-panelled floors upstairs and darker, cheaper rooms downstairs. Shared bathrooms. Homely atmosphere, friendly and helpful with management who speak good English. Tours to caves and waterfalls also arranged. Motorbike rental ฿200.

Around Chumphon

There are a number of hotels and bungalow operations at Hat thung Wua Laen Beach – the Chumpon Cabana is the most upmarket and right on the beach. At weekends local Thai families descend on the beach drinking beer and partying late into the night – it can be noisy.

Chumphon Cabana Resort $$$-$$
69 Moo 8, T077-560245-7, www.cabana.co.th.
Some nicely decorated a/c bungalows set in attractive gardens and 2 hotel blocks all with a/c and hot water. The newer buildings have all been designed on energy-saving principles in keeping with the owner's environmental concerns. The resort has all the usual

facilities including a pool, good watersports (including a PADI dive centre), a very peaceful location and a great view of the beach from the restaurant and some of the bungalows.

Chuan Phun Lodge $$-$
54/3 Moo 8, Thungwualaen Beach, T077-560120/230.
Attractive en suite rooms in this newish lodge/ hotel – the ones at the front have sea-facing balconies. Good value.

Clean Wave $$-$
54 Moo 8, Thungwualaen Beach, T077-560151.
Some rooms with a/c. Cheaper fan-cooled bungalows. Set in a big compound just back from the beach you're pretty much guaranteed your peace and quiet here. Friendly and efficient.

Baan Tanaya $$-$
16 Moo 8, T08-95927382.
Run by a friendly family who speak little English, the a/c, en suite rooms, each with a small balcony, open directly on to a nice stretch of the beach. They also serve some pretty good Thai food and have a small shop.

Sea Beach Resort and Bungalow $
4/2 Moo 8, Thungwualaen Beach, T077-560115.
Clean, cheap bungalows, some a/c, some fan, at this friendly resort, a favourite of the kitesurfing community.

Surat Thani

Southern Star $$$-$$
253 Chonkasem Rd, T077-216414.
The most luxurious hotel in the centre of town. The 150 rooms are tastefully decorated and are well equipped with satellite TV and minibar. There are 2 restaurants, one on the 16th floor which, in spite of great views over the city, is not recommended. For those looking for nightlife, the Southern Star is also home to the largest disco in the south.

100 Islands Resort and Spa $$-$
19/6 Moo 3, T077-201150-8, roikoh.com.
An attractive resort-style hotel on the highway, diagonally opposite the Tesco Lotus and Boots, right out of town. Some of the pleasant rooms open out directly on to the pool. There's a restaurant, jacuzzi, sauna and karaoke. Good value and recommended despite location.

Phongkaew Hotel $
126/3 Talat Mai Rd, T077-223410.
Small rooms, complete a/c, hot water, free Wi-Fi and cable TV, make this one of the best deals in town. Friendly and in a good location near the TAT office.

Bandon $

*268/2 Na Muang Rd, T077-272
167.*

The entrance is through a busy
Chinese restaurant. Clean, tiled
rooms, some a/c, all with private
shower rooms. Rooms get quite
stuffy though even with the fan
at full throttle. Good value and
quiet.

Nakhon

Twin Lotus Hotel $$$-$$

*97/8 Hatankarn- khukwag Rd,
outskirts of the town centre,
T075-323777.*

Nearly 400 a/c rooms with TV
and minibars, and a good-sized
swimming pool and fitness
centre. The usual services
expected for a top-end hotel.
The reasonable tariff includes a
buffet-style breakfast. A well-run
and well-maintained hotel.

Grand Park Hotel $$-$

*1204/79 Pak Nakhon Rd,
T075-317666-73.*

Opposite the Nakhon Garden
Inn, this is a bit of a block
architecturally and doesn't really
live up to its grand name, but it
has adequate rooms and is
centrally located with lots of
parking. A/c, hot water, bathtubs,
TV, minibar. One of the better
hotels in this category.

Thaksin Hotel $$-$

*1584/23 Si Prat Rd. T075-342790,
thaksinhotel.com.*

Comfortable, good-value rooms,
with cable TV, en suite and a/c.
Decent location, friendly and
some English spoken.

Nakhon Garden Inn $

1/4 Pak Nakhon Rd, T075-344831.
One of the nicest mid-range
places to stay – a rustic feel for
Nakhon, with 2 brick buildings
on either side of a large garden
compound with clean a/c rooms
and hot water. The rooms have
been nicely decorated – rather
dark, but good value and a bit
different from most of the places
in the city centre.

Thai Lee $

*1130 Rachdamnern Rd,
T075-356948.*

Large, bright, clean rooms with
fan and attached bathroom
(Western toilet), best-value
accommodation in the lower
end of the market.

Nai Phlao beach & Khanom

Khanom Golden Beach Hotel $$$-$$

*59/3 Moo 4, Ban Na Dan,
T075-326690, khanom@nksrat.
ksc.co.th.*

Hotel block with pool, snooker
room, children's room, tour desk,
restaurant and rental of windsurf
boards, sailing dinghies and
bicycles. Friendly and

professional staff. Rooms are
rather characterless but clean
and comfortable. The larger
more expensive suites are very
spacious and well equipped.

SuparRoyal Beach Hotel $$$-$$

*51/4 Moo 8, Hat Nai Phlao,
T075-528417.*

Hotel block under same
management as the Supar Villa.
Clean rooms, tiled floors,
generally very characterless but
every room has a sea view.

Alongot Resort $$

Khanom beach, T075- 529119.
The promising exterior of these
bungalows is ruined by very drab
interiors. The location is great –
right in the middle of Khanom
beaches' long sweep. They sell a
decent array of food as well.

Khao Luang National Park

The bungalows $$$ at the park
office of the Karom Waterfall
sleep up to 10 people. Camping
is possible if you have your own
gear. The second park office at
Krung Ching Waterfall,
T075-309644-5, has 2 guest-
houses $$$$-$$ and a campsite.
For homestay, see Activities and
tours, page 139.

Eating

With the Gulf Coast being a more popular destination for Thais and several of the resort towns being established long before tourists arrived the food options here are more varied than in other coastal areas. As with other beaches in Thailand many hotels, guesthouses and bungalows serve food.

Hua Hin

Try the central market for breakfast. Good seafood is widely available particularly at the northern end of Naresdamri Rd. Most of the fish comes straight from the boats which land their catch at the pier at the northern end of the bay. There is also a concentration of restaurants and bars geared to *farang* visitors along Naresdamri Rd and surrounding lanes.

Brasserie de Paris $$$
3 Naresdamri Rd, T032-530637.
A French restaurant with a great position on the seafront sandwiched between the squid piers. Attentive and prompt service. The speciality of Hua Hin crab is absolutely delicious.

Palm Pavillion $$$
Sofitel Central, 1 Damnoenkasem Rd.
1900-2300.
This seafood restaurant is probably the best in Hua Hin. Don't expect the usual range of Thai dishes; the chef is French.

Hua Hin Brewing Co $$$-$$
33 Naresdamri Rd, T032-512888.
0900-0200.
A partly open-air chaotic seafood restaurant serving good barbecued food. Also serves 3 home brews. Under-staffed during busy periods.

Lo Stivale $$$-$$
132 Naresdamri Rd, T032-513800.
1030-2230.
The best Italian restaurant in town although the pizzas are pretty standard. The house speciality of short pasta with crab meat and tomato sauce is recommended. Terrace and indoor seating available. Good and prompt service. Popular with foreign families.

Chao Lay $$
15 Naresdamri Rd, T032-513436.
Daily 1000-2200.
This place with its blue and white checked cloths on a stilted building jutting out into the sea is hugely popular with Thais. It has 2 decks and is a great place from where to watch the sunset. Fruits of the sea including steamed squid, huge seabass, rock lobster and prawns, are served up with military precision.

Maharaja $$-$
25 Naresdamri Rd, T032-530347.
Reasonable prices at this highly a/c Indian which is all peach decor, flower fabrics and fake chandeliers. Great naan bread and curries. Attentive service.

Veranda Grill $$-$
Veranda Lodge, 113 Hua Hin 67, Phetkasem Rd, T032-533678, verandalodge.com.
0700-2300.
Enjoy terraced dining on lapis lazuli blue tiles overlooking the beach. The basil air-dried squid is worth savouring.

Jeak Peak $
On the corner of Naebkhaehat and Dechanuchit roads.
This small shophouse is one of Hua Hin's most famous and longest standing noodle shops. Renowned for its seafood noodles and pork satay, this shop has been in the same location for 63 years and has lots of olde worlde charm. It's often packed but the queues are worth it.

Cafés & bakeries
Museum and tea shop
Sofitel Central, see Sleeping.
Take colonial tea here for a taste of old-world charm. Earl Grey followed by ham buns, scones, jam and cream, biscuits and peach tarts is a treat for ฿315.

World News Coffee
Naresdamri Rd, next to the Hilton.
Daily 800-2230.
Bagels, cakes, coffee and newspapers – at a price. Internet access too.

Foodstalls
There is an excellent food market opposite the Town Hall on

Damnoenkasem Rd. The night market just off Phetkasem Rd does the usual selection of cheap Thai food as well as seafood that is so fresh that they have to tie the crabs' and lobsters' pincers shut.

Cha-am

There are plenty of seafood restaurants along Ruamchit Rd, mostly serving the same dishes, including chilli crab and barbecued snapper with garlic. On the road into town from the highway you'll find dozens of places selling excellent grilled pork and Isaan-style food.

Moo Hang Nai Wang $
Almost opposite the KS golf sign on the road in from the highway.
This small shack, with Thai signage only, is arguably the best purveyor of authentic Isaan food on this stretch. Succulent grilled pork and chicken come with spicy papaya salad and sticky rice. It might require a bit of asking but this place is highly recommended for those wishing to be more adventurous in their culinary choices.

Neesky Café $
Almost on the corner of the beach road and the road linking to the highway.
This small, thatched place serves Thai food, steaks and supposedly the best burger in Thailand.

Prachuap Khiri Khan

Prachuap is famous for its seafood and there are a number of excellent restaurants (as well as some more average ones) in the centre of town and along the seafront. If you venture to Ao Manao there are a couple of open-air food courts selling excellent Thai food.

Laplom Seafood $$$-$$
North of the river.
Offers an extensive range of seafood, probably the best selection in town, reasonably priced and friendly.

Shiew Ocha II $$$-$$
On the seafront towards the north of the town.
Good seafood and meat dishes.

Mong Lai $$-$
2.5 km north of Laplom the north end of the bay below the mountain.
Country-style restaurant that is well known for its spicy dishes.

Panphochana $$-$
in the centre of town, 2 doors down from the Hadthong Hotel, T032-611195.
Open 1000-2200.
Welcoming, English-speaking owner, offers a vast range of seafood, pork and chicken. Breakfasts also served. Interior and outdoor dining possible with great views of the bay.

Plern Samut $$-$
on the seafront next to the Hadthong Hotel, T032-611115.
Daily 0900-2200.
One of the most famous restaurants in town the food here is awesome. Very friendly owner Khun Narong and his family have been running this place for more than 30 years – the squid and prawn are divine. Great location too, with outside seating looking over the bay.

Aroijung Steak $$-$
On main road to Ao Manao.
Daily 0800-2100.
Serves up great steaks and tasty Thai food (look for the sign). Very friendly and incredibly cheap.

Gossip A
Susuek Road.
Thu-Tue, 1030-2100.
Small, cute café set in an old wooden shop. Good for coffee, waffles and ice cream. Also serves up a few Thai dishes.

Chumphon

Farang Bar and Travel Agency $$-$
Tha Tapao Rd, T077-501003.
0430-0100.
Thai-style soups and salads, noodles, spaghetti dishes and baguettes. Porridge for breakfast too. Cocktails are served at ฿100. Drink and eat while watching a movie. The night staff here are a lot friendlier than the day staff.

Save your lunch from the local monkeys.

Puean Djai Restaurant $$-$
Opposite the railway station.
Open 1000-0200.
This restaurant is in an attractive garden setting. Very tasty pizzas using cheese from an Italian cheese factory in Prachuap Khiri Khan. Pasta, crêpes and Thai cuisine also concocted.

Lanna Han Isaan $
Set near the railway tracks in a cute garden.
Delicious, cheap Isaan food that is very popular with locals. The food here is very spicy so ask for *pet nit noi* (a little spicy).

Spaghetti House $
188/132 Saladaeng Rd,
T077-507320.
0900-2200.
A comfortable a/c restaurant serving tasty and filling spaghetti at reasonable prices. Also delicious smoothies and ice

creams with some unusual offerings: Japanese cucumber and durian ice creams. There's also a coffee house inside.

Foodstalls
There are 2 night markets on Krom Luang Chumphon Rd and on Tha Taphao Rd.

Around Chumphon

There are several restaurants spread along the length of Hat Thung Wua Lean Beach road but opening times can be erratic and depend on how busy things are.

Ok Mai $$
Next to Chuan Phun Lodge.
0830-2100 (when beach is quiet likely to be shut during day).
Excellent Western-style breakfasts and awesome pancakes. One of the best places to eat on the beach front.

Sabai Sabai $$-$
Far end of the beach.
From breakfast through to late but tends to open less during quiet periods.
French-run bar-cum-restaurant that serves up good burgers, fries and the like. Also has a pool table and plays good sounds.

Apple Cafe $$-$
Middle of the beach.
Normally 0800ish-1700ish.
One of the best and only places for coffee and tea and cake on the beach. Run by a friendly Canadian and his Thai wife.

Surat Thani

Lucky $$
452/84-85 Talat Mai Rd,
T077-2703267.
Open 0900-2200.
Lots of fried fish served up in the airy dining room with its faux-ranch ambience. Friendly, English-speaking staff.

The Pizza Company $$-$
Na Muang Rd, T1112, is close to Swensen's in a large building.
It serves what you'd expect but is recommended for being able to get a stab at a decent salad.

Swensen's $
Na Muang Rd, next to the Sahathai Department Store.
Open 1000-2200.
Sells dozens of ice creams in a/c coolness.

Noodle Shop $
Next to Phongkaew Hotel on Talat Mai Rd.
One of the most popular noodle shops is found here run by a friendly and slightly eccentric Thai-Chinese man. The beef noodle soup is superb.

Foodstalls
Foodstalls on Ton Pho Rd, near to the intersection with Na Muang Rd, sell delicious mussel omelettes. There's a good night market on Na Muang Rd, and on Ton Pho Rd and vicinity. There's a plentiful supply of fruit and *khanom* stalls along the waterfront. Market next to the local bus terminal (Talat Kaset I).

Nakhon

Prawns are Nakhon's speciality and farms abound in the area. Good seafood (including saltwater prawns) is available at reasonable prices in most of the town's restaurants. Roadside stalls sometimes sell a Nakhon speciality: small prawns in their shells, deep fried in a spicy batter and served as a sort of prawn pattie. **The Bovorn Bazaar,** in the centre of town off Rachdamnern Rd, is a good place to start in any hunt for food. It has restaurants, a bakery, a bar and a coffee shop.

A & A Restaurant $$
T075-311047.
Open 0700-2400.
A/c restaurant just down the road from the Nakhorn Garden Inn and marked with flags boasting fresh coffee. Serves Thai-style toasted bread with jam, marmalade, milk and sugar, excellent coffee, and tasty Thai food. It also does Western breakfasts for a reasonable price. Try the pork rib noodle soup and the chicken noodles.

99 Rock Bar and Grill $$-$
Bovorn Bazaar, Rachdamnern Rd, T075-317999.
Open 1100-1400, 1600-2300.
A Western-style bar with cold beer and a menu including pasta, pizzas, baked potatoes and grilled chicken.

Hao Coffee Shop $
Bovorn Bazaar, off Rachdamnern Rd.
It is charmingly decorated with antiques and assorted oddities and is like a museum piece with display cabinets everywhere.

Krour Nakorn $
At the back of Bovorn Bazaar off Rachdamnern Rd next to the massive trunk of an Indian rubber tree.
Pleasant eating spot, with open verandas, art work, wicker chairs and a reasonable line in seafood and other spicy dishes. You get given an entire tray of herbs and vegetables to go with your meal.

Bakeries
Ligo
Rachdamnern Rd and Bovorn Bazaar.
A good selection of pastries and doughnuts.

Sinocha (sign only in Thai)
Down the narrow alleyway by the Thai Hotel.
Perhaps even better than Ligos, it sells Danish pastries, doughnuts, as well as a good range of dim sum.

Foodstalls
Nam Cha Rim Tang is a stall in the Bovorn Bazaar, which sets up early evening and produces good banana *rotis*. Lining Rachdamnern Rd, along the wall of the playing fields, there are countless stalls selling *som tam*, a chilli-hot papaya salad from Thailand's northeastern region usually served with grilled chicken (*kai yaang*).

Khanom & Nai Phlao beaches

There are lots of foodstalls in Khanom town on Tambon Rd. On the beaches the only food is provided by the hotels, resorts and bungalows operators.

Entertainment

Beyond sunbathing and eating it's hard to find much to entertain Western travellers along the Gulf Coast. There is a smattering of festivals, a few traditional Thai activities such as Nakhon's shadow plays, but it's pretty thin stuff. Some of the busier beach spots will have restaurant-cum-bars.

The towns along the Gulf Coast are not particularly noted for their nightlife. Most of the top-end hotels will house bars of some description.

It's a fact

Shadow plays mostly relate to tales from the Ramakien and the Jataka tales. Narrators sing in ear-piercing falsetto accompanied by a band comprising *tab* (drums), *pi* (flute), *mong* (bass gong), *saw* (fiddle) and *ching* (miniature cymbals). There are two sizes of puppets. *Nang yai* (large puppets) which may be 2 m tall, and *nang lek* (small puppets). Shows and demonstrations of how the puppets are made can be seen at the workshop of Suchart Subsin, 110/18 Si Thammasok Soi 3 (take the road opposite Wat Phra Mahathat, turn left – at the top of the *soi* Suchart Subsin's house is signposted – and walk 50m). This group has undertaken several royal performances.

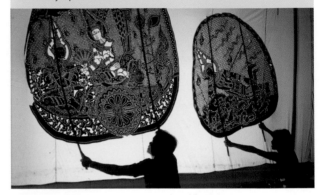

Hua Hin

Bars & clubs
The *sois* between Poonsuk and Naresdamri roads are stuffed, cheek by jowl, with bars catering to most tastes. The Hua Hin Brewing Co (see Eating, page 132), has a vast cavern-like pub with a giant screen for sports, open until 0200.

Festivals & Events
Hua Hin Jazz Festival
Jun
huahin jazzfestival.com.
Organized by the Hilton. Stages are set up in front of the Sofitel Central and railway station.

The King's Cup Elephant Polo tournament
Sep
thaielepolo.com.
Takes place at the Som Dej Phra Suriyothai military ground, south of Hua Hin.

Surat Thani

Festivals & events
Rambutan Fair
Aug (movable).

Chak Phra Festival
Oct-Nov (movable).
Marks the end of the 3-month Buddhist Rains Retreat and the return to earth of the Buddha. Processions of Buddha images and boat races on the Tapi River, in longboats. Gifts are offered to monks as this is also *krathin*, celebrated across Buddhist Thailand.

Nakhon

Festivals & events
Hae Pha Khun That
Feb.
A 3-day event when homage is paid to locally enshrined relics of the Buddha.

Tenth Lunar Month Festival
Sep-Oct (movable).
A 10-day celebration, the climax of which is the colourful procession down Rachdamnern Rd to Wat Phra Mahathat.

Shopping

Apart from the usual run of markets – many are listed in the guide text – shopping is not one of the Gulf Coast's high points.

Hua Hin

The most distinctive buy is a locally produced printed cotton called *pha khommaphat*. The usual tourist shops and stalls can be found lining most streets in the town.

Night market
Dechanuchit Rd, close to the bus station.
Dusk-2200.
Sells a range of goods including Tibetan jewellery, paper dragons, T-shirts, cassettes, watches and silk scarves.

Books
Bookazine
116 Naresdamri Rd, T032-532071.
Open 0900-2200.
English-language books, magazines and stationery.

Silk
Jim Thompson shop
In the Sofitel Central or the Hilton. Rashnee Thai Silk Village, 18/1 Naeb- khehehars Rd, T032-531155.
Open 0900-2100.
Allows visitors to see the full silk-making process from worm to finished product.

Nakhon

Nakhon is the centre of the south Thai handicrafts industry. Nielloware, *yan liphao* basketry (woven from strands of vine of the same name), shadow puppets, Thai silk brocades and *pak yok* weaving are local specialities.

Handicrafts
Shops on Tha Chang Rd, notably the Thai Handicraft Centre (in the lime green wooden house on the far side of the road behind the tourist office), Nabin House and Manat Shop. With the exception of the Thai Handicraft Centre, silverware predominates.

Shadow puppets
From the craftsmen at Suchart Subsin's House, Si Thammasok Rd, Soi 3 (see Entertainment, above) and stalls around Wat Phra Mahathat.

Activities & tours

Hua Hin

There are watersports and horse riding along the beach.

Golf
There are 5 championship golf courses close to Hua Hin including the Royal Hua Hin, the Springfield Royal Country Club, the Palm Hills Golf Resort and Country Club, Lake View and Majestic Creek Country Club. Royal Hua Hin Golf Course, behind the railway station, T032-512475, royal_golf@ hotmail.com. Designed in 1924 by a Scottish engineer working on the Royal Siamese Railway, it is the oldest in Thailand. Open to the public daily 0530-1930. Green fees ฿1500 at the weekend and ฿1200 during the week.

Muay Thai (Thai boxing)
Muay Thai Boxing Garden
8/1 Th Phunsuk, T032-515269.
Every Tue and Sat, 2100, ฿300 plus free drink.

Therapies
Mandara Spa
The Marriott, see Sleeping, page 127, T032-511881, ext 1810, mandara spa.com.
Open 0800-2000.
A heavenly experience. Its signature treatment is a red mud body detox (฿3100). Aroma-stone therapy (฿5520). Thai massage (฿2400) and body scrubs (exotic lime and ginger salt glow, ฿3300) are also offered.

Six Senses Earth Spa
The Evason, see Sleeping, page 126.
Awesome treatments, every-thing from reiki to basic Swedish massage, are available at this award-winning spa. The Earth Spa is sited in environmentally friendly mud huts designed to stay cool without a/c. Prices are high (฿2500-6000) but this is one of the most approachable and luxurious spas in Hua Hin.

The Spa
The Hilton, see Sleeping, page 126.
Open 1000-2100.
Has a large menu of different massages, facials using Guinot products, Thai fruit wrap (฿1850) and ancient Thai massage (฿1090). Twin share packages enjoy a 20% discount.

Tour operators
Tour operators are concentrated on Damnoenkasem and Phetkasem roads.

Western Tours
1 Damnoenkasem Rd, T032-533303, westerntours huahin. com.
Daily tours, THAI agent, transport tickets.
Its trip to Khao Sam Roi Yod (฿900) is recommended. Kayaking, elephant riding and golf tours organized.

Chumphon

Diving
Easy Divers
Ta Taphao Rd, T077-570085, chumphoneasydivers.net.
Takes divers to sites around the 41 islands off Chumphon.

Nereides Diving & Sailing Centre
T077-505451, nereidesthailand@ yahoo.com.
Located on Hat Thung Wua Laen beach this small, French-run dive shop organises tailor-made trips to most of the nearby dive sites, as well fishing tours and boat rental.

Kitesurfing
The beach at Chumphon is fast becoming one of the premier kitesurfing locations in the country. At the moment there is only one operator offering classes.

Kite Thailand
Chumphon in an office next to Seabeach Bungalows, T08-1090 3730 (mob), T08-9970 1797 (mob), kite thailand.com.
The friendly Dutch owner also runs sessions for all levels – a taster day, including equipment costs ฿4000 per person, a full 3-day course about ฿12,000.

Tour operators
Fame Tour and Service
118/20-21 Salad-aeng Rd, T077-571077, chumphon-kohtao. com.
Open 0430-2400.
Tours, boat tickets (taxi to pier included).. Sells tours including trekking to Pak Lake (buffaloes, elephants and monkeys), long-tailed boat cruises.

Farang Bar and Travel Agency
Tha Tapao Rd, T077-501003, farangbar@yahoo.com.
Friendly staff offering lots of information and selling all tickets. Free taxi to train station offered.

Kiat Travel
115 Tha Tapao Rd, T077-502127, chumphonguide.com.

New Infinity Travel Agency
68/2 Tha Taphao Rd, T077-570176, T08-1687 1825 (mob), new_infinity@hotmail.com.
Open 0600-2400.
Offers all tourist services, including a guesthouse, run by the very helpful manager.

Transport

Songserm
Tha Tapao Rd, next to New Infinity Travel, T077-506205.

Surat Thani

Tour operators
Phangan Tour
2000, 402/2 Talat Mai Rd,
T077-205799.
Office hours 0530-2200.
Travel to Koh Phangan.

Phantip Travel
293/6-8 Talat Mai Rd,
T077-272230.
A well-regarded and helpful agency dealing with boats, buses, trains and planes.

Samui Tour
*346/36 Talat Mai Rd,
T077-282352.*
Office hours 0600-1700.
Deals with Raja ferries to Koh Samui and Phangan and provides the bus transfer to Don Sak.

Nakhon

Khao Luang National Park
Khiriwong Agro Tourism Promotion Center, Moo 5, Tambon Kam Lon, Amphoe Lan Saka (near the park office), T075-309010, T08-1229 0829 (mob).
Offers tours to Krung Ching Waterfall, including whitewater rafting. Can organize homestays and guides.

Hua Hin

Air
There are daily flights with SGA who run a 12-seat Cessna from Bangkok. A taxi from the airport is ฿40-50, a local bus costs ฿10.

Train
Trains from from Bangkok take three hours and there are onward connections to all points south.

Bus
The bus terminal is quite central and provides regular connections with Bangkok and many southern towns.

Cha-am

Air-conditioned buses from Bangkok drop you right on the beach but other buses from Phetburi or Hua Hin stop on the Phetkasem Highway at its junction with Narathip Road. Motorbike taxis from here to the beach cost ฿20.

Prachuap Khiri Khan

There are regular bus and/or train connections with Bangkok, Hua Hin, Chumphon and Surat Thani.

Chumphon

Boat
There are boats to Koh Tao from two piers, one 10 km southeast of the town, the other 30 km away at Thung Makham Noi. Tickets for these boats can be bought at all the travel agents in town.

Bus
Buses and minibuses to Phuket, Ranong, Bangkok, Surat Thani and other points north and south. Regular train connections with Bangkok and all stops south.

Surat Thani

Air Asia (airasia.com) and **THAI** (thaiair.com) have regular flights to Bangkok.

Train
There are regular trains to Bangkok and points en route and south to Trang and the Malaysian border. There are a number of travel agents selling tickets and who can offer up-to-date timetabling (see Tour Operators).

Nakhon

Air
There is an airport north of town with daily flights to Bangkok. **Air Asia** (airasia.com) and **Nok Air** (nokair.com).

Bus
There are bus connections with Bangkok and most destinations in the south.

Taxi
Shared taxis leave from Yommarat Rd and connect to Phuket, Krabi and Trang, Surat Thani.

Contents

Gulf Islands

Temple of the Big Buddha on Koh Samui.

Introduction

I n just a couple of decades Thailand's Gulf Islands of Kohs Samui, Phangan and Tao have transformed from virtually unknown travellers' paradises into internationally recognised destinations. This transformation is best exemplified by Koh Samui's journey from backpackers' haven to sophisticated palm-studded tropical island beach resort. Its popularity is certainly deserved as it boasts some beautiful bays with sandy beaches hemmed by coconut palms seducing many a traveller. On the smaller Koh Phangan, which has equally gorgeous beaches, fame has been achieved via the world's largest outdoor party – the legendary Full Moon celebration- with the sands at Hat Rin playing home to up 10,000 people who flock to dance and drink the night away. Further north is the dive mecca of Koh Tao which is rimmed by remote bays guarded by huge granite boulder formations and surrounded by perfect tropical seas. Here, with the shallow waters, corals and diverse marine life, is one the planet's most popular places to learn to dive.

What to see in...

...a weekend
Koh Samui, with its better transport links, is the best destination for a short break. You can party in the bars and clubs in **Chaweng** or just relax on **Mae Nam** or **Bophut** beaches. Take in a *muay thai* kick boxing contest at the local stadium or relax eating fine sea food.

...a week or more
People can get stuck on the Gulf Islands for months – **Koh Phangan** is famed for its chilled out vibe, full moon parties and meditation centres. If you want to learn to dive, **Koh Tao** is Thailand's dive capital and has some excellent dive sites and schools.

The Christmas Tree Worm.

Koh Samui

The largest in an archipelago of 80 islands, only six of which are inhabited, many of Koh Samui's original inhabitants were not Thai, but Chinese from Hainan who settled on the island 150 to 200 years ago. Today, about 60,000 people live on Koh Samui with the annual number of visitors many times this figure. The first of these foreign tourists began stepping ashore on Samui in the mid-1960s. At that time there were no hotels, electricity (except generator-supplied), telephones or surfaced roads, just an over-abundance of coconuts. This is still evident because, apart from tourism, the mainstay of the economy is coconuts; two million are exported to Bangkok each month. These days most visitors end up on one of the island's two most popular beaches at Lamai and Chaweng, both on the east side of the island. They are the longest uninterrupted beaches on Samui, with good swimming and busy nightlife. If you want something a little more laid back then head to Mae Nam or Bophut, on the north shore, while there are several other smaller places scattered around the island.

Koh Samui.

While Nathon is Koh Samui's capital, and is where the ferry docks, the island's main attractions are its wonderful beaches; most people head straight to one, and remain there until they leave. Samui's capital is now completely geared to tourists, with travel agents, exchange booths, clothes stalls, bars and restaurants lining the three roads running parallel to the seafront, with two main roads at either end linking them. Although Nathon is used mainly as a transit point, it still has a friendly feel.

Throughout the island some evidence of the immigration of Hainanese is still reflected in the traditional architecture. Houses, though they may also incorporate Indian, Thai and Khmer elements, are based on the Hainanese style. The use of fretwork to decorate balconies and windows, the tiled, pitched roofs and the decoration of the eaves make the older houses of Samui distinctive in Thai terms. Sadly, it is unlikely that many will survive the next decade or two. They are being torn down to make way for more modern structures, or renovated and extended in such a way that their origins are obscured.

Two thirds of the island is forested and hilly with some impressive waterfalls (in the wet season). Hin Lad Waterfall and Wat are 3 km south of Nathon and can be reached from the town on foot, or by road 1 km off Route 4169. It's a 45-minute walk from the car park. Na Muang Waterfall, in the centre of the island, has a 30-m drop and a good pool for swimming. As the only waterfall on the island which is accessible by paved road it is busy at weekends and on holidays.

Tip...

March to June is hot and fine with a good breeze and only the occasional thunderstorm. At this time of year good discounts are available on accommodation.

Essentials

❶ Getting around *Songthaews* circulate during daylight hours and stop when flagged down – prices start at ฿50 per person but are often inflated – haggling may be required. Occasional night-time *songthaews* run from 1830 and charge double. Taxis do not use their meters. On average a fare from Nathon–Chaweng and from Bophut–Chaweng is ฿500. There are scores of places renting out motorbikes and jeeps but note that the accident rate on Koh Samui is horrendously high.

❷ ATM ATMs/exchange booths are available all over the island with the highest concentration on Chaweng Beach Rd.

⊕ Hospital 24-hr emergency clinic at Samui International Hospital, Chaweng, T077- 422272, sih.co.th (also has a dental clinic). Best to take injured to hospital as ambulance can be slow. In Big Buddha, Hyperbaric Services, 34/8 Moo 4, at Big Buddha, T077-427427, T08-1084 8485 (mob), ssnsnetwork.com

⌕ Post office Nathon Post Office, to the north of the pier, Mon-Fri 0830-1630, Sat-Sun 0830-1200. Lamai Post Office, south end of the main road.

❶ Tourist information TAT, 370 Moo 3, T077-420720, daily 0830-1630.

North coast

Still relatively undeveloped, Samui's northern run of bays and beaches is home to some good, low-key resorts.

Bang Po (Ban Poh) is a quiet, secluded and clean beach which is good for swimming making it one of the better options for those wanting to escape the buzz of Chaweng and Lamai.

Mae Nam offers a clean, serene beach with lots of coconut palms and fringed with coral reefs to tempt swimmers and snorkellers. It is a popular spot and a number of new, beautifully designed resorts have opened here. **Bophut** is one of the few places on the island where there are still traditional wooden Samui houses with Chinese lettering above the doors. It has grown increasingly popular in the last few years and there are now currency exchanges, bookshops, yoga schools, bars, restaurants and good watersports facilities.

Restaurants and bars light up Chaweng beach.

The beach is straight and narrow and lacks the sweeping expanse of Chaweng, or the quiet intimacy of Laem Set, yet the place maintains a refined, friendly village atmosphere with the string of restaurants making the beachfront a popular evening location. Most hotels offer fishing, snorkelling and sightseeing charters, although there are also plenty of independent outfits. As with most of the more remote beaches on Samui, the *songthaews* that are allotted for the beach run rather infrequently. It is possible to charter them and there are always motorcycle taxis around.

Big Buddha (Bang Ruk) is a small bay that has been a stomping ground with expats and travellers. Accommodation is cramped and it tends to be noisy as the bungalows are squashed between the beach and the road. However, the beach is quiet and the water is good. During the choppier weather from October to February, this sheltered cove is popular with fishing boats. **The Temple of the Big Buddha** sits on an island linked to the mainland by a short causeway, near Bophut beach. This unremarkable, rather featureless, modern seated image is 12 m high. In recent years the site has been smartened up and made into a 'proper' tourist attraction; there are now 50 or so trinket stalls at the entrance and several foodstalls.

Samrong Bay is set at the far northeastern corner of the island, this spot is also known as 'Secret Beach'. But it is not a secret any longer as there are two major resorts here.

Choeng Mon, at the northeast of the island is arguably the prettiest bay on the north coast. The crescent of extremely fine white sand has an island at its eastern end, attached to the mainland by a sandbar, traversable at low tide. While in places it is rocky underfoot in the centre of the bay, the sand continues well out to sea. The restaurant scene is pretty lively, particularly in the centre of the beach where bamboo tables with oil lamps reach right down to the water's edge and there are a couple of beach bars at the eastern end. The beach is most popular with couples and families. There is a *songthaew* station at the far eastern side of the area, behind the beach.

East coast

The east coast is the busiest part of the island and where most tourists – particularly those coming to Samui on a package deal – will end up. It has its charms though might not be for those who are looking for a quiet, secluded beach.

Chaweng is the biggest beach on the island and is split into three areas – north, central and Chaweng Noi. The latter is to the south, round a headland, and is home to of the most expensive hotels on the island. Central Chaweng is an attractive sweep of sand with lovely water for swimming and is lined with resorts, bungalows, restaurants and bars. The town that has grown up here is entirely geared towards tourists and in recent years it has become swamped. Along the road behind the beach there is a further proliferation of bars, clubs, tourist agencies, restaurants, fast-food chains, stalls and watersports facilities. However, the infrastructure has not kept pace with the concrete expansion and the drains stink in the searing heat. In comparison to the other beaches on the island it is crowded and getting more resort-ridden by the year, but it's still Samui's most popular and by far the busiest beach.

Lamai, Samui's 'second' beach, is 5 km long and has a large assortment of accommodation. The beach is nice but rugged and not as attractive as Chaweng with rocks in many places. Cheaper accommodation can be found more readily here than on Chaweng. Just south of Lamai, there is a cultural hall and a group of phallic rock formations known as Grandmother and Grandfather rocks (Hinyai and Hinta). There's an array of tourist shops leading up to it. Companies along the main road parallel to the beach offer fishing and snorkelling trips around the islands. The sea at Lamai can be wild and challenging during the early months of the year, and suitable only for the most competent of swimmers. Due to the tide there are not as many watersports here and the sea can appear murky, particularly at the northern end. Many hotels and restaurants are geared to the German market.

South coast

The small, often stony, beaches that line the south coast from Ban Hua Thanon west to Thong Krut are quieter and less developed with only a handful of hotels and bungalows, although construction continues at a breathless pace and the area is littered with endless 'land for sale' boards. While most tourists head for the white sands and sweeping shores elsewhere, there are some beautiful little coves peppered along this southerly stretch.

Ban Hua Thanon is an attractive rambling village with wooden shophouses and *kway tio* (noodle) stalls – and the only Muslim community on Koh Samui. The forebears of the inhabitants come from Pattani in Thailand's far south. With its stony beach being the biggest anchorage for fishing boats on the island, this village is quiet and rarely visited by tourists. North of the village are a couple of restaurants, well situated with cooling sea breezes.

Na Khai is a small beach with just a handful of resorts. The swimming can be rocky, but if you are looking for a quiet place to stay and don't require a classic sweep of golden sand, then this is an option. **Laem Set** is not really much of a beach compared with Chaweng and Lamai. However, it is quiet, clean and palm fringed and there is some reasonable snorkelling.

Samui Butterfly Garden T077-424020, 0830-1730, ฿170, is set on the side of the hill behind Laem Set Inn opposite Central Samui Village. It features a screened butterfly garden with a limited collection of butterflies, a display of (dead) insects, moths and butterflies, a few beehives, a hillside observatory, observation platforms for views of the coast, a glass-bottomed boat for viewing a coral reef and a restaurant.

Thong Krut Bay and the hamlet of **Ban Thong Krut** are at the southern extremity of the island. The stony beach is around a kilometre long and the swimming is average but there are excellent views from here and it is peaceful and undeveloped with just a handful of shops including a little supermarket and The Beach, Java and Green Ta'Lay restaurants. Boat trips to a couple of nearby much smaller islands or to fish and snorkel can be arranged through various companies in the village. Nearby, is the **Samui Snake Farm**, 88/2 Moo 4, T077-423247. Shows are held at 1100 and 1400. The commentary is hilarious. Not for the squeamish.

West coast

Like the south coast, the western coastline south of Nathon is undeveloped with secluded coves and beautiful sunsets. **Phangka**, near the southwest tip of the island, has good snorkelling in the quiet waters of a small bay; **Thong Yang**, further north, is an isolated beach, relatively untouched by frantic development. The vehicle ferry from Don Sak, on the mainland, docks here.

Diving in the Gulf

With its numerous dive schools and excellent conditions for beginners Koh Tao is now one of the busiest places on the planet for learner-divers. The reason for this is simple – Koh Tao has diving just seconds from the beach. There's plenty to see including resident green and hawksbill turtles although over-development has caused problems both for the turtles and the reefs. There is some positive news though. Around Koh Tao, there are several deep water pinnacles that provide some of the best diving in the region. Conditions in the Gulf are highly variable which is why serious divers tend to stick to the Andaman Sea. Even in peak season visibility can be as low as three metres, but will clear to an incredible 40 m in an instant. The shallow seabed and current patterns are such that sediment never has the opportunity to disperse to deeper waters.

Koh Samui also has a plethora of dive schools but the better diving is at least an hour away in the Ang Thong National Marine Park where hidden lagoons and sheer limestone cliffs reflect the style of the underwater scenery. The waters here are rarely more than 10 m deep and the visibility is never crystal clear due to fresh water run-off from the mainland. However, these are ideal conditions for novices. The reefs are pretty, the diving is pleasant but not too challenging and it's great for snorkellers.

The largest fish on the planet, the whaleshark is one of the biggest reasons experienced divers head to Koh Tao and the Chumphon Pinnacle. Growing up to 12.2 m (40 ft) in length and weighing up to 13.5 tonnes, these humungous aquatic behemoths feed mostly on plankton, filtering these microscopic creatures out of the water in much the same way whales do. Most often they are solitary creatures but occasionally they will group at a particularly abundant feeding station. They are also incredibly slow moving, only reaching 5 kph (3 mph), meaning that they can be easy to track. Whalesharks are also known for their friendly and peaceful posture towards divers – there have been no recorded cases of attack. The best time to see whalesharks in the Gulf is March and April.

Sail Rock

One of the most famous dive trips is to Hin Bai or Sail Rock. Jutting out of the water 18 km off Samui's north shore, and about halfway between Phangan and Tao, this rock rises from 30 m below to just above the surface. It is covered in beautiful green and yellow corals and frequented by large marine animals like reef sharks and rays. Its unique feature, though, is the spectacular journey upwards through an underwater chimney that is flooded with beams of sunlight. It feels like ascending inside a cathedral spire. Visibility here is some of the best in the Gulf as the pinnacle is an exposed site and the currents keep plankton and sediment on the move.

Chumphon Pinnacle

The best dive in this area is undoubtedly Chumphon Pinnacle, where tales of big marine mammals have hit legendary status. A massive granite pinnacle soars from 40 m to about 16 m below the surface and is surrounded by a group of smaller ones. Diving here is a bit like a wander through an underwater mountain range. There are large plateaux covered in healthy hard corals, sponges and seawhips which lead back up the pinnacles to reveal a huge variety of life. Giant groupers and batfish are always hovering around while white-eyed morays reside amongst the colourful coral gardens. Not only are huge schools of jacks spotted regularly, but occasionally there are also whalesharks and sailfish. Even whales have been seen.

White Rock

Ko Nang Yuan is said to be the only place in the world where three islands are joined together by sandbars. The islands are ringed by a variety of shallow dive sites and there are some beautiful arches to swim through. The most exciting dive is probably White Rock, which is actually two submerged granite boulders sitting 12 m apart. The site is a great place for finding all sorts of reef creatures like stingrays and butterflyfish. Being quite shallow, it also makes a good night dive. However, its main claim to fame is local personality, Trevor, the terrible triggerfish. This giant trigger is a chap with an attitude problem and, despite being a permanent resident on a fairly busy dive, has been known to nip at unwary divers' fins.

Tip...

The best diving and facilities are, without doubt, accessed from Koh Tao. There are a few liveaboards with schedules best described as flexible - if the boat isn't full it won't go. Be sure to check the operators' policy on this.

Koh Phangan

The Gulf's party island, Phangan is world renowned for its Full Moon Party that attracts thousands of young people looking for the night of their life on the sands at Hat Rin. The pace of development on the island has been rapid and while still partly unspoilt it is not as beautiful as parts of Koh Samui and Koh Tao. The beaches at Hat Rin and some along the east coast are attractive and – except for Hat Rin – uncrowded. The water is good for snorkelling, particularly during the dry season when clarity is at its best. Between May and September the tide is out all day between Mae Hat and Hat Rin. Fishing and coconut production remain mainstays of the economy, and villages still have a traditional air – although tourism is now by far the largest single industry.

A young coconut palm.

Thong Sala & around

Koh Phangan's main town is the port of **Thong Sala** (pronounced Tong-sala) where most boats from Koh Samui, Surat Thani and Koh Tao dock. Thong Sala has banks, ATMs, telephone, internet access, travel agents, a small supermarket, dive shops, motorbike hire and a second-hand bookstore. Humming during the day with all the departures and arrivals, this can be a bit of a ghost town during the evenings, although it's a pleasant place to spend the night, with some good restaurants.

On the coast to the east of Thong Sala, outside Ban Tai, is **Wat Khao Tum** and the **Vipassana Meditation Centre** – all-inclusive fees are ฿4500 for 10 days, contact Wat Khao Tum, Koh Phangan, Surat Thani, for more information, or watkowtahm. org, where they provide a contact and booking facility. There are views from the hilltop *wat* to Samui and the Ang Thong Islands. Ten-day meditation courses are held every month with 20-day courses and three-month retreats also available. All the courses are conducted in English.

The rest of Phangan offers natural sights such as waterfalls, forests, coral and viewpoints but little of historical or cultural interest. Sometimes the best way to explore the island is on foot, following tracks that link the villages and beaches, which cannot be negotiated by *songthaew* or motorbike. It is possible to walk on a trail from Hat Rin up the east coast to Hat Thien, although other paths are swiftly swallowed up by the forest.

The interior

Phaeng Waterfall is to be found about 4.5 km from Thong Sala and 2 km from the village of Maduawan. The walk east to Hat Sadet runs parallel to a river along which are three waterfalls and the carved initials of several Thai kings who visited here, including King Chulalongkorn (Rama V), who was so enamoured that he reportedly came here on 10 occasions between 1888 and 1909, and the present King Bhumibol (Rama IX), who came in

Essentials

❶ **Getting around** There are regular boats connections to/from Samui, Tao, Chumphon (see page 116) and Surat Thani (see page 117). For more detailed travel information see page 171. *Songthaews* run from the pier to any of the bays served by road. A trip to Hat Rin from Thong Sala is ฿80-100. At Hat Rin *songthaews* wait close to the Drop in Club Resort. For a few beaches this is the best option. For remote beaches it is often easiest to travel by long-tailed boat or walk. Motorbikes and mountain bikes are available for hire though roads are dangerous.

❺ **ATM** ATMs and exchange booths are concentrated on the main road in Thong Sala, in Hat Rin and also throughout the island.

⊕ **Hospital** Koh Phangan Hospital, about 2.5 km north of Thong Sala, offers 24-hr emergency services. Bandon International Hospital, in Hat Rin, T077-375471, is a 24-hr private clinic with English-speaking staff. Facilities are better in Samui or Bangkok.

❷ **Post office** Hat Rin, close to pier, Mon-Fri 0830-1640, Sat 0900-1200.

❶ **Tourist information** There is no official tourist information on the island. The TAT office on Koh Samui, see page 145, is responsible for the island. See kohphangan.com and phangan.info, for information.

1962. The waterfalls can be reached on foot or on mountain bikes. Other waterfalls include **Ta Luang** and **Wang Sai** in the northwest corner, **Paradise** in the north (near the Paradise Resort), and **Thaan Prawet** and **Wung Thong** in the northeast corner. The highest point is **Khao Ra** (627 m). A path runs to the summit although visitors have reported that the trail is indistinct and a guide is necessary.

South coast

The stretch of beach from **Ao Bang Charu** to **Ao Hinsong Kon** is unpopular with visitors due to its proximity to Thong Sala and as a result accommodation is good value and bungalows are well spread out and quiet. The beach shelves gently and is good for children, but the water is a little murky.

Around the region

The beach between **Ban Tai** and **Ban Khai** may not be as good as at Hat Rin and there is a lot of wood debris about, but this is more than made up for by cheaper accommodation and less noise. Some snorkelling and good swimming is possible and it is generally quiet, although on the monthly black moon parties the beach comes alive with techno beats. The area is also well-located for the twice-monthly half moon parties in the nearby jungle and the Wat Po herbal sauna. In July and August the tide is out all day.

Hat Rin

Hat Rin is home to the world-famous **Full Moon Parties** when thundering bass-lines rock the beach and the streets are awash with alcohol (see box, opposite). There are also Half Moon Parties, Black Moon Parties, Pre-Full Moon Parties – in fact any excuse for a party – on the beach so it has become famous for almighty blow outs.

Hat Rin is at the southeastern tip of Koh Phangan and has the best and most popular beach on the island with some good snorkelling. It also has the greatest concentration of bungalows which are packed close together (except on the hillsides). The 'east' beach, **Hat Rin Nok**, is more attractive and is cleaned every morning. During the day it is packed with sunbathers, coloured blow-up lilos, a small number of hawkers, volleyball nets and the water is crammed with long-tailed boats. The 'west' beach, **Hat Rin Nai**, is smaller and almost non-existent at high tide; accommodation is slightly cheaper here. The two beaches, less than 10 minutes' walk apart, are both wonderfully quiet until about 1300, as most people are sleeping off the night's excesses. At night the noise from generators and the bars can be overpowering on Hat Rin Nok but a few minutes' walk away from the action towards Hat Rin Nai, the music, incredibly, is inaudible – this applies on full moon nights too. Theft has become a real problem in the area, use safety deposit boxes for valuables and secure bungalows with extra locks wherever possible – especially when sleeping.

Hat Rin.

East coast

The beaches and coves from **Hat Thien** to **Hat Sadet** are only accessible by boat. The stretch of stony coastline at Hat Thien doesn't afford much for those hoping to lie and fry, but its rocky, tree-lined character makes it an attractive and rugged area. It's not a bad option at all: there are cheap guesthouses and it's possible to walk over the headland to Hat Yuan where the beautiful and popular white-sand beach is much more palatable to sun worshippers.

Ao Thong Nai Pan Noi and **Ao Thong Nai Pan Yai** is a double bay boasting some of the most beautiful, quiet, white-sand beaches on the island, romantically hemmed in by the mountains and with among the highest recurring visitor rates. Yai has more palms leaning over the beach but Noi has a wider beach and is a bit more bustling. It is said to have been Rama V's favourite beach on the island, and it's not hard to see why – plenty of people come here for a short holiday and end up staying for months. It remains fairly off the beaten tourist track and is more a place to relax for those whose main aim is not to party. The journey by truck from Thong Sala takes almost an hour and the road is muddy in the rainy season.

Full Moon parties

Unfortunately, over the past few years rape and violent robbery have badly tarnished the friendly atmosphere. Many people do attend without any problems but caution is highly recommended. There have also been several stories of post-party boats to Koh Samui being dangerously overloaded with deaths occurring – it is recommended that you avoid these services completely.

On full moon night, if you are not planning to party till dawn, it is advisable to stay on Hat Rin West or elsewhere on the island, unless you feel you can sleep to the boom of the bass from the beach. Up to 10,000 people turn up on Hat Rin East every month to dance, watch the jugglers, fire eaters and firework displays and drink themselves into oblivion.

Don't bring valuables with you; if a safety deposit box is an option at your bungalow, leave everything there. Don't leave anything of value in bungalows that are easily broken into. Do not eat or drink anything that is offered by strangers.

Wear shoes. The beach gets littered with broken glass and some people suffer serious injury from this.

Carry the business (name) card of your bungalow in case you get lost. Don't take drugs. Plainclothes policemen regularly arrest a number of Westerners who are only released on bail if they can pay the stiff fine/bribe. Otherwise they will be held for five to six weeks prior to trial.

Further information can be found on the following websites: fullmoon.phangan.info; halfmoonfestival.com; and kohphangan.com.

North coast

About 5 km northwest of **Thong Nai Pan**, **Ao Hat Kuat**, more commonly known by its English translation '**Bottle Beach**', is even more isolated, with a beautiful beach. Staff at the bungalows here are not as friendly as they could be. Despite developing a reputation as a bit of a British ghetto and a huge new development here, it retains its escapist appeal.

Along a rutted track, **Ao Hat Khom** is another relaxed place and many stay for weeks. The bay is fringed by a reef offering some of the best snorkelling on Phangan; however, because the seabed shelves gently, swimming is sometimes only really possible at high tide and getting out to the reef can be tricky.

Hat Salat is one of the most peaceful parts of the island, though due to its picturesque bay it is also one of the fastest-developing spots. **Ao Mae Hat** has a super beach with a sandy bank extending outwards. There are palm trees, a few bungalows and good snorkelling.

West coast

Ao Hat Yao is an attractive curved, clean beach on the west coast with good swimming and snorkelling, 20 minutes by *songthaew* from Thong Sala. Bungalows are spread out and quiet.

To the south of Ao Hat Yao, **Ao Chaophao** is a relatively quiet and undeveloped bay with just a handful of places to stay. The perfect crescent of sand and sunsets make the bay particularly attractive. There is also good swimming because the seabed shelves steeply before reaching the reef around 100 m offshore where there is good snorkelling. At the southern end is a lagoon and the coast here also has some remnant mangroves.

Ao Sri Thanu is a long but rather narrow beach, 15 minutes by *songthaew* from Thong Sala. It is a peaceful spot to spend a few days and is sparsely settled but is not very attractive. Behind the beach is a freshwater lake fringed by pine trees which is ideal for swimming.

North of Thong Sala and south of Ban Sri Thanu, the beaches at **Ao Wok Tum** are average and the swimming is poor. Accommodation is good value though. The beaches between **Ao Hin Kong** and **Ao Nai Wok** aren't that striking and swimming is difficult as the seabed shelves so gently. However, it is quite attractive with shallow boulders near Cookies and it is not rocky underfoot for the first 10 m or so. Accommodation is good value.

Koh Tao

A boat hop from Phangan is Koh Tao, the smallest of the three famous Gulf of Thailand islands. It is a big dive and snorkelling centre with plenty of shallow coral beds and tropical fish. The waters – especially in the south and east – are stunning, a marbling of turquoise blue, sapphire, emerald and seaweed green. For non-divers this small island offers a surprisingly high number of independent upmarket resorts, with the added bonus of quiet beaches. Over the last few years Koh Tao has transformed itself from unknown destination to one of the most popular places to learn to dive on the planet. The accessibility of interesting marine life at depths available to beginners, the fairly gentle currents and the low costs have all contributed to this popularity. The presence of giant manta rays and whalesharks means that more experienced divers will also find something of interest here. The name Koh Tao, translated as 'turtle island', relates to the shape of the island.

The waters around Kao Tao are home to some interesting marine life.

Ban Mae Hat & the west coast

The harbour is at the island's main village of **Ban Mae Hat**. On both sides of the harbour there are small beaches with a few resorts. These areas have easy access to the town. There are numerous shops from fashion boutiques to bookstores and supermarkets and some of the best restaurants as well as a burgeoning nightlife, post office, money exchanges, dive shops, tour operators, transport and foodstalls.

To the north of Ban Mae Hat on the west coast, is the white-sand curved beach of **Hat Sai Ri**. Stretching to around 2 km, it is the longest beach on the island with the sweep of sand only interrupted by the occasional large boulder. It has the widest range of accommodation, and many restaurants, shops, dive centres and bars. Although it is a bustling beach with some great bars, the debris – plastic bottles, rotting wood and the like – left by the retreating tide is really unsightly.

North coast

The little cove of **Ao Mamuang** is only accessible by boat so it remains quiet and unfrequented. It is a great place for solitude and there is some good snorkelling.

Off the northwest coast of Koh Tao is **Koh Nang Yuan**. Once a detention centre for political prisoners, this privately owned island consists of three peaks and three connecting sandbars, making it a mini-archipelago. It's surrounded by crystal-clear water and some wonderful coral. Lomprayah runs boats to the island at 1030, 1500 and 1800, returning at 0830, 1330 and 1630.

East coast

Ao Hin Wong is a peaceful bay with fantastic views but no beach. However, you can swim off the rocks and boulders and there is some great snorkelling – turtles have been spotted here. The accommodation consists of simple huts tumbling down the steep hillsides.

Essentials

❶ **Getting around** There are regular boat connections to/from Samui, Tao, Chumphon (see page 116) and Surat Thani (see page 117). For more detailed travel information see page 171.

There's only one surfaced road on Koh Tao. Motorbike taxis and pick-ups are the main form of local transport and the island is great for walking. Long-tailed boats can be chartered to reach more remote beaches. You can also rent motorbikes (the tracks and roads are not for novices) and mountain bikes.

❸ **ATM** ATMs and exchange booths can be found near the pier in Ban Mae Hat – a few more are scattered around the island.

⊕ **Hospital** Badalaveda Diving Medicine Centre, Sai Ri, T077-456664; Koh Tao Physician Clinic, Sai Ri T077-456037, T081-737 5444, 0800-1900; Koh Tao Health Centre, Mae Hat, T077-456007.

➋ **Post office** Thongnual Rd, Mae Hat, straight up from the pier and turn left, Mon-Fri 0830-1630.

❶ **Tourist information** There is no official tourist information on the island. Try kohtao.com or the free quarterly Koh Tao Info magazine, kohtaoinfo.tv.

The wooden chalets of Rock View, Koh Tao.

Tip...

Avoid bringing any plastic bottles or tin cans to Koh Tao as these are difficult to dispose of. Some environmentalists advise people to drink cans rather than bottles of beer as few businesses find it economically viable to recycle bottles and simply dump them. In addition, due to reduced rainfall in recent years, water is now a great problem on the island, and much of it is imported from the mainland. Visitors should use it sparingly.

Koh Tao boat trips.

South of Ao Hin Wong, the bay of **Ao Mao** has just one resort and some great snorkelling, particularly at the Laem Thian pinnacle. It is among the more remote and secluded places to stay on Koh Tao.

Continuing south, the bay of **Ao Ta Not** is served by a poor road but vehicles brave the conditions to ferry guests. This is one of the more remote bays and it has a good beach. Although it is not as pretty as Hin Wong, it is wider, has boulders, and more facilities, more expensive accommodation, restaurants, watersports and diving (see page 169).

Lang Khaai Bay is littered with dozens of boulders which are reached from a steep slope. The bay is good for snorkelling but there is only a tiny slither of beach.

The beach at **Ao Leuk** shelves more steeply than most of the others around Koh Tao and so is good for swimming and has some of the best snorkelling on the island. This is a quiet beach in spite of visiting groups.

South coast

Next to **Ao Chalok Ban Kao, Ao Thian Ok**, also known as Shark Bay, is a beautiful, privately owned bay with the Jamahkiri Spa and Resort set on one hillside. The sea is a stunning mix of blues and greens while the attractive beach is lined with a strip of coconut palms. The bay is known for the black-tip reef sharks that congregate here.

The area of **Taa Toh** 'lagoon' is on the south coast and consists of three beaches, the largest of which is **Hat Taa Toh Yai**. There is good snorkelling on the far side of the lagoon from Hat Taa Toh Yai with reef sharks and more. There is easy access from here to **Ao Chalok Ban Kao** where a gently shelving beach, enclosed within a horseshoe bay on the south coast is capped with weirdly shaped giant boulders. It has a good range of accommodation, restaurants and nightlife. This large bay also has the highest concentration of diving resorts.

Hat Sai Nuan is an isolated bay, only accessible by long-tailed boat or by a pleasant 30-minute walk around the hilly headland. There are just a handful of places to stay and a relaxed atmosphere. It is arguably the best spot on the island.

Sleeping

Bophut Village
The Waterfront $$$$-$$$
71/2 Moo 1, T077- 427165, thewaterfrontbophut.com.
Modern and attractive bungalows set around a small pool close to the beach but still in the village itself. Renovated and expanded by its British owners in 2003, it has a cosy atmosphere and is popular with families. Rooms have kettles and DVD player. Free childminding and Wi-Fi. The low-season prices are a bargain.

The Red House $$$
T077-425686, design-visio.com.
A delightful place with 4 boudoirs with balconies that are elegantly furnished with Chinese textiles in deep reds and attractive furniture. The 4-poster beds look over the sea.

Bophut Beach
Anantara $$$$
101/3 Bophut, T077-428300, anantara.com.
With resorts and spas throughout Thailand, Anantara's well-designed Samui resort is chic and comfortable with a luxurious yet traditional feel. The striking lobby is dominated by a cluster of lanterns and doors imprinted with golden stencilling. This opens out onto a stunning, rectangular lotus pond. The infinity pool overlooks a well-kept section of the beach.

The spa (1000-2200) is a cool oasis in the grounds. The Italian full moon restaurant occupies a stylish raised platform with superb views.

Chalee Villa $$-$
Western tip of the beach, T078-857884.
This is a blast from the past with simple Thai-style beach bungalows spread leisurely along the shore a few metres from the waves. Basic, but clean and comfortable with friendly staff and a relaxed ambience – the best of the strip's budget accommodation.

Big Buddha
Shambala $$-$
23/2 Moo 4, T077-425330, samui-shambala.com.
A well-kept bohemian beach resort with 14 cute, bright, blue, fan bungalows amid a sweet garden with flourishing bougainvillea. A good choice for those looking for a serene, budget option and relaxed atmosphere. There's a great chill-out area with books and games and a detailed information board. Run by friendly and helpful Brits.

Samrong Bay
Sila Evason Hideaway $$$$
T077-245678, sixsenses.com.
Ultra-chic and exclusive resort and spa with cool, calm and minimalist lines. 66 hidden villas with rectangular private pools and luxury sundecks. There are 2 restaurants, a gym, shop and Six Senses Spa (1000-2200). The massage rooms overlook the sea. The Drinks on the Hill bar has cracking cocktails – especially the bellinis.

Arayaburi, formerly Bay View Village $$$$-$$$
6/14 Moo 5, T077-427500, samui- hotels.com/arayaburi/.
Offers 65 villas, with small private terraces that are fairly closely packed. Superior rooms are nice and light and there are flowers on all beds. Garden view bungalows do not get much of a view. Beachside pool, bike, motorbike and canoe hire available. It shares a private beach with the Sila Evason Hideaway.

Choeng Mon
Sala Samui $$$$
Suratthani office: 10/9 Moo 5, Baan Plai Lam Bo Phut, Suratthani 84320, T077-245888, Bangkok office: 19/F Thaniya Plaza Building Zone A/1, 52 Silom Road, Suriyawong, Bangrak, Bangkok 10500, salasamui.com.
Stunning luxury hotel with award-winning design. The beachside pool is surrounded by decking and hidden private villas that have pools, raised relaxing platforms and outdoor bathtubs, all with a Mediterranean feel. The Mandara spa is open 1000-2200.

The White House $$$$-$$$
Centre of the beach, 59/3 Moo 5, T077-245315, hotelthe whitehouse.com.
Set in a delightful shady tropical garden, this is a small collection of large white houses with Thai details. The refined hotel also has a medium-sized pool in a cosy position just behind the beach and restaurants.

Koh Samui East coast

Chaweng
Poppies $$$$
T077-422419, poppiessamui.com.
Beautifully designed to maximize space, these a/c Thai-style houses have open-air bathrooms and are set in a tropical garden with water running through it. There is an excellent, popular open-air restaurant (see Eating, page 165) and a small pool. The Swiss management offers outstanding service and one of its marketing gimmicks has been to set up a live video cam overlooking Chaweng beach 24 hours a day.

Corto Maltese $$$$-$$$
119/3 Moo 2, T077-230041, corto-samui.com.
Interestingly designed small resort, next to the beach, far removed from the generic hotel room design. The bright blue huts have playfully sculptured interiors, which are very comfortable, with a/c, fridge and TV as standard. Spilt level flooring

separates the lounge from the sleeping area and bathroom. Swimming pool, jacuzzi and beachfront restaurant.

Beach Love $$$
Next to Impiana, T077-422531, beachlovesamui@hotmail.com.
Modern building built on stilts so that all four rooms have sea views. The rear backs on to the road. Cool urban interiors with concrete screed flooring, pale blue colour scheme and sleek white sanitary ware. TV, a/c, fridge, bay window and balcony.

Lamai
Spa Resort $$$$-$$$
T077-230855, spasamui.com.
As far as holistic health resorts go, this is excellent: the services provided are good value, the staff welcoming and award-winning restaurant. Run by an American and his Thai wife, it has a sauna, steam room and a small pool and offers daily yoga, t'ai chi and meditation. The cheaper bungalows with attached bathrooms are excellent value. The rocky, shallow beach here is busy with boats. Book ahead.

Bill Resort $$$$-$$
T077-424403, bill resort.com.
A fabulously quirky and stylish retreat with excellent standards of service and accommodation on an attractive and fairly secluded beach. The resort, with its range of well spaced, elegantly designed and

Tip...
Over full moon most places insist on a 7-night stay at inflated prices – don't turn up expecting to find a room in Hat Rin.

well-furnished rooms, climbs a hillside giving it a slightly magical village feel. Pool, jacuzzi, restaurant and travel services.

Lamai Coconut Resort $$
124/4 Moo 3, T077-232169.
With 33 immaculate bungalows close to the beach, this resort has some of Lamai's best-value rooms. With shiny wooden floors, linen, fridges, elegant furniture and large windows, the bungalows feel luxurious despite the modest fan-room rate.

New Hut $
Next to Beer's House, T077-230437.
Simple, but good quality, 'A' frame bamboo huts, slap bang on the beach, with mattress on the floor, mosquito net, fan and shared bathroom. There are also bungalows with bathroom inside available. Funky restaurant.

Koh Samui South coast

Laem Set
Kamalaya $$$$
102/9 Moo 3, Laem Set Rd, T077-429800, kamalaya.com.
This 'wellness sanctuary and holistic spa' is the latest,

distinctly upmarket place to cater for Samui's spiritual tourists. Oriental and Western healing practices influence treatments. The excellent hillside spa is centred around a monk's cave and commands spectacular views. A range of exceptionally stylish rooms are available overlooking the small sandy bay. The service is unbeatable and both restaurant and poolside *shalas* offer detox specialities as well as indulgent delights at reasonable prices. Non-residents are welcomed.

Thong Krut
Emerald Cove $
62 Moo 4 Taling Ngam, Phanga Beach, T077-334100.
Although isolated and poorly signposted, this attractive spot on the southwest corner of the island is worth seeking out. 10 en suite bungalows, with the more expensive rooms featuring a rock-lined bathroom, TV, fridge, kitchen sink and oddly dated decor.

Koh Samui West coast

Wiesenthal Resort $$$$-$$$
227 Moo 3 Taling Ngam, T077-235165, sawadee.com/ hotel/samui/wiesenthal/.
Standing out among its competitors on the west of the island, this German-owned business is clean, excellent value and sits directly on an attractive beach with great views out to sea. The spotless octagonal a/c rooms have TVs and fridges.

Koh Phangan South coast

Phangan Beach Resort $$$-$$
112/1 Moo 1, Bang Charu & Ao Hinsong Kon, T077-238809, phanganbeachresort@ hotmail.com.
Very cosy a/c and fan bungalows. Spacious and clean with a sliding door leading to an open-air bathroom. Comfortable with nice finishes. Set in a garden that leads straight to the beach.

Ban Tai & Ban Khai
Phangnan Rainbow $$$-$
25/3 Moo 4, T077-238236.
Comfortable fan rooms. The cheapest bungalows have a shared bathroom. Location and size determines the price, some have a sea view. A family-friendly resort. Restaurant. Make sure the taxi driver takes you to Ban khai Beach and not Hat Hin, where there is another resort of the same name.

Triangle Lodge $$-$
Ban Tai, T077-377432, phangan.info/trianglelodge.
The more expensive bungalows on the beach sport nicely carved wooden balcony decoration. The restaurant has a wide and imaginative menu and the staff are friendly. Bikes for rent.

Lee Garden Resort $
Ban Khai, T077-238150, lees_garden@yahoo.com.
A scattering of bungalows set in a garden next to the beach with balconies and hammocks in a quiet location. There are funky tunes, a giant tree swing, good food and great views. Well run.

Hat Rin Nok
Palita Lodge $$$$-$$$
T801-375170, kohphanganlodge.com.
The management have moved upmarket with the construction of 10 suites with rock bath tubs that fill from a fountain and rain showers, 2 seating areas.

Hat Rin Nai
Phangan Buri Resort & Spa $$$$-$$$
T077-375481, phanganburiresort.net.
A more expensive resort away from the crowds with a lovely beachfront pool and another further back. Bungalows are attractively furnished and are nicely spaced in rows leading down to the beach. Non-guests can use the pool for ฿100.

Listings

Koh Phangan East coast

Hat Thien to Hat Sadet
The Sanctuary $$$$-$
*Hat Yuan, T08-1271 3614 (mob),
the sanctuary-kpg.com*
Renowned for its post and
pre-party 'detox and retox'
programmes and unbeatably
bohemian beach atmosphere.
Managed by Westerners it offers
everything from fasts and
colonic-cleansing courses to a
treat-heavy menu, cocktails and
wine in the boulder-strewn café.
Accommodation ranges from
dorms for under ฿250 to palatial
open-plan hilltop houses. The
vegetarian and seafood
restaurant with its home-grown
produce and bakery is pricey but
top quality. Self-development
courses in yoga, meditation and
massage run year round. Only
accessible by boat or a long walk
through jungle.

Ao Thong Nai Pan Yai
Dolphin Bungalows $
*Bar & Restaurant, southern end
of the beach,
kimgiet@hotmail.com.*
Enjoys almost legendary status
with guests returning year after
year. A lovingly landscaped
jungle-garden houses the
beachfront bar and restaurant
(see Eating, page 166) and
further back, hides the wooden
fan bungalows, which are all en
suite with hammocks on the
balcony. Designed with genuine
care for the environment.

White Sand $
*At the southern end of the beach,
T077-445123.*
This is one of the beach's best
budget options. Serves some of
the best Thai food on the beach,
reasonably priced and the staff
are friendly.

Ao Thong Nai Pan Noi
Star Hut $$$-$
*T077-445006,
star_hut@hotmail.com.*
The largest and most popular
place on the beach. The wood
and bamboo huts are attractive
although too close together.
Some are fan only and others
have a/c. The good restaurant
serves cheap Thai and Western
food. It is well managed. A bus
runs 3 times daily to Thong Sala.

Koh Phangan North coast

Ao Hat Kuat
Bottle Beach $$-$
*Bungalow No 1, T077- 445152,
bottlebeach@hotmail.com.*
The first and most upmarket of 3
resorts run by the same family,
this is the smartest of the Bottle
Beaches and features polished
wood bungalows under coconut
palms. The bungalows are set in
a nice garden with little platform
verandas right on the beach. The
wooden ones have a Swiss feel.
All have shower and fan. More
expensive rooms have 4 beds.

Smile $
T077-445155.
Blue-roofed bungalows set up
amongst the boulders reached
by little stone paths and rooms
with jungle views are particularly
peaceful. It has an attractive
restaurant with hanging shell
mobiles and newspapers. There's
a tree swing and sofa swings on
the beach.

Ao Hat Khom
Ocean View Resort $$-$
T077-377231.
Up on the headland with a great
view and a range of bungalow
options – the creatively designed
more expensive ones with views
are a particular bargain. The
restaurant also has lovely sea
views and serves good
vegetarian food.

Ao Chao Lok Lum
Chaloklum Bay $$$$-$$$
*T077-374147-8,
chaloklumbay.com*
Attractive beachfront bungalows
on stilts with a/c and hot water
or fan. There are also a couple of
large, attractive beach houses for
groups or families. Shop on site.

Hat Salat & Ao Mae Hat
Salad Hut $$$
*T077-349246, salad_hut@
hotmail.com.*
A smaller cluster of attractive
bungalows including 4 family
rooms. The bungalows facing
the beach have nice big rooms
with carved balconies complete

with a day-bed and 2 hammocks. There's a restaurant, snorkelling and boat trips.

Island View Cabana $
Ao Mae Hat, T077-374172.
One of the oldest places on the island, set in a wide part of the beach where a sandbar stretches out to Koh Ma which provides good snorkelling. Simple huts, some have attached shower rooms with Western toilets. The restaurant serves good, cheap food, pool table. This is a popular, well-organized place.

Koh Phangan West coast

Ao Hat Yao
Long Bay A$$$-$$
T077-349057, long-bay.com.
A classy option with swish, modern a/c rooms and some cheaper fan options all with relative luxuries such as dressing tables and wardrobes, set around a swimming pool by the sea.

Sandy Bay $$$-$$
T077-349119.
A good selection of spacious a/c and traditional fan bungalows on the beach. All are kept clean and have large verandas with hammocks or wood furniture. This is a popular place with tables and chairs on the sand and the best restaurant on the beach which mainly serves cheap Thai food. Kayaking and island trips offered. Movies shown. Haad Yao Divers attached.

Ao Chaophao
Seaflower $$$-$$
T077-349090.
Prices vary with distance from the beach. Run by a Canadian-Thai couple, well-laid out wooden bungalows, with high peaked thatched roofs set in a mature, shady garden. Camping expeditions, snorkelling (equipment is free for guests), fishing, cliff diving and caving trips. Restaurant has an interesting menu.

Jungle Huts $$-$
T077-349088.
Offers large and airy huts with attached shower rooms ranging from the cheapest with just fans to those with a/c. Hammocks on the large verandas. Restaurant specializes in cocktails, plus Thai and Western dishes. Motorbike rental available.

Ao Sri Thanu
Laem Son $$-$
T077-349032.
Family-run bungalows set back off the beach. There are no rocks and the sea is sandy underfoot. One of the nicest places on the stretch. Popular.

Tip...

If diving, you should head straight for the dive shops where they will find you a place to stay in affiliated accommodation – often at a subsidized rate on the days when you are diving.

Ao Hin Kong & Ao Nai Wok
Moo 6 $$$
Moo 6 Hinkong Beach, T077-238520.
Absolutely stunning villas with kitchen, lounge area and bathroom. Finished to a high standard with a/c, cable TV and hot water showers. Across the road from the beach. Restaurant coming soon. Discount for stays longer than a week.

Cookies $$-$
Ao Plaay Laem, T077-377499, cookies_bungalow@ hotmail.com.
30 attractive bamboo bungalows, set in a green garden with a small splash pool. Some have shared bathroom, some have a/c and DVD players. The restaurant has a raised platform and the beach is secluded and attractive. Run by the friendly Aom and An. The watersports club offers windsurfing, kayaking and laser boats.

Blue Sea Bungalows $
69/4 Moo 4, Ao Plaay Laem, T08-1844 7736 (mob).
This resort has just 5 sturdy and spacious bungalows at an angle facing the sea. This is a very quiet spot attracting a more mature crowd not interested in partying. All have bathrooms inside. Restaurant.

Charm Churee Spa.

of this quiet resort popular with couples and families. The pool is close to the beach with sun loungers and the restaurant is on the beach. The sea is beautiful at this northern end of the beach. Dive centre attached, coralgrand divers.com.

Koh Tao Ban Mae Hat & west coast

Ban Mae Hat

Charm Churee Villa and Spa $$$$-$$$
Jansom Bay, T077-456393, charmchureevilla.com.
The island's most stylishly upmarket resort, in an exquisite cove, just south of Mae Hat. Bungalows on stilts are perched on the hillside, amongst coconut trees, with wonderful sea views from the balconies. Seafood restaurant, beach bar and spa. Tranquillity guaranteed.

Crystal Dive Resort $$$-$$
Just left of the pier on the beach, T077-456106, crystal dive.com.
One of the longest-standing dive centres on the island and awarded the prestigious PADI Gold Palm 5 star IDC Resort qualification for its excellent facilities. A range of rooms and

bungalows is available with good rates for divers. Pool, restaurant, bar with large screen movies shown, yoga school attached.

Hat Sai Ri

Koh Tao Cabana $$$$
T077-456505, kohtaocabana. com.
33 villas built into the headland at the northern end of the beach including 10 attractively designed white circular villas – which have a Mediterranean feel – climbing up the hillside. Bathrooms are open-air and built into rock faces. There are pleasant gardens with attractive wooden sun loungers.

Koh Tao Coral Grand Resort $$$$-$$$
T077-456 431, kohtaocoral.com.
Large, dusty pink cabins with wooden floors, TVs, fridges, coffee-making facilities and shower rooms dot the landscape

Thipwimarn Resort $$$$-$$$
T077-456409, thipwimarnresort.com
Beyond the northern end of the beach on the northwest headland, this beautiful, relatively new place has 11 bungalows perched on the rocks. Its infinity pool enjoys spectacular views. The deservedly popular restaurant overlooks Sai Ri Bay and the sea.

Ban's Diving Resort $$$$-$$
T077-456466, amazingkohtao.com.
This resort offers everything from gorgeous a/c luxury rooms with silk furnishings and large balconies to plain fan rooms around the pool for divers. Partial views of the sea. As well as diving, wake-boarding, waterskiing and kayaking are offered.

Here & Now $$$-$
Sai Ri Beach, T077-456730,
hereandnow.be.
12 simple rooms with a spiritual
bent, blocked off from the main
route to the water by ropes
strung across the path. Fairly wild
surrounds. Shared and private
showers. This is the last
establishment on the northwest
headland of the island, north of
Sai Ri beach. You can swim off
the rocks into the sea. The
restaurant has a great view of
Nang Yuan Island, which
apparently inspired the novel *The
Beach*.

$$-$ In Touch Resort
T077-456514.
Very funky resort with an equally
cool beach-front restaurant.
Brightly coloured individual huts
have lots of character. Arranged
in a garden opposite the beach,
the fan option are the best
designed. The cheapest huts are
wooden bungalows with
open-air bathrooms.

**Blue Wind Bakery and Resort
$$-$**
*T077-456116, bluewind_wa@
yahoo.com.*
A small, friendly and attractive
place with excellent value fan
and a/c rooms and a charming
beach restaurant. Pretty wood
bungalows nestled in a beautiful
mature garden. Their bakery
serves pastries, pasta and ice
cream. Daily yoga classes.

Koh Tao North coast

**Nangyuan Island Dive Resort
$$$$-$$$**
Koh Nang Yuan
T077-456088, nang yuan.com.
The only bungalow complex on
this trio of islands has a/c rooms.
PADI dive courses and diving trips
arranged. Facilities and
atmosphere are excellent but it's
a little overpriced. Guests receive
a transfer to Koh Samui.

Koh Tao East coast

Ao Hin Wong
Hin Wong Bungalows $$-$
T077-456006.
The newer wooden huts with
verandas overlooking the sea are
pretty. Reasonably priced
restaurant, snorkelling
equipment and canoes for hire.
Discounts available after 3
nights. Electricity available
1800-0600.

Ao Ta Not
**Tanote Family Bay Dive
Resort $$$-$$**
T077-456757.
At the northern end of the bay,
spread out amid the rocks, this
resort offers cheap, dark fan
rooms or more expensive
brighter rooms with balconies.
All have tables and chairs. No
special rates for divers,
calypso-diving-kohtao.de. Taxi to
main island pier twice a day.
Restaurant open 0700-2200.

Diamond Resort $$-$
40/7 Aow Tanote,
T077-456591.
The cheaper rooms are excellent
value; they have cold water
showers but are comfortable and
spacious with plenty of windows.
Only fan available. Next to a very
quiet beach. Restaurant, with
others within walking distance.

Mountain Reef Resort $
At the southern end of the bay,
T077-456697/9.
A family-run resort which will
take guests out fishing for their
dinner. Larger rooms are more
expensive – go for the ones
overlooking the beach which get
great sunrise views. There's a
daily taxi to the island pier.
Friendly and welcoming staff.

Lang Khaai Bay
Snorkelling Point Resort $
*Next to Pahnun View, T077-
456264.*
Wooden bungalows with views
of the bay. Comfy beds and a
hammock on the balcony.
24-hour electricity. Restaurant.
Owner speaks good English.

Ao Leuk
Nice Moon Bungalows $$-$
*T077-456731, nicemoon43@
hotmail.com.*
About 200 m south of the beach
on cliffs overlooking the bay. Free
snorkelling equipment, friendly
and informative. Restaurant.

Eating

Ao Thian Ok

Jamahkiri Spa & Resort $$$$
T077-456400, jamahkiri.com.
A well-designed private resort which incorporates large boulders into the fabric of the buildings. The handful of boutique rooms with floor to ceiling windows and balconies all sit on stilts looking out to sea. Free pick-up for the resort, restaurant and spa. There's car, kayak and snorkel hire.

New Heaven A$$$-$$
T077-456462,
newheavenkohtao.com.
Dark teak bungalows with tropical-looking bathrooms. Restaurant has sweeping views of the bay. The newer bungalows have a/c. From this cliff-side setting, the sea, which is good for snorkelling, is a short walk away.

Rocky Resort $$-$
T077-456035.
It's all about the stunning location in this beautiful bay. Bungalows, though a little weathered, are built around the boulders and many have balconies over the sea with tables and chairs. Basic, but well spaced out and friendly with reasonably priced food.

Ao Chalok Ban Kao

Bhora Bhora $$$-$
T077-456044,
bhorabhora.com.
21 spacious rooms with mosquito screens on the windows. The resort takes pride in its relaxed, traveller-style atmosphere and unique rooms, some including sections of granite boulders as part of the walls and the wooden rooms having bathroom walls made of glass bottles set in concrete. Restaurant 1800-2400. Rates include breakfast.

View Point Resort $$
T077-456444, viewpoint.com.
The large bamboo and thatch rooms are clean, attractive and quiet, with views. The cheapest have shared showers. Good bargains for divers.

Hat Sai Nuan

Sai Thong Resort and Spa $$$-$
T077-456476.
A special and secluded spot, well worth taking the trip off the beaten track for. Accommodation ranges from cheap hillside huts with shared bathrooms to slightly overpriced but romantic beach-front bungalows. The simple outdoor spa has a distinctly bohemian appeal, set among jungle and offering relaxation treatments in a small saltwater pool. Relaxed restaurant with cushions, hammocks, a garden and small private beach.

Eating out on Koh Samui has improved greatly with some high-class establishments offering excellent dining options – most of the top-end hotels and resorts will house good restaurants. There's also the regular smattering of street-food places serving up noodles and other basic Thai food.

Nathon

Sunset $$
175/3 Moo 3, T077-421244. Open 1000-2200.
South end of town overlooking the sea. Great Thai food, especially fish dishes.

Coffee Island $$-$
T077-423153.
Open 0600- 2400.
Open-fronted café right opposite the pier with good Colombian, Brazilian and Ethiopian coffee and a full range of cakes as well as steaks, shakes, curry and seafood.

Tip...

There are increasing numbers of restaurants in virtually every village. Word-of-mouth recommendations are the best guide; new ones open all the time.

North coast
La Sirene $$$-$$
65/1 Moo 1, Bophut, T077-425301.
Open 1000-2300.
A delightful little restaurant run by a friendly Frenchman. The seafood is fresh and locally caught and displayed outside the restaurant, the coffee is excellent too. French and Thai food offered.

Starfish & Coffee $$
51/7 Moo 1, Bophet, T077-427201.
Open 1100-0100.
Another lovely setting for a meal or a quick drink on the outside terrace in this big airy building. Plenty of seafood and international cuisine in the maroon-themed restaurant with wrought-iron and leopard-print decor.

BBC (Big Buddha Café) $$$-$
202 Moo 5, right next to the wat, Big Buddha, T08-1788 9051 (mob).
Open 0900-2300.
High-quality Thai and international food, reasonably priced in this island-style open-plan layout; an enjoyable place to sit and watch the sunset.

Honey Seafood Restaurant and Bar $$
At the most easterly tip of Choeng Mon beach.
Great seafood.

East coast
Poppies $$$
Chaweng, T077-422419.
An excellent Thai and international restaurant, one of the best on the beach. Live classical guitar accompaniment on Tuesday, Thursday and Friday and a Thai night on Saturday. Booking recommended.

Lamai
Will Wait Bakery $$
Lamai, T077-042 4263.
Delicious pastries, croissants and pizzas. A popular breakfast joint.

The Spa $$-$
Spa Resort Lamai (see sleeping, page 158).
Award-winning restaurant serving a range of vegetarian and Thai food, as well as healthy specialities and seafood. Well-priced menu, friendly service and a relaxed ambience.

Koh Phangan

Many visitors eat at their bungalows and some serve excellent seafood. Prices are standard though it's worth checking on your tab to avoid a shock at the end of your stay.

Thong Sala & around
Absolute Island $$
T077-349109.
A cliff-top restaurant with gorgeous views and a romantic ambience which serves up great Thai food and seafood.

Hat Rin
Lucky Crab $$
T077-375124.
The original seafood place in Hat Rin, on the main road between east and west. Full of 'unlucky' crabs, since its popularity and extensive menu means they're eaten at a rate of knots. It is usually packed every night but often under-staffed, leading to excruciatingly inefficient service. Punters eat at long tables in a party atmosphere. The soups and salads are also excellent.

Nic's Restaurant & Bar $$
Moo 5, T08-7007 3769, nics-restaurant.com.
1700-late.
A welcome stylish addition to the area, serving reasonably priced tapas, pasta, pizza and Thai food. After beach specials 1800-2000, 50% off listed drinks. DJs from KL play funky house around the time of the Full Moon Parties. Chill out areas and big screen showing sporting events.

The Rock $$
Run by Paradise Bungalows.
The Rock has unbeatable views of the beach, and dishes out exquisite seafood, an unusual range of bar snacks including the ever-popular garlic bread and salads, imported organic coffee, super cocktails and higher quality wine than you'll find anywhere else. Relaxing music makes for a welcome break from the booming tunes elsewhere.

Nira's Bakery $
T077-375109.
Open 24 hrs.
A bakery selling a gorgeous range of cakes, pastries, brownies and bread. The spinach and feta pastries and spinach muffins are recommended. The next door café (0800-2400) does great coffee, spirulina shakes and breakfasts. Watch BBC World out the back or sit roadside on wooden picnic tables and chairs.

Om Ganesh $
At Hat Rin pier, T077-375123.
An old favourite for Indian food, offers delicious traditional tandoori, curries and thalis. Also the Himalayan Art Gallery next door with art for sale.

East coast
Dolphin Bar & Restaurant $$
See Sleeping, page 160.
Breakfast and lunch, tapas served in the evenings. Excellent range of food served at seating areas from raised platforms to cabanas hidden in the jungle. The ingredients are of the highest quality and the food here is amongst the best on the island.

Su's Bakery $$
Thong Nai Pan Yai, first shop on the left as you enter the village.
Fantastic thin-base pizzas are definitely worth the walk from the beach to the village. Very popular with regulars. Fresh coffees, brownies and banana cake are also a big hit.

Memory $
Thong Nai Pan Yai, opposite Nu Bar.
Serves some of the best Thai food on the beach. Very friendly owner, Nat.

North coast
Sheesh $$-$
Chao Lok Lum, T077-374161.
A funky addition to the north coast catering for this craze that has seized Phangan and Koh Tao. International food, cocktails, dance floor, sun deck and private outdoor booths for sucking on a variety of fruity tobacco flavours.

Tip...

Most guesthouses on Koh Tao have restaurants attached but guests have sometimes been evicted from their bungalows if they have not been spending enough in the restaurant so it is worth enquiring if there is a minimum expenditure before checking in.

Koh Tao

Ban Mae Hat
Café del Sol $$
Mae Hat Sq, T077-456578.
Open 0800-2300.
Great place for breakfast, also serves sandwiches, bruschetta and coffee. For dinner the French/Italian chef prepares salmon or steak and other international cuisine.

Hat Sai Ri
Papa's Tapas $$$
Opposite Siam Scuba Dive Center, Sai Ri village, T077-456298.
Open 1900-late.
A sophisticated addition to the island and Thailand's only absinthe bar. Be sure to sample wonderfully concocted Asian fusion tapas with attention to detail.

Entertainment

Thipwimarn Restaurant $$$
On the northwest headland,
T077-456409.
Open 0700-2200.
This has become a popular spot for fashionable dining due to the views over Sai Ri bay and excellent Thai and seafood.

Coffee Boat $
On the main road just before the
main drag down to the beach in
Sai Ri village, T077-456178.
A cheap and cheerful authentic Thai diner and bakery. Ample portions of tasty, hot Thai food.

Ao Ta Not
Poseidon $$
T077-456735.
Open 0730-2200.
Restaurant serving fried fish, veggie dishes and unusual milkshakes – including cookie vanilla flavour and prune lassis.

Ao Chalok Ban Kao
New Heaven $$
Rather a climb, at the top of the
hill, T077-456462.
Evenings only.
A bit pricey but good food and fantastic views over the gorgeous Thian Og Bay.

Viewpoint Restaurant $
Beyond the Bubble Dive Resort at
the eastern end of the beach,
T077-456777.
Open 0700-2200.
Wide menu of Thai and some Western food. Perched above the sea it enjoys great views.

Koh Samui

Bars & clubs
Frog and Gecko
91/2 Moo 1, Bophut, T077-425248.
Open 1200-0200.
The first of several English pubs/ sports bars on the beachfront. The music and Thai food is good.

The Tropicana
Bophut, T077-425304.
The Tropicana makes a refreshing change from the sports bars.

Chaweng
Most of the bars in **Chaweng** are at the northern end of the strip, which is also home to a variety of go-go bars mixed in with the occasional European-style pubs.

Green Mango
On the main road.
Western DJs play garage and house. Also hosts live bands.

The Reggae Pub
Chaweng lagoon, T077- 422331.
This bar, club and live music destination is a little out of town is popular as a party destination.

Tropical Murphys
14/40 Chaweng Rd, opposite
McDonald's in Central Chaweng,
T077-413614.
Open 0900-0200.
An Irish pub and the only place on the island serving draught Guinness and Kilkenny.

Lamai
Most bars in Lamai are located down the *sois* which link the main road and the beach. **Bauhaus** is a large, popular venue consisting of a pub, restaurant and discotheque.

Koh Phangan

Koh Phangan's Full Moon Parties are world famous – see box on page 153 for more details. Clubs and bars open and close with great frequency – we've provided a general run-through of the most established places – The 3 best and loudest clubs on Hat Rin Beach East are **Vinyl Club**, **Zoom Bar** and the **Drop in Club**, dropinclub.com.

What the locals say

Although perhaps not a particularly well-kept secret, I can't fault Mint Bar on Koh Samui (Green Mango, Chaweng, mintbar.com) for consistently booking quality local and international DJs playing real electronic music while the surrounding nightlife scene continues its infatuation with pop and tired hip hop.

Matt Crook, freelance journalist

Bars & clubs

Backyard Club
On Hat Rin West.
Infamous for its Full Moon after-parties which start at 1100 with the best of the DJs.

Cactus Club
Further down the beach with a bar right on the beach, plays hip hop, R'n'B and rock.

Esco Bar
Positioned on rocks overlooking the sea at Hat Rin West between the Siam Healing Centre and the Phangan Buri Resort.
Open 1200-2400.
Reggae seems the order of the day at this great little bar.

Nargile House
Close to the Drop in Bar on Hat Rin East.
Open until late.
Smoking the sheesha at tables costs ฿300 at this road-side bar.

In **Thong Nai Pan Noi** there's the hip **Flip Flop Pharmacy**, on the beach, then along the road there's **Jungle Bar**, **Rasta Baby**, the Mexican bar and restaurant **Que Pasa** and the **Hideaway Bar**, decorated in bunting.

The Pirate's Bar
Ao Chaophao, accessed through the Seatanu Bungalows.
Hosts the moon set party, 3 days before full moon. The bar in the shape of a ship is set in a tiny cove accessed by a bridge.

Koh Tao

Whitening
On the road to the Sensi Paradise Resort, Ban Mae Hat.
The staple diver's after-hours spot with a bar on the beach.

Dragon Bar
Pier Rd.
Wooden tables spill onto the street from this bar playing different music every night.

Pure
South Sai Ri beach.
The hippest place in town scattered with big bean bags. Open every night until 0200.

Cabaret
Cabaret Christy's
Chaweng.
Drag cabaret acts. Performances start around 2300.

Star Club
200/11 Chaweng Rd, T077-414218.
Puts on a hilarious show at 2230 nightly. No admission charge, customers must buy drinks.

Muay Thai (Thai boxing)
At Chaweng Stadium T077-413504, free transfers.
8 fights from 2100.
And at Lamai's new stadium. Fights 2-3 times weekly during high season, ฿500.

Also held in Thong Sala, Hat Rin and on Tong Nai Pan Noi. Look out for flyers for fight days.

Shopping

Shopping is not high on the list for most people visiting the Gulf Islands. In fact, for many, the islands afford an opportunity to escape consumerism for at least a few days. Consequently most shops sell the usual run of gifts, beach items with the occasional book shop thrown in. There are also a number of tailors on Koh Samui.

Koh Samui

Nathon is a good centre for shopping on the island. It is worth a visit to browse through the stalls and take a walk down the main road, past the fresh market on the left and on down to the 'hardware' market on the right. The stalls provide the usual T-shirts, CDs/DVDs, watches and handicrafts. The inner road – Angthong Rd – is worth walking down too. There are a number of shops along the main road of **Bophut**. There is a good German, English and French bookshop, and shops selling art, gifts, clothes and produce from around Thailand, Laos and Cambodia.

The main shopping centre on the island, **Chaweng** caters for the visiting crowds, providing necessities in the supermarkets, pharmacies and opticians, along with plenty of tourist tat and upmarket designer clothes/swimwear stores. A plethora of tailors pepper Chaweng, including Armani International

Activities & tours

Suits, Joop! and Baron Fashion. Bookazine, which sells newspapers, magazines and books, is next to Tropical Murphy's on the beach road. For genuine branded surfwear, including Quiksilver and Roxy, try the shops next to McDonald's in the centre of town.

In **Lamai**, jewellery, beachwear and clothing boutiques are along the main road.

Koh Phangan

Shops selling leather goods, funky fashions and books abound in Hat Rin. **JD Exotic** sells swish shirts for men and **Napo-po** sells stylish boho fashions, accessories and photographs. **Fusion** offers funkier, contemporary fashions.

For a more in-depth guide to diving near the Gulf Islands see page 148-149.

Cookery courses
Blue Banana
2 Moo 4, Big Buddha Beach Koh Samui, T077-245080.
Classes with 'Toy'.

Diving
Captain Caveman
Shambala Resort, Big Buddha, and on Chaweng Beach Rd, T08-6282 2983 (mob), samuireef.com.
Office hours 1000-2100, closed Sun morning.
A 5-star PADI dive centre. Prides itself on small classes. Snorkelling trips to Ang Thong Marine National Park, ฿3750, to Koh Tao and Nangyuan and Mango Bay, ฿2500.

Chaloklum Diving
Chao Lok Lum Village, Koh Phangan, T077-374025, chaloklum-diving.com.
One of the longest-standing operations on the island with an excellent reputation. Its small-group policy guarantees personal attention.

Crystal Dive
Hat Rin Koh Phangan T077-375535, crystaldive.com.
This booking branch of the respected dive resort in Koh Tao is run by Backpackers Information Centre.
Diving is popular year round on

Koh Tao. It is said to be the cheapest place in Thailand to learn to dive. There's a decompression chamber in Ban Mae Hat – T077-456664.

A PADI Open Water course costs roughly ฿9000 and a fun dive for qualified divers is around ฿1800. Remember that you shouldn't compromise on safety when diving – plenty of accidents occur on Koh Tao due to poor equipment, too many divers per instructor and diving while intoxicated. Check the reputation of the school, the equipment and ratios of students to instructors before handing over your cash. Recommended dive schools include:

Big Blue
Ban Mae Hat, T077-456050, or Hat Sai Ri, T077-456179, bigbluediving.com.

Buddha View Dive Resort
Chalok Ban Kao, T077-456074, buddhaview-diving.com.

Crystal Dive Resort
Ban Mae Hat and Sai Ri, T077-456107, crystaldive.com.

Easy Divers
Ban Mae Hat, T077-456010, www.thaidive.com.

Siam Scuba Dive Center
Sai Ri village, T077-456628, scubadive.com.

Transport

Spas & therapies

Samui Dharma Healing Centre
63 Moo Tee 1, Ao Santi Beach, near Nathon, Koh Samui, T077- 234170, dharmahealingintl.com.
Runs alternative health programmes. Fasting courses are directed according to Dharma Buddhist principles in alternative health. Many other therapies and accommodation available.

Thalasso Spa
Samui Peninsula Spa & Resort, Koh Samui, T077-428100, samuipeninsula.com.
Professional treatments in attractive rooms; mud treatments are the speciality.

Chakra
Hat Rin, off the main drag leading up from the pier, Koh Phangan, T077-375401, chakrayoga.com.
Good body, face and foot Thai massages, reiki, reflexology and acupressure treatments.

Monte Vista Retreat Centre
Thong Sala, Koh Phangan, T077-238951, montevistathailand.com.
The latest addition to the island's holistic health scene.

Wat Pho Herbal Sauna
Close to Ban Tai beach on the southwest coast of Koh Phangan.
This herbal sauna uses traditional methods and ingredients.

Jamahkiri Spa & Resort
Ao Thian Ok, Koh Tao, T077-456400. Free pick-ups available. Open 1000-2200.
Indulge in 1 of the reasonably priced packages available at this spa in grounds overlooking the sea. Steam sauna and a variety of massages are available.

Tour operators

One Hundred Degrees East
23/2 Moo 4, Big Buddha, Koh Samui, T08-6282 2983 (mob), 100 degreeseast.com.
Charter trips run by Ivan Douglas who runs Captain Caveman. Private charters. A direct charter from Samui to Tao is ฿18,000.

My Friend Travel Agency
14/62-64 Mo 2, Chaweng Beach Rd, Chaweng, Koh Samui, T077-413364. Open 1000-2300.
Run by the friendly and Amporn who speaks English.

Thong Sala Centre
44/13 Thong Sala Pier, Koh Phangan T077-238984, jamareei@hotmail.com.
Can organize boat, train, plane tickets and offer sound travel advice. Trustworthy.

Backpackers
Hat Rin, Koh Phangan T077-375535, backpackersthailand.com.
An invaluable source of information and the only TAT-registered independent travel agent on the island.

Koh Samui

Air
The airport is in the northeast of the island, T077-428500 and is owned by **Bangkok Airways**. There are multiple daily connections with Bangkok and regular flights to Krabi, Chiang Mai, Phuket and U-Tapao (Pattaya) with **Bangkok Airways** (bangkokair.com, T02-2706699). THAI (thaiair.com T02-3561111) offer daily connections to Bangkok. Bangkok Airways also connect to Singapore and Hong Kong. Koh Samui is the only airport on the Gulf Islands.

Transport to town or the beach is by a/c minibus to Bophut, Mae Nam, Chaweng, Choeng Mon, Lamai and Big Buddha. There's also a limousine service at domestic arrivals, T077-245598, samuiaccom@hotmail.com. (Minivan ฿150 to Chaweng, ฿300 to Lamai, ฿150-300 to the north coast).

Boat
There are numerous daily boat options. Schedules, journey times and prices change according to the season. Several of the companies also provide private onward travel to mainland destinations such as Phuket, Krabi, Bangkok, Hua Hin. Tickets from travel agents will cost more but include scheduling advice and transfers.

Lomprayah, main road, Mae Nam, on the corner of the road to the Baan Fah Resort (office Mon-Sat 0800-1700), T077-427765, lomprayah.com. Daily service departing from Wat Na Phra Lam pier to Koh Phangan, Koh Tao and Chumphon (฿900). They also sell combined bus tickets to Hua Hin and Bangkok. Price includes transfer to pier.

Songserm Travel, seafront road, Nathon, T077-420157, office hours 0800-1800. Runs express passenger boats daily. These boats leave from the southern pier in Nathon to Surat Thani, Koh Phangan and Koh Tao.

Seatran (office on pier, daily 0500-1700, T077- 426001-2) operates hourly boats to Surat Thani from the main northerly pier in Nathon.

The slow overnight boat to Surat Thani leaves Nathon at 2100, arriving in Don Sak at around 0300/0400.

Bus/train
Buses and trains from Bangkok to Surat Thani/Chumphon are easy to link to ferry services to and from Koh Samui – speak to a local travel agent or for more details see page 139.

details see page 139.

Koh Phangan

For bus, train and air information see Koh Samui above.

Boat
Most boats dock at the pier at Thong Sala. Many of the companies listed below also provide onward connections and ticketing to mainland destinations.

From Thong Sala to Koh Samui: with **Songserm** (T077-377704) to Nathon pier, Mae Nam beach with **Lomprayah** (T077-238411), Big Buddha pier with **Seatran** (T077-238679). Speed Boat Line to Bophut, Koh Samui.

To Koh Tao from Thong Sala with Seatran, Lomprayah and Songserm.

To Surat Thani from Thong Sala with Songserm, Raja Ferry; prices include bus ticket to bus and train stations. The night boat leaves Koh Phangan for Surat Thani at 2200 (although times can vary, so it's worth checking in good time). To Chumpon with **Lomprayah**.

Koh Tao

Boat
There are boats of various speeds and sizes going to and from Koh Tao. The best connections are with Chumphon (see p139) from where trains and buses connect to other mainland destinations.

To Chumphon with **Lomprayah**, T077-456176, office hours 0830-1900, with **Songserm**, T077-456274, 1430; with **Seatran**, T077-456907; with **Ko Jaroen**, T08-1797 0276 (mob), the nightboat at 2200, 5 hours.

To Koh Samui, **Lomprayah** is the most comfortable, with a/c and TV and shortest journey time; with **Songserm**, T077-456274; with **Seatran**, T077-456907.

To Koh Phangan with **Lomprayah**, **Songserm** and **Seatran**. To Surat Thani with **Songserm** day and nightboat; with **Seatran**, free transfer from Bang Ruk pier to Nathon on Samui for boats to Surat Thani.

Contents

Phuket town.

Phuket & North Andaman Coast

Introduction

The northern stretch of the Andaman coast presents a startling cultural mosaic, from Ranong's cheroot-smoking Burmese through to Phuket's numerous Muslim communities, Chao Le sea gypsies and Chinese traders.

This region's main hub is Phuket, one of the busiest tourist destinations in the whole of Southeast Asia. In Phuket you'll find a fantastic array of 5-star resorts and upmarket restaurants. There's a string of good beaches with gaudy Patong providing a contrast to the sleepy charms of Cape Panwa while the island's increasingly sophisticated capital of Phuket City is filled with striking Sino-Portuguese villas.

The beaches of Khao Lak that run up Route 4 along the Andaman coast north of Phuket are re-inventing themselves after the horrors of the 2004 tsunami and host some perfectly languid spots to lose yourself in.

Further north up Route 4 towards Ranong, a handsome town that offers hot springs and an important transport hub, is a run of soporific islands that are seducing visitors into weeks of lazy hammock non-activity. These islands, particularly Kohs Chang and Phayam, are idylls for world-weary travellers.

This stretch of coast also provides easy jump-off points to some superb diving and snorkelling options with the Similans and Surin being the two most important sites. Inland, stunning Khao Sok national park is easily reached and is justifiably popular with visitors to the region.

Left: Long-tail boat, Phuket.

What to see in...

...a weekend
Phuket is one of several de-facto weekend break destinations for the hardworking and well-heeled citizens of the cities of Bangkok, Kuala Lumpur and Singapore – the range of luxury available means that its title as Thailand's Riviera is well-deserved.

...a week or more
Travel into **Ranong** absorb the hot springs and Chinese vibe before heading south beach, island and forest hopping via **Koh Phayam**, **Khao Lak**, **Khao Sok**, before swinging down through **Phuket** and on to stunning **Phangnga Bay**.

Phuket Island

Known as 'the Pearl of Thailand', Phuket lies on the west coast of the warm Andaman Sea and is connected to the mainland by the 700-m-long Sarasin causeway. It is a fully developed resort island with hundreds of hotels and restaurants and some gorgeous beaches.

Phuket was first 'discovered' by Arab and Indian navigators around the end of the ninth century. Always a rich island – known for its pearls, fish and fruit – Phuket proved irresistible to the Burmese who carried out a surprise attack in 1785. The previous governor's young widow Chan and her sister Mook immediately disguised all the women of the town as men and had them pose as soldiers. Fearing the worst from the fierce-looking ranks, the Burmese retreated. Chan and Mook were honoured for their bravery and today, on the road to the airport, you can see the Heroines' Monument to the two sisters. Much of Phuket's considerable wealth derived from tin and the island was dubbed 'Junk Ceylon' in the mid-16th century. In 1876, during the reign of King Rama III Chinese workers flooded the island to work in the mines. The slave conditions that ensued later led to rebellion but conditions improved and in 1907 modern tin-mining methods were introduced by Englishman Captain Edward Miles. Phuket Town became so wealthy that paved roads and cars appeared. These days, tourism is the big earner, with rubber, coconut and fisheries also contributing to the island's wealth. A third of the island's 200,000 population now lives in Phuket City. While around 30% of these are Chinese descendants, the rest are indigenous Thais, Sikhs, Hindus, Malay Muslims and Chao Le sea gypsies.

Phuket City was given city status in 2004, although most islanders still call it "Phuket Town". Treated largely as a stopover, Phuket City is now anxious to revamp its image and pull in a more sophisticated crowd. So, in addition to its Sino-Portuguese architectural heritage, which is reminiscent of Georgetown in Malaysian Penang there is a burgeoning arts and literary scene and even a foreign film festival once a year. What will aid Phuket City is that there are still some old and grand buildings left, rare in Thailand, and a magnet for those with an eye for architecture.

At the end of the 19th century, Phuket Town, one of the richest settlements in the country, saw a flowering of Sino-Portuguese mansions built by tin barons revelling in their wealth. In **Old Phuket** you'll still find houses and shops in styles similar to that of Penang and Macao and dating back 130 years.

Featuring complex latticework, Mediterranean coloured ceramic tiles, high ceilings and wooden interiors, these architectural dreams, remain cool in the summer and free of damp during the monsoon. Once a year at the end of the Old Phuket Town Festival in mid-December, these houses are open to the public. The best examples are along **Thalang, Yaowarat, Ranong, Phangnga, Krabi, Dibuk, Rassada, Soi Romanee and Damrong roads**.

A particularly notable example of one of Phuket's finer older buildings is **Government House**, which stood in as the 'American Embassy' in Phnom Penh in the classic film – *The Killing Fields*.

Tour boats around Phangnga Bay.

Essentials

❶ Getting around *Songthaew* buses run from the market on Ranong Road, Phuket City throughout the island roughly every 30 mins between 0600-1800. Fares range from ฿20-30. There are also numerous places to hire cars/jeeps and motorbikes. Tuk-tuks can be found around the island but are pricey – Patong from Phuket City and vice versa should cost you about ฿450.

❷ Airport Phuket International Airport is in the north of the island, about 30 km from Phuket City. From the airport take the airport bus (T076-232371, airportbusphuket.com), into Phuket City. Metered taxis, cars (known as limousines) and vans service the airport. Despite being metered, the taxis only offer flat fares; from the airport to Phuket City shouldn't cost more than ฿500. A trip from the airport to Phuket City by minivan should cost about ฿150.

❸ Bus station The main bus terminal, Phangnga Rd, T076-211480, is in Phuket City.

❹ ATM ATMs and exchange booths are easy to find on all the major beaches and in Phuket City along Rasada, Phuket, Phangnga and Thepkrasatri roads there are branches of all the major banks.

❺ Hospital Bangkok Hospital Phuket, 2/1 Hongyokutis Rd, T076-254421, phukethospital.com; **Phuket Ruampaet Hospital**, 340 Phuket Rd, T076-217964; **Vachira Hospital Phuket**, Yaowarat Rd, T076-212150, vachiraphuket.go.th.

❻ Pharmacy You'll find pharmacies and basic medical care on every major beach.

❼ Post office Phuket City, Montri Rd (at the corner of Thalang Rd).

❽ Tourist information TAT, 73-75 Phuket Rd, T076-212213, tathkt@phuket.ksc.co.th, 0830-1630. Also try the Phuket Gazette, phuketgazette.net.

Tip...

The driest and sunniest months are November to April. May to October are wetter with more chance of overcast conditions, although daily sunshine still averages five to eight hours. August is when the monsoon begins and red flags appear to warn swimmers not to venture out because of powerful and fatal currents.

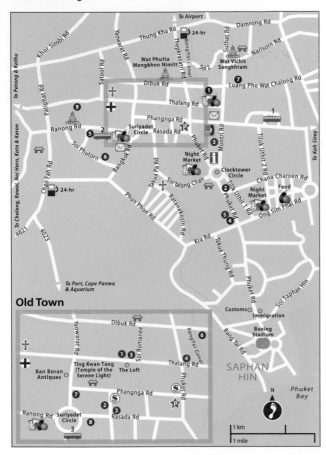

Phuket City listings

❶ Sleeping
1 Ban Suwantawe *1/10 Dibuk Rd*
2 Crystal Inn *2/1-10 Soi Surin, Montri Rd*
3 Forty-three *43 Thalang Rd*
4 Phuket 346 *346-348 Phuket Rd*
5 Phuket Backpacker Hostel *167 Ranong Rd*
6 Raya Thai Cuisine *48 Deebuk Rd*
7 Sino House *1 Montri Rd*
8 Taste Phuket *16-18 Rasada Rd*
9 Thalang Guesthouse *37 Thalang Rd*

❶ Eating & drinking
1 Baan Talang *65 Thalang Rd*
2 Ka Jok See *26 Takua Pa Rd*
3 Kanda Bakery *31-33 Rasada Rd*
4 Kow-Tom-Hua-Pla *Phuket Rd*
5 La Gaetana *Phuket Rd*
6 Natural *Soi Phutorn*
7 Nong Jote Café *16 Yaowarat Rd*
8 Santana Coffee *54/8-9 Montri Rd*

Preservation orders have been placed on all buildings in Old Phuket. Among the finer ones are the **Chartered Bank THAI office,** Ranong Rd opposite the market, and the **Sala Phuket.** Damrong Rd. Less grand, but quietly elegant, are the turn-of-the-20th-century **shophouses** on, for example, Thalang Road. There has been considerable renovation of buildings on Dibuk, Thalang and Krabi roads but nearby there are still side streets with some lovely examples of traditional shophouses. **Soi Romanee,** the island's former red-light district, in particular is such a street with traditional merchant houses on both sides of the road, a few with fading paintwork on the walls.

Some of the renovation has introduced smart new restaurants, cafés, art galleries and antique shops. Notably, **The Loft,** which sells expensive Southeast Asian antiques and Chinese porcelains and received an award for its efforts in conserving traditional architecture. At the same time there are still plenty of more traditional hardware stores, small tailors, stationery shops and the like, that clearly cater to the locals.

Another sight worth visiting in the old town is the **Temple of the Serene Light,** Phangnga Rd, the entrance is marked in English and Thai – there are signs telling the story of the place in English. Believed to be 110 years old, this is a small Taoist temple, filled with paintings and religious artefacts, that was rebuilt following a fire. There are night markets on **Ong Sim Phai** and **Tilok Uthit 1.** These are excellent places to buy street food on a nocturnal prowl through the old town. **Khao Rang Viewpoint** is a romantic spot atop a large hill.

Post-tsunami recovery

The tsunami of 26 December 2004 hit Phuket at a peak time for tourism, with the infamously raucous Patong Beach suffering tremendous loss of life - indeed, much of the televised footage came from here. Phuket's beaches have now largely recovered with the grand sweep of Patong touted as a minor miracle. Of Phuket's other beaches, Bang Tao, Kamala, Kata, Karon, Nai Harn and Phuket Fantasea all suffered damage. Land grabs by developers in the wake of the disaster forced out many small businesses but, on the whole, the island has bounced back in terms of tourism and visitor numbers are higher than ever.

Around Phuket Island

Patong beach

Phuket's busiest spot is sited on the west coast at **Patong beach** which began to metamorphose from a hippy paradise into a commercial centre during the 1970s. It is now a mass of neon signs advertising hotels, massage parlours, restaurants, straight bars, gay bars, nightclubs and the plain peculiar. While families may not be able to avoid vulgarity, they will be able to bypass ladyboys and devious side-street deals by choosing from a range of excellent family hotels. Patong still offers the widest selection of watersports on Phuket and, in spite of hotel development, it is still possible to snorkel on the reef at the southern end of the bay.

Karon & Kata beaches

Heading south from Patong the horseshoe-shaped **Karon and Kata beaches** are divided by a narrow rocky outcrop. Karon started tourist life as a haven for backpackers; it is now well developed, with a range of hotels and bungalows and a wide selection of restaurants. Although there is a tiny hippy/alternative corner at the southern end of the beach, tipped off by a reggae bar, on the whole, prosperous Scandinavians dominate now. Karon's major drawback, physically, is the overly exposed beach despite its cosy curve. Nonetheless, there are good mid-range places to stay, and the slower

Boys will be girls

Katoeys, transvestites or, as they tend to be known by *farang* in Thailand, 'ladyboys', are larger in number than one might expect. They are also part of a long tradition of transvestites in Southeast Asia. Many bars and clubs will have *katoeys* working for them, whether as bar 'girls' or in shows of one sort or another. They are often very beautiful and extraordinarily difficult, if not impossible, to tell apart from the real thing. Patong Beach on Phuket is famous for its *katoey* population.

pace of life here will appeal to many. Kata consists of two beaches: **Kata Yai (Big) and Kata Noi (Little)**, divided by a cliff. Both bays are picturesque with rocks along the edges and sweeping fine pale yellow sands in the centre. Descending a winding hill, Kata Noi comes as a pleasant surprise, offering an adorable little bay with a small and perfect beach. The snorkelling is good at the south end of Kata Noi and around **Koh Pu**, the island in the middle of the bay. Kata Yai, just the other side, is a

sprawling mass of development: hotels, souvenir shops and roadside restaurants abound. It provides excellent facilities for the holidaymaker, including numerous options for watersports and a lot of choices for nightlife down the rambling streets running inland from the coast.

Nai Harn to Rawai

Nai Harn, a small, gently sloping beach – home to the prestigious **Phuket Yacht Club** – is one of the island's most beautiful locations, renowned for its spectacular sunsets. The slopes of the bay are steep so, to reach most accommodation, you'll need to climb numerous steps. From Nai Harn it is possible to walk to **Promthep Cape**, the best place to view the sunset. Near the highest point there is a shrine covered in gold leaf and surrounded by wooden elephants.

To the north of Promthep Cape, up the eastern side of the island, the first beach is **Rawai**, which was 'discovered' by King Rama VII in the 1920s. This crescent-shaped beach is now relatively developed

Patong beach.

although not to the same degree as Patong or Karon, being more popular with Thai and Southeast Asian tourists, particularly during Chinese New Year and Songkran. The bay is sheltered and it is safe to swim throughout the year, but the beach, although long and relatively peaceful, is rather dirty and rocky

Chalong

The next beach up the east coast and south of Phuket City is **Chalong**. The beach isn't great but there are a few decent places to eat and the **Royal Pewter Showroom**, 61/16 Moo 6, Soi Baan Nai Trok, T076-281001, phuketroyal pewter.com, which has some interesting displays and a showroom. There is also the opportunity to make something out of tin under the watchful eyes of an instructor (฿350).

About 6 km south of Phuket City, just north of Chalong junction, is the ostentatious **Wat Chalong**, best known for its gold-leaf encrusted statues of the previous abbots, Luang Pho Chaem and Luang Pho Chuang. The former was highly respected for his medical skills, which proved to be particularly valuable when Phuket's Chinese miners revolted in 1876. Visible from almost anywhere around the south of Phuket City is Phuket's own **Big Buddha Statue**. Your reward for scaling the enormous and steep **Nakkerd Hill** is a great view of Chalong Bay and an up-close glimpse of a 45-m seated Buddha. To get to the Buddha driving from Phuket City, go past Wat Chalong and look for the sign pointing out the right-hand turn to the statue.

Cape Panwa

South of Phuket City, down Sakdidej Road which becomes Route 4023, in the grounds of the **Cape Panwa Hotel**, is **Panwa House**, one of Phuket's finest examples of Sino-Portuguese architecture. Panwa House was formerly inhabited by a fishing family from Phuket and, later, by the hotel's official coconut picker. The picker's job was to remove coconuts from the trees so the guests would not be concussed. The house is now filled with curious artefacts, like the coconut scraper in the shape of an otter. At the tip of Panwa Cape is the **Marine Biological Research Centre and Aquarium**, T076-391126, 1000-1600, ฿20. The air-conditioned aquarium is well laid out with a moderate collection of salt- and freshwater fish, lobsters, molluscs and turtles and some other weird species. Watching the sun set along the paved seafront is recommended. Heading north from here up the east coast of Phuket island, apart from a couple of piers, there is little of note.

Koh Tapao Yai, a small island off the cape, is home to a few hotels (see page 201) and around 200 hornbills. Baby brother of Koh Tapao Yai, **Koh Tapao Noi** is another small island, secluded and devoid of almost everything except flora, fauna and hornbills. There is also a lighthouse that was built in 1890. Other than that, enjoy the beach and the sea while you can. To get there, take a boat from Ao Makham Pier (6 km from Phuket City).

Kamala to Surin

On the west coast just north of Patong is **Kamala Beach**, fringed by coconut trees, which hosts a sedate Muslim fishing village – modest clothing should be worn. There is little tourist development with the north of the beach offering the best swimming. Between Kamala and **Surin** is a

Cape Panwa.

Tip...

There are regular public *songthaews* every hour from the market on Ranong Road in Phuket City to Cape Panwa and the aquarium.

Nai Yang beach.

Tip...

To get to this wildlife park turn east off the main road in Thalang and follow signs for Ton Sai Waterfall. The beautiful, peaceful road winds through stands of rubber trees and degraded forest.

little-known beach by the name of **Laem Sing**. It's one of the less crowded beaches on the island and the sand is clean and the water is clear. The only problem is the onslaught of jet skis that noisily zip around dangerously close to where people are swimming. Laem Sing is also where you'll find Soundwave Sundays, the most happening Sunday night party in Phuket. **Surin Beach** is quite dirty. It is lined with casuarina trees and open-$ir restaurants, patronized mostly by Thais. The seabed shelves away steeply from the shoreline and swimming can be dangerous. There is a short golf course but no hotels on the beach. **Pansea Beach** has soft sand in a steeply sloping bay just north of Surin, with two exclusive hotels.

Nai Yang National Park

To get to Nai Tang, take a bus from the market on Ranong Rd in Phuket City.

The attractive and often empty forest-lined beach of **Nai Yang** lies next to the airport and is part of the **Nai Yang National Park**. It is the ideal place to pass a few hours before an early evening flight. Further south, there is more activity, with a range of luxury hotels and bungalows. The park encompasses Nai Yang and **Mai Khao** beaches,

which together form the longest beach on the island (13 km). The area was declared a national park in 1981 to protect the turtles which lay their eggs here from November to March. Eggs are collected by the Fisheries Department and young turtles are released into the sea around the second week of April (check on the date as it changes), on Turtle Release Festival Day. The north end of the beach (where there is good snorkelling on the reef) is peaceful and secluded. There is no accommodation in the national park, although camping is possible.

Mai Khao is Phuket's northernmost and largest beach – still with no proper development. Instead there is the village of Had Mai Khao and the **Sirinath National Park**. Again, sea turtles nest on this beach, including the huge leatherbacks, and the Turtle Release Festival is in mid-$pril. The community effort to conserve the turtles involves collecting the eggs and keeping a hatchery. The beach is steeply shelved so swimming isn't recommended and it is unsuitable for children.

Phuket's Vegetarian Festival

The first four days of the Ngan Kin Jeh (Chinese Vegetarian Festival) are comparatively ordinary. It is during the last five days that events, for most foreigners, turn really weird. Devotees show their commitment and the power of the gods by piercing their bodies with an array of objects apparently chosen by the gods. The processions end in a large field where razor ladders, cauldrons of boiling oil and pits of burning coals await the supplicants. Tourists have tried to take part and ended up severely injured but locals say those successfully possessed by the spirits feel no pain, unless the gods leave them while the object is still embedded. Islanders insist the festival's real message is to eat healthy food and do good deeds but this is often hard to square with the image of people strolling down the street with a chair, model battleship, miniature Eiffel Tower or potted plant through their cheek. Details of the festival can be found here phuketvegetarian.com.

Khao Phra Thaeo Wildlife Park

The **Khao Phra Thaeo Wildlife Park,** T076-311998, 20 km north of Phuket City, 0600-1800, ฿200, supports wild boar and monkeys and the last of the island's natural forest ecosystem. During the dry season, a walk around the park is a lot of fun and not particularly gruelling. The primary nature trail has 14 stations where you can stop and learn a bit about the park. There isn't much wildlife to be seen, although you may come across a monitor lizard, gibbon or even wild boar. The park's two waterfalls, Bang Pae Waterfall and Ton Sai Waterfall, are not up to much during the dry season when there isn't any water. When there is water, visitors can paddle in the upper pool. There are bungalows, a lakeside restaurant and a number of hiking routes here.

The road east from Ton Sai Waterfall becomes rough and can only be negotiated on foot or by motorbike; it leads to **Bang Pae Waterfall** 0600-1800. Alternatively, the falls can be approached from the other direction, by turning off Route 4027 and driving 1 km along a dirt track. There is a lake, refreshment stands, forest trails, and bathing pools. Just south of the waterfall (follow signs off Route 4027) is a **Gibbon Rehabilitation Centre,** T076-260492, 1000-1600, free, donations welcome as it is run by volunteers, funded from the US and apparently the only such initiative in Southeast Asia for these endangered animals.

Phangnga Bay

P hangnga Bay is best known as the location for the 1974 James Bond movie *The Man with the Golden Gun*. Gorgeous limestone karsts tower out of the sea (some as high as 100 m) and boats can be hired to tour the area from Tha Don, the Phangnga customs pier.

The poor relation to its neighbouring tourist hotspots of Phuket and Krabi, Phangnga town is often overlooked by visitors. Its relaxed, authentic Thai feel, dramatic setting and interesting day-trips make it an excellent place to pass a few days. There is one main road that goes through the centre of town which nestles narrowly between striking limestone crags. If you want urban sophistication and multiple culinary options, then Phangnga may disappoint. It is a non-tourist Thai experience, and Phangnga folk come across as almost grumpy with tourists – a relief after the feigned jollity of so many of Thailand's tourist-drenched resorts.

Sited in the bay itself Koh Yao Noi and Koh Yao Yai, are the two most important islands in the 44-strong cluster of islands known as Koh Yao, to the east of Phuket. They are so close to each other that it only takes around eight minutes by long-tailed boat to cross between the two. Consistently untouched by tourism – due to a strong Muslim and Chao Le community who wanted to retain control over what could have become a rampaging beast, Yao Noi is home to one of the best run homestay programmes in Thailand.

James Bond Island, Phangnga Bay.

Essentials

⊖ **Bus station** Phangna town bus station is on Petkasem Rd, near the centre of town. Motorcycle taxis and *songthaews* will wait at the bus station to take passengers to town and the surrounding villages.
⊗ **ATM** ATMs are available in the town centre along Petkasem Rd.
✚ **Pharmacy** Pharmacies are available on Petkasem Rd but for medical services it is best to head to Phuket.
❶ **Tourist information** There is no formal tourist information service in town – you could ask at the Phangnga Inn.

Phangnga town & around

Due to the limestone geology, there are a number of caves in the vicinity. The most memorable are at **Wat Thomtharpan Amphoe Muang**, the so-called 'Heaven and Hell Caves', around 2 km to the south of town on the road to Phuket. It's hard to see where Heaven is in this Buddhist depiction of Hell, designed to teach youngsters about the consequences of sinning. Cheap plaster models of humans are burned on spits, chopped in half, sent through a mangle, torn apart by birds and gutted by dogs. Hideously distorted demons with metre-long tongues and outsized genitalia glare down on the visitor. Eat before you arrive at this eerily deserted compound.

Just on the outskirts of town on Route 4 towards Phuket, on the left-hand side, is the **Somdet Phra Sinakharin Park**, surrounded by limestone mountains; it is visible from the road and opposite the former city hall. Within this park are **Tham Luk Sua** and **Tham Ruesi Sawan**, two adjoining caves with streams, stalactites and stalagmites. **Tham Phung Chang** is a little closer into town on the other side of the road, within the precincts of **Wat Phraphat Phrachim Khet**. To get to the arched entrance to the wat, take a *songthaew*. In this long dark cave, again dripping with stalactites and stalagmites, there is a spring, Buddha images and a small pool.

Several kilometres out of town, and a right turn off the Krabi road, the **Sra Nang Manora Forest Park** (probably best reached on a rented motorbike) offers a delightful break from the midday heat. The forest is free to enter and offers an easy, shaded 90-minute walk past several caves and sheer limestone cliffs..

Wat Tham Khao Thao is 12 km from Phangnga on Route 4152 to Krabi, on the left-hand side of the road, under a cliff wall (buses travel the route). Views of the plain can be seen from a stairway up the cliff face. The road here passes through nipa palm which then becomes an area of mangrove.

Tip...

In the centre of town, behind the Rattanapong Hotel is the fresh produce and early morning market while along the main street near the Thaweesuk Hotel are some remaining examples of the Chinese shophouses that used to line the street.

Sunrise at Phangnga Bay.

Phangnga Bay National Park

Park entrance fee, ฿200 (check to make sure it is included in the tour price). To get there take a *songthaew* to the pier, ฿10, from Phangnga town. 7 km along Route 4 there is a turning to the left (Route 4144 – signposted Phangnga Bay and the Ao Phangnga National Park Headquarters) and the pier is another 3 km down this road.

Relaxed boat tours of **Phangnga Bay** can be booked from one of the travel agents in the town's bus station. They cost up to ฿1100, and include the park entrance fee, accommodation, meals and a guided canoe tour, where someone does the paddling for you. The trips are just sightseeing tours as the boat drivers speak little English.

The standard tour winds through mangrove swamps, which act as a buffer between land and sea and nipa palm, and past striking limestone cliffs before arriving at **Tham Lod Cave**. This is not really a cave at all, but a tunnel cut into the limestone and dripping with stalacites that look like petrified chickens hanging upside down. From Tham Lod, the route skirts past **Koh Panyi** – a Muslim fishing village built on stilts which extends out into the bay, its most striking feature being a golden mosque and the sheer peak rearing up behind it. Through the narrow lanes, the main transport is bicycle. There are also overpriced seafood restaurants in this village.

Other sights include **Khao Mah Ju**, a small mountain near Koh Panyi. There is also **Khao Khian** or 'Mountain of Writings' with ancient depictions of animals and sea life dating back more than 3000 years. **James Bond Island** or **Koh Tapu** lies in the little bay of **Koh Phing Kan** or 'Leaning Mountain' which is a huge rock split into two parts with the smaller part having slid down so that the taller section appears to be leaning. The limestone karst stack that sticks up out from the sea just off this island is called Koh Tapu (Nail Island). The famous rock, like a chisel, seems much smaller than it should be, and the tiny beach and cave are littered with trinket-stalls (refreshments available) and other tourists. Recently, erosion of Koh Tapu caused by the wash from the hundreds of boats visiting the island has led to a declared intent to limit the numbers of visitors.

Koh Yao Noi & Koh Yao Yai

From Koh Yao Yai to Phuket: to Laem Hin Pier, 0800; to Tien Sin Pier, 0800 and 1500; Rassada Port, Thu and Sun 0830, Sat 1430; to the village of Bang Rong, return at 0700, 1000 and 1500.

In 2002, **Koh Yao Noi** gained recognition from eco-tourists when it received the **World Legacy Award** for Destination Stewardship from Conservation International and National Geographic Traveler magazine jointly for its **eco-friendly homestays**. Eco-activities include a rubber plantation and fishing demonstrations, kayaking, hiking and snorkelling. In keeping with the eco-theme, there are a few sensitively designed resorts on Koh Yao Noi – visitors need to remember that the Muslim locals prefer outsiders

Boat times

Boats from both Koh Yao Yai and Koh Yao Noi to Krabi and Phangnga depart from around 0700. Times vary; you need to check with your bungalow or resort. From Phuket there are many boats to Koh Yao Yai, ฿50, with vessels leaving from Laem Hin Pier at 1400, 1 hour 20 minutes. From Tien Sin Pier at 1000 and 1400. From Rassada Port on Thursday and Sunday only at 1400 and Saturday at 0600. Boats from Bang Rong leave at 1230. Five boats a day from Phuket to Koh Yao Noi leave Bang Rong Pier, 1 hour, ฿50.

Bird's nest soup

The tiny nests of the brown-rumped swift (Collocalia esculenta), also known as the edible-nest swiftlet or sea swallow, are collected for bird's nest soup, a Chinese delicacy, throughout Southeast Asia. The semi-oval nests are made of silk-like strands of saliva secreted by the birds which, when cooked in broth, softens and becomes a little like noodles. Like so many Chinese delicacies, the nests are believed to be an aphrodisiac and the soup has even been suggested as a cure for Aids. Collecting the nests is a precarious business and is only officially allowed twice a year – between February and April and in September. The collectors climb flimsy bamboo poles into total darkness, with candles strapped to their heads. In Hong Kong a kilogramme of nests may sell for US$2000 and nest concessions in Thailand are vigorously protected.

to dress modestly and not to drink alcohol outside resorts or restaurants.

Traditional ways and handicrafts still persist, as with the inventive 'fish-scale flowers' by the housewives of Koh Yao. These flowers – usually roses, geraniums and bougainvillea – are created from dried fish scales. The unusual rural heritage is seen in other ways too. Although expensive resorts are appearing on Koh Yao Yai, there are still wooden houses, rubber plantations and wandering buffalos. A partially paved road encircles Koh Yao Noi, with its village in the middle and huts scattered throughout the island. For little trips there are beautiful beaches, especially on **Koh Nok**, and a dreamy lagoon on **Koh Hong**.

Koh Yao Yai, the larger of the two islands, has better beaches for swimming but fewer places to stay, most of which tend to be overpriced. There's a spectacular view where the road ends on the west side of the island, overlooking **Klong Son Bay**. Koh Yao Noi is considerably more advanced than its bigger sister, with better facilities, including a hospital and internet shops. Mobile phones operate throughout both the islands. On the northern tip of this island and best reached by boat, is an enormous tree, the trunk of which takes 23 men to span. Hire a bike for a delightful few hours taking in the beauty of the island while negotiating the (sometimes difficult) roads. The main attraction is the peace and quiet. It has become a bit of a hotspot for alternative travellers, who have bagged the place as good for retreats ranging from yoga to healing crystal workshops.

Fishing boat at Koh Yao Noi.

North towards Khao Lak & Ranong

From Phuket all the way up to Prathong Island near Takua Pa (south of Ranong), virtually the entire western Andaman coast comprises great long sandy bays with the occasional peninsula or rocky headland. This collection of excellent beaches make up Khao Lak, a place devastated by the 2004 tsunami but which is now recovering some of its former glory.

Khao Lak.

Khao Lak & around

Head north along Route 4 from Phuket and you'll soon reach a string of beaches and small towns known collectively as Khao Lak built entirely to serve tourists – the central area focuses on **Nang Thong** beach which is set 500 m from Route 4. Before the 2004 tsunami that devastated Khao Lak killing 1000s, this area was being touted as Thailand's next big thing with several major developers moving in. The tsunami stopped that effort in its tracks and while some new resorts are springing up the area has never recaptured its previous boom-town vibe. One of the possible reasons for this is that the deeply superstitious Thais may not be keen to invest in a place they would consider to be filled with the troubled ghosts of tsunami victims. Some of the beaches at the northern end of Khao Lak, such as **Ao Thong**, are stunning, yet abandoned half-destroyed resorts still remain amid the swaying palms creating a genuinely eerie feel. Even the planned tsunami museum and memorial seems to have been completed reluctantly; a metal sculpture tucked away on a scrub of land behind a row of shops is the supposed memorial, while the only effort to create a museum is a community-run single room known as the International Tsunami Museum containing a few photographs, on the main road, daily 0930-2030, suggested donation ฿100. Round the back of this is the Thai Navy patrol boat that was washed a good 600 m inland by the encroaching tsunami wave.

There are, however, a few plus points – you should still be able to find some space on one of Khao Lak's long beaches – head to the far end of **Khuk Kak** beach or **Bang Sak** and the aforementioned Ao Thong just to the north. Given its proximity to the Koh Similans, Khao Lak is now becoming something of a dive mecca and there are a few excellent dive operators based here. Note that many buses now travel on a new road which bypasses Khao Lak and goes straight to Phangnga town, and then on to Phuket. Check that your bus passes through Khao Lak if you want to get off here.

Essentials

❶ **Getting around** Some *songthaews* run along the main road – the best choice to reach the more remote beaches is to rent a motorbike. Check with your resort/bungalow.
❺ **ATM** There are some ATMs in the main hubs along the main road.
⊕ **Pharmacy** You will find pharmacies on the main road but for medical services head to Ranong or Phuket.

Beach at Khao Lak.

Khao Lampee-Had Thai Muang National Park

Park Visitor Centre, Thai Muang District, Phangnga Province 8210 (along the coast past Ban Thai Muang along 14 km of beach, 6 km from Thai Muang town), T077-395025, ฿200 for entry for 3 days, children ฿100.

This relatively small national park, 72 sq km, comprises two distinct geographical zones: the **Thai Muang Beach** and the **Khao Lampee** area. The western portion, Thai Muang Beach, has 14 km of undisturbed beach lined with casuarina trees. The park continues inland for about 1 km and

Khao Sok National Park

Khao Sok National Park has limestone karst mountains (the tallest reaches more than 900 m), low mountains covered with evergreen forest, streams and waterfalls, and a large reservoir and dam. The impressive scenery alone would be a good enough reason to visit, but Khao Sok also has a high degree of endemism and an exceptionally large number of mammals, birds, reptiles and other fauna.

The list of 48 confirmed species of mammals include: wild elephants, tigers, barking deer, langur, macaques, civets, bears, gibbons and cloud leopards. Of the 184 confirmed bird species, perhaps the most dramatic include: the rhinoceros hornbill, great hornbill, Malayan peacock pheasant and crested serpent eagle. The plants to be found here are also of interest. The orchids are best seen from late February to April. If you visit between December and February, the rafflesia Kerri Meijer is in flower. This parasitic flower has an 80-cm bloom – the largest in the world – with a phenomenally pungent odour so that it can attract the highest number of pollinating insects. It also has no chlorophyll. Besides the astounding rafflesia, there are also at least two palms endemic to the Khao Sok area.

In the centre of the park is the Rachabrapah Reservoir. Near the dam there is a longhouse of sorts, and several houseboats. The best location for animal spotting is near the reservoir where grassland at the edge of the water attracts animals. In addition to camping, canoeing and walking tours, you can take elephant treks at Khao Sok. The routes taken must be outside the park, however, as elephant trekking is not permitted within the confines of the park.

khaosok.com, entry ฿200.

Getting to Khao Sok

Buses from Phuket and Khao Lak to Surat Thani stop near the road that leads to the park entrance – guesthouses are 2 km from here. Make sure your bus takes this route. Many tour operators in the south offer trips to Khao Sok but if you have your own wheels it can be done in a day from Khao Lak. Various tours with park rangers are available from the guesthouses.

Listings

Sleeping
Khaosok Las Orquideas Resort $$$-$$
343 Moo 6, T08-72693359 (mob), khao-sok-resort.com

Set up a drive on the road into the park, this small and beautifully tended guesthouse is the pride and joy of friendly its Spanish owner, Francisco. A set of small bungalows clings to a hill-side, each one complete with marble flooring, views across the treetops and en-suite bathrooms. The price includes an awesome breakfast and bicycle hire – a little bit more expensive than some of the other places here but with massive added value make this place highly recommended.

Art's Riverview Lodge $$$-$$
T08-6470 3234 (mob), artsriverviewlodge@yahoo. co.uk, or write to Art's Riverview Jungle Lodge, PO Box 28, Takua Pa, Phangnga 82110.

Art's is long-running, stylish and popular so book ahead. Its 30 rooms include lodges with balconies overlooking the river and many rooms have a spare bedroom and dining room. There is no hot water. The restaurant is beside the river near a swimming hole with a rope providing endless entertainment. Impertinent monkeys congregate at sunset to be fed bananas by residents.

Serves up great coffee, Thai and western food from a spot overlooking the swimming hole.

includes mangrove forest along the edge of the sea inlet, some swamp forest (*pa samet*) and freshwater lagoons from the old mine works from which Thai Muang derives its name (*muang* in this case means mine). The inland eastern portion covers several waterfalls and surrounding forested hills. Turtle Beach, entrance fee ฿20, is a 20-km-long beach where turtles, including the giant leatherback, come ashore at night to nest from November to February. Young turtles can be seen hatching from March to July. Hawksbill and Olive Ridley turtles are currently being raised in ponds near the parkheadquarters. There is an office in the Khao Lampee area, but the park headquarters are based in the Thai Muang area near the entrance.

Ranong & around

Carry on up the coast and you'll reach Ranong, a hub to visit everything from hot-springs through to some of Thailand's sleepiest island getaways, places like Koh Chang and Koh Phayam. Ranong's proximity to the Similan and Surin islands makes it an ideal stopover for divers – certainly, as the gateway to Richelieu Rock and the Mergui archipelago, it is hard to beat. Surrounded by forested mountains, Ranong is a scenic place to stay for a day or two. It is a small and unpretentious provincial capital and an important administrative centre. Increasingly, it is being eyed up as a spa/hot spring location but is currently still more popular with Southeast Asian tourists than those from further afield. The free municipal hot springs just outside the town are a charming spot, where the area's varied population gather day and night to get warm, floppy and relaxed in the ever hot water. It offers an excellent way to watch all levels of Thai society at their most lethargic while warming yourself after one of the town's many thunderstorms. There are waterfalls here, one of which, Punyaban, can be seen from the road as you approach the town. It is also the jumping-off point for a number of beautiful islands in the Andaman Sea.

Ranong town contains excellent **geo-thermal mineral water springs** (65°C) at **Wat Tapotharam**, 2 km east of the town and behind the **Jansom Thara Hotel** (free). To get there, walk or take a *songthaew* along Route 2; ask for '*bor nam rawn*' (hot water well). Surrounded by dramatic forested hills, the spa water bubbles out of the ground hot enough to boil an egg and cools sufficiently to allow the city's residents to enjoy a free hot bath and take refuge in its cosy depths during Ranong's frequent thunderstorms.

Hot spring at Ranong.

Essentials

On the roadside near Ranong.

⊗ Airport There is an airport 20 km south of town – Air Asia fly here from Bangkok (airasia.com).

⊖ Bus station The bus terminal is on the edge of town, Highway 4, near the Jansom Thara Hotel. However, the buses stop in town on Ruangrat Rd before the terminal.

⊛ ATM On Tha Muang Rd there are branches of **Bank of Ayudya, Siam Commercial Bank, Thai Farmers Bank** and **Thai Military Bank**, all with ATMs and/or exchange facilities.

⊕ Hospital At the junction of Permphon Rd and Kamlungsab Rd.

⟳ Post office Chon Rao Rd, near the junction with Dap Khadi Rd.

❶ Tourist information There is a small tourist office on Kamlungsab Rd.

Tip...

Bring an umbrella – Ranong province is the first southern province bordering the Indian Ocean and it is Thailand's rainiest (often in excess of 5000 mm per year), narrowest and least populated province.

The valley also has a luxurious **hot spring and health club**, offering a jacuzzi, gym, steam room, sauna and massages from ฿300, but it lacks the natural setting and village green feel of the municipal springs across the road. Around the park are several seafood restaurants and food stands. The springs also provide the Jansom Thara Hotel with thermal water for hot baths and a giant jacuzzi. There is a small park with a cable bridge over the river, a tiny cave containing a small Buddhist shrine and a number of municipal bathing pools. The *wat* here contains a footprint of the Buddha.

Continuing along Route 2 for another 6 km or so, the road reaches the old tin-mining village of **Hat Som Paen**, which is worth a visit to see the numerous giant carp, protected because of their supposed magical qualities. Deep in the hills, a few kilometres further up the road, is **Ranong canyon**, where city folk escape to recline in pretty *shalas* above the water, swim or feed countless hungry catfish.

Port of Ranong lies 3 km from town. Each morning the dock seethes with activity as Thai and Burmese fishing boats unload their catches. Boats can be hired, at a pontoon next to the dock, to tour the bustling harbour and look across the Kra River

estuary to the Burmese border (approximately ฿400). Border officials can be touchy so carry your passport. Ranong is an important point of contact between Burma and Thailand. Like Mae Sot, there are more intensive searches and check points as you leave the area. Do not be surprised if the military come on to your bus up to three or four times on the way out to check documents. This intensifies in line with the guerrilla operations in Burma and the drug wars.

Laem Son National Park

There are a number of notable beaches and islands in the neighbourhood of Ranong, many within the limits of the Laem Son National Park. The water here is warm and a pleasure to swim in, especially around the reefs. The park and the islands effectively lie at the outer limits of the Kra River estuary – so don't expect coral on all islands or excellent visibility. Mangroves fringe many of the islands and because of the high rainfall in the area the natural vegetation is tropical rainforest. While

Getting there

Ranong tour operators arrange tours and tickets to the national park. *Songthaews* run the 43 km south of Ranong along Route 4 from where there's a 10-km turn-off that leads straight to the park – take a motorbike taxi from the roadside.

For the islands daily boats run from the Saphan Plaa island pier in Ranong to Koh Chang and Koh Phayam. The quickest and cheapest way to explore the smaller islands closer to Laem Son is to charter a long-tailed boat once almost in the national park. Negotiating directly with the fishermen operating from Hat Bang Baen (turn off left just before the park entrance) should cost about ฿1000, while Wasana Resort offers a worthwhile day trip.

Passenger long-tailed boats at Ranong.

the islands may not have the best snorkelling and water, they hide some wonderfully white sand and secluded beaches and they do have good birdlife (there are around 138 bird species in the park). The best birdwatching months are December to February with many migrating birds and optimum weather conditions. On the mainland is **Hat Bang Baen** a delightful, relatively untouched, enormous beach lined by forest with lovely shells and fine sand. You can also organize boat trips here to nearby islands.

Unlike the larger Koh Chang on Thailand's east coast, Ranong's tiny **Koh Chang** has more to offer birdwatchers than beach lovers, but is best known for its distinctly laid-back ambience. Commonly sighted birds are kites, sea eagles and the endearingly clumsy hornbill. And, in the forest along the coast, monkeys and deer can be spied – and heard. The beaches here are mediocre at best and grim at worst, with streaks of black and dubious grey-yellow sand. The island also hibernates from June to mid-October when the monsoon rains lash down with even locals shifting to the mainland, leaving Koh Chang almost empty. But what this island lacks in beach bounty, it makes up for in the chill-out stakes. While there is a burgeoning backpacker tourist industry replete with yoga and dive schools, beach bars and

tattooists, the economy still depends on fishing and plantations of rubber, palm and cashew nut. Self-generated electricity remains sporadic and there is no sign of cars, with most people getting around on motorbikes through tracks to the beaches. But, while the beaches are never going to be used in an ice cream advert, the swimmable **Ao Yai** on the west coast is well worth a visit. Koh Chang survived the tsunami remarkably well, thanks to other islands acting as a breaker for the waves. Only its market was destroyed along with a few bungalows.

Buffered by Koh Similan, **Koh Phayam**, along with Koh Chang, were the only inhabited islands on the Ranong coastline not to suffer any deaths from the tsunami. Koh Phayam has no cars and boasts only narrow rutted roads, many that are more like big lanes which run through cashew nut plantations. There are, however, a series of small tracks around the island for walking, cycling or motorbiking. Perfect for lounging are the long and curving white sand beaches at **Ao Yai 'Sunset Bay'** or **Ao Khao Kwai 'Buffalo Bay'**. These days, Koh Phayam has become a quiet hit for the laid-back diving and snorkelling set. If you are not the diving sort, the island is also home to wonderfully diverse wildlife with hornbills, while further inland away from the white sandy beaches are monitor lizards,

Treehouse, Koh Phayam.

boar, deer, monkeys and snakes. There is also a tiny fishing village on the east coast of the island and a sea gypsy settlement to the west. Though still a relatively sleepy island, Koh Phayam's guesthouses, especially on Buffalo Bay, have developed steadily since the tsunami, flourishing as the Koh Surin islands, which are easily accessible from Phayam, become ever more popular. Ecological awareness is high on the island agenda, recycling is common, as is solar power and conservative use of electricity (bring a torch). It is possible to hire motorbikes (฿200 per day) but be warned that the roads are sometimes treacherous, narrow and uneven.

Koh Khang Khao (25 mins from Hat Bang Baen) is the stuff of dreams – it has a relatively small white sand beach for sunbathing and rocks for picnics, sheltered by trees that continue to grow thick, fast and jungle-like up the steep mountainous slopes. A sandy shelf means there's about 7 m of shallow swimming – ideal for families – before the bed falls away to deeper, rockier territory with some reefs providing good snorkelling. The more adventurous could try to circumnavigate the island by clambering over the countless rocks that fringe the rest of the coastline.

Koh Khao Khwai (30 mins from Khang Khao) is another beautiful island boasting a long stretch of beach and azure water, with lots of tiny crabs scuttling over the sand and the parched skeletons of long-dead trees lying further up the beach. The longer of the two beaches sweeps from the west along the southerly curve of the island. It's easy to walk from the west to the east side, or take a short path from the southern tip of the beach through the rich vegetation and into a dreamy cove, with white sands, set against the impressive backdrop of mountainous rainforest. The water is bath-like in temperature, but beware of the stony bottom. This cove is, however, overlooked by some national park bungalows, which have information leaflets.

Koh Similans

Getting there

Boats depart from Thap Lamu pier, 20 km north of Thai Muang near Khao Lak (3-5 hrs) to the Similans, 40 km offshore. Boats also leave from Ao Chalong and Patong Beach, Phuket with Songserm Travel (T076-222570), Tuesday, Thursday and Saturday from December-April. Boats also leave from Ranong.
The best time to visit is December-April.

Bungalows are now available on Koh Ba Ngu by the time of publication. Reservations can be made at the Similan National Park Office, Thai Muang, or at Tap Lamu Pier, T076-411914. Camping may also be possible on Koh Ba Ngu. Bring your own tent. They also serve basic food at the park office.

For experienced divers the best way to visit the Similans is via a liveaboard boat with fully inclusive dives, food, transport and accommodation.

Sea Bees runs the comfortable Genesis 1 and Marco Polo, 1/3 Moo 9 Viset Road – Ao Chalong, Phuket – they also have an office in Khao Lak T076-381765, sea-bees.com.

Mermaid Liveaboards have two very nice boats, 3 Sawatdirak Road, Patong, Phuket T08-72748348 (mob), mermaid-liveaboards.com

Jonathan Cruiser is a well-run budget boat, Scuba Venture Co Ltd. 43/63 Moo 5, Viset Road, Rawai Phuket T076-281529, jonathan-cruiser.com.

The Similan Islands lying 80 km northwest of Phuket and 65 km west of Khao Lak are some of the most beautiful, unspoiled tropical idylls in Southeast Asia. The national park consists of nine islands (named by Malay fishermen, who referred to them as the 'Nine Islands' – *sembilan* is Malay for nine). The water surrounding the archipelago supports a wealth of marine life and is considered one of the best diving locations in the world, as well as a good place for anglers. A particular feature of the islands is the huge granite boulders. These same boulders litter the seabed and make for interesting peaks and caves for scuba divers. On the west side of the islands the currents have kept the boulders 'clean', while on the east, they have been buried by sand.

Richelieu Rock – dive site

The idea of describing the splendour that is Richelieu Rock in a paragraph or two is more than a challenge, it's nigh on impossible. This isolated, submerged hill is without doubt the dive site that has it all. From the tiniest of tiny critters to the ultimate in grace, size and beauty: the whaleshark. Entering over the top of the rock it's worth heading straight down to the base where there are masses of healthy, colourful soft corals and several enormous groupers. Back on the slopes there is a wealth of smaller creatures to admire – lionfish, seasnakes, cowries and trumpetfish – every surface seems to house yet another fascinating resident.

But at all times, keep an ear out for the sounds of manic tank banging. This is the signal that a whaleshark has been seen and you should make a mad dash towards the sound. When the conditions are right, you may be really lucky and see several in a day. Both adults and juveniles are attracted to the Rock and this is one of the few places in the world where you can still dive with them. Pay them the respect they deserve.

Sleeping

Phuket has hundreds of places to stay, largely at the upper price end. During the low season (Jun-Oct) room rates may be as little as half the high season price. All rates quoted are peak season. Advance booking is recommended during high season (particularly at Christmas and New Year).

Phuket City

There are some good guesthouses in the old part of town.

Sino House $$$
1 Montri Rd, T076-221398, sinohousephuket.com.
Another modern hotel in town, this time with a Chinese twist. The rooms are large and all have Wi-Fi access, a fridge, a/c and cable TV. A decent breakfast is included. Located in a quiet area of town, opposite O'Malleys Irish bar if you fancy a drink. They also have a spa that comes highly recommended for massages.

The Taste Phuket $$$
16-18 Rassada Rd, T076-222812, thetastephuket.com.
Decent upmarket hotel in a converted shophouse. Rooms come with hot water rain shower, a/c, cable TV and large double bed. The expensive rooms have massive TVs, DVD players and gardens. The Taste is dubbed a 'lifestyle venue', which means it has a café and bar where you can chill while listening to jazz and drinking cocktails. The staff can offer advice on places to go in Phuket and organize bookings.

Phuket 346 $$$-$$
346-348 Phuket Rd, T076-256128.
Hip little guesthouse with only 3 rooms in a converted Sino-Portuguese shophouse. There is lots of art around the place making it quaint and chilled. Rooms have high ceilings, comfortable beds, lovely linen and a/c. You'll feel more like you're in someone's home than a guesthouse. There's also a café and art gallery.

Baan Suwantawe $$
1/10 Dibuk Rd, T076-212879, baansuwantawe.co.th.
Serviced apartments and hotel, opposite Lemongrass restaurant. The rooms are clean and comfortable and there is a large outdoor swimming pool. Breakfast is not included. Rooms have access to broadband and overlook the pool. The accommodation here really stands out from other choices in Phuket. Cable TV and a/c.

Crystal Inn Hotel $$
2/1-10 Soi Surin, Montri Rd, T076-222 7756, phuket crystalinn. com.
Comfortable, trendy rooms conveniently close to Surin Circle. There are 54 rooms in total and the hotel also has a lobby bar. Rooms come with twin beds or a large double bed. TV, a/c and artwork come as part of the package. Stylish accommodation at a reasonable price.

Raya Thai Cuisine $$
48 Deebuk Rd, T076-218155.
Offers 5 simple rooms in a 70-year-old Macao-style house set off the road. Part of the Raya Thai Cuisine restaurant (see Eating, page 206). Quirky in the nicest possible way. The rooms themselves are simply furnished and decorated, but the setting is romantic, with a bridge leading to the rooms from the restaurant. Friendly owners full of tales about Old Phuket. The food is also good.

Thalang Guesthouse $$
37 Thalang Rd, T076-214225.
A pleasant house with an old-world charm, large windows, wood floors, double-panelled doors and ceiling fans. 13 rooms on 3 floors. Varying prices and standards. Some rooms look on to a brick wall. Rooms 3 and 21 are best, though a little more expensive – they have balconies overlooking the street. This is an excellent base to explore the old town. The owner, Mr Tee, has a good reputation with guests who are encouraged to leave notes and drawings on the landing. As well as Japanese customers, it attracts students, backpackers and divers.

Phuket Backpacker Hostel $$-$

167 Ranong Rd, T076-256680, phuket backpacker.com.

By day, Ranong Road is home to a lively market, but by night the street has a strange empty charm about it. The hostel may look gloomy from the outside, but inside it's everything you would expect from decent, budget accommodation. There are dorms and rooms with or without air conditioning. The standard rooms are a little pricey for true backpackers (฿900 or ฿1000), but they are clean and the lounge is a cool place to hang out. This place is dubbed a 'boutique hostel', if such a thing is possible.

Forty-three $

43 Thalang Rd, T076-258127.

Tucked away on Thalang Rd is this gem. There are 4 room types, with the most snazzy having private gardens or balconies, as well as outdoor showers. Definitely worth a look if you're in Phuket City on a budget.

Around Phuket Island

Patong Beach
Safari Beach $$$$

136 Thaweewong Rd, T076-341171, safaribeachhotel.com.

A/c rooms only, restaurant attached. Small hotel set around pool in leafy compound just north of Soi Bangla. The location remains sought after as it is on the beach and the standard rooms are spacious and of a decent quality.

Sunset Beach Resort $$$$

316/2 Phrabarame Rd, T076-342482, sunset phuket.com.

What better place to feel safe than a hotel with the tsunami warning tower on the roof? This is another mega-hotel with a double kidney-shaped pool snaking its way between terraced, balconied wings. From the upper floor rooms you can see the sea. There is also a decent spa and good but predictable meals. A 5-minute tuk-tuk ride from Bangla Rd.

Thavorn Beach Village $$$

6/2 Moo 6, Nakalay Bay (between Kamala and Patong beaches, on the Kao Phanthurat Pass, 5 km from Patong), T076-290334-42, thavornbeachvillage.com.

Giant vulgar concrete Hindu cobras spring from the fountain in front of the reception at this otherwise attractively designed resort of Thai-style villas, with 4 rooms each (2 ground floor, 2 first) many with verandas beside the large lagoon-like pool. A secluded spot on a sparsely populated beach – Nakalay Bay (rocky at low tide). It also offers extras like Thai cooking courses and scuba-diving. The restaurant overlooks the sea.

Karon & Kata beaches
Boathouse Inn $$$$

T076-330015, boathouse.net.

Southern end of Kata Beach, a/c, pool. This establishment, also known as Mom Tri's Boathouse, is clearly a labour of love. Its creator, Mom Tri Devakul, is an architect and artist, and there's an art gallery supporting local Phuket artists. The villa also has a saltwater pool and a professional health spa. Thai cookery classes are offered and there's even a customized Boathouse Cookbook. The wine cellar is one of the nicest surprises with over 400 wines – a rarity in the land of whisky and beer.

Katathani Resort and Spa $$$$

14 Kata Noi Rd, T076-330124-26, katathani.com.

Stunning location in this quiet cove. All rooms have a seafront balcony and there are even louvred panels in the bathroom that can be opened if you want to gaze at the sea from your bath. For even greater luxury, there is a natural rain shower and bathtub in the Grand Suite while the Royal Thani Suite has floor-to-ceiling windows.

SouthSea Resort $$$$

36/12 Moo 1, Patak Rd, T076-370888, phuket-southsea.com.

A/c, restaurant, pool, nearly 100 rooms in this low-rise, intimate boutique resort. Rooms feature teak wood and Thai silks and are cool and minimalist. Some bathrooms need renovation. Attractive central pool, gym could be better equipped. You have to negotiate a busy street to reach the beach although a security guard is there to help pedestrians across the road.

P&T Kata House $
104/1 Koktanod Rd, T076-284203.
One of several cheap guest-houses at the southern end of Kata Beach set back a few hundred metres from the shore, past a 7-11, offering some of the island's cheapest rooms outside Phuket City. The rooms are clean with fresh linen and many overlook a garden, and are of similar quality to competitors which charge 3 times as much. There is no hot water but a/c rooms are available.

Nai Ham to Kawai
Baan Krating Jungle Beach $$$$
11/3 Moo 1, Witset Rd, T076-288264, baankrating.com/phuket/.
Remote, attractive position, has a long and good track record. Accessible through Le Royal Méridien Phuket Yacht Club, this is on Ao Sane Beach, which is nicknamed Jungle Beach for the foliage around it. There are 30 villas, all with sea views from the balconies and a pool overlooking Nai Harn Bay. The rooms have a rustic feel, picked up again by

the presence of a pool table and big screens in the relaxation area. If you like to explore, your own transport is a good idea here as it is an isolated spot.

Evason Phuket Resort and Spa, formerly Phuket Island Resort $$$$
100 Witset Rd, Rawai Beach, T076-38010-7, six-senses.com/evason-phuket/.
On the tip of Laem Ka with stunning views across to the nearby islands and over Chalong Bay. While the buildings are quite large, the rooms are exquisite with a cool, airy feel. There are tennis courts and a refined spa. To make up for the poor quality of the beaches on the main island, the resort has its own island in the bay – Koh Bon. Set in 26 ha of garden facing the Andaman Sea, this is definitely intended to be a place of escapism as the resort, though large – 285 rooms – is flanked by 2 inland lagoons and surrounded by extensive foliage.

Cape Panwa
Cape Panwa $$$$
27 Moo 8, Sakdidej Rd, T076-391123, capepanwa.com.
Beautifully secluded, good variety of accommodation including bungalows for families or friends, tennis courts, fitness centre, beauty salon, flower arranging and Thai cookery courses. For a touch of exclusivity take the Mercedes electric tram

down to the beach which can only be accessed through the hotel. There is also a coral reef 40 m offshore. Leonardo Di Caprio stayed here in Room E301 which has a double balcony and the best view of the sea and the bay. Other famous guests include Catherine Zeta Jones, Pierce Brosnan and Elizabeth Taylor. The choice of restaurants include Italian and Thai fusion and there's an excellent cocktail bar. Good breakfast buffet. While you may never wish to leave the hotel, there is also a shuttle service into Phuket Old Town.

Sri Panwa $$$$
Cape Panwa, T076 371000, sripanwa.com.
Run by one of the youngest management teams in Thailand, this resort is beginning to set the pace for up-and-coming designer luxury. Each of the enormous pool villas are brilliantly put together and clustered together in a small community on a hillside with gorgeous views over the cape. You could easily spend your entire holiday here with occasional forays down the hill onto Panwa's promenade. All the cutting edge facilities you'd expect, with ipods and players in each room, giant plasma screens, day beds, giant bath tubs and even kitchens in the bigger villas. No beach though.

The Kantary Bay Hotel
$$$$-$$
31/11 Moo 8, Sakdidej Rd,
T076- 391514,
thebay-phuket.com.
A seafront hotel 15 minutes' drive from Phuket. Rooms have sofa and dining table, stereo and large balcony. There is a gym, 2 pools and a garden. Selection of studios and suites make this place excellent value.

Phuket Paradise Resort $$$
T076-211935, phuketweb.com/ pprh/index.html.
The idiosyncratic ambience of this resort on Koh Tapao Yai is largely due to the presence of hornbills which can be seen between 0600 and 1800 as they fly around the hotel (dawn is the best time to catch the shy birds). In 1986 there were a mere handful of these colourful heavy-beaked birds, until hornbill fan and manager Khun Aroon insisted that everyone take care of the birds. There are now over 200 on Koh Tapao Yai. The rooms are set in the hillsides, some with a seaview. There is a free daily boat trip and car service to town and golf trips can be arranged.

Kamala Beach
Papa Crab Guesthouse
$$$-$$
93/5 Moo 3 Kamala Beach,
T076-385315, phuket papacrab. com.
Ten air-conditioned rooms and 3 bungalows at this unusually named guesthouse. Basic accommodation next to the beach. Has tour information and can arrange a taxi to the airport. Cosy little place. The rooms are simple, clean and with comfortable beds. Everything is very white, so it all looks a bit post-modern.

Surin & Pansea beaches
Amanpuri Resort $$$$
118/1 Pansea Beach, T076-324333, amanpuri.com.
A/c, restaurant, pool; the more expensive rooms are beautifully designed Thai pavilions, with attention to every detail. Superb facilities include private yacht, watersports, tennis and squash courts, fitness centre, private beach, library, undoubtedly the best on Phuket. Guests include political leaders.

Chedi Phuket (formerly Pansea Resort) $$$$
118 Moo 3, T076-236550, phuket.com/chedi.
South of Amanpuri. Chic, exclusive resort set into the hillside above a perfectly secluded sandy white beach. There is a range of beautifully designed traditional thatched Thai cottages sleeping 2-10 people, professional staff, superb facilities, including watersports, cinema, library, games room, a/c, restaurant, pool. Rooms can be somewhat small and monastic. The small pool appears almost black due to the dark stone used.

Nai Yang &
Nai Yang National Park
Nai Yang Beach Resort
$$$-$$
T076-328300, phuket.com/ naiyangbeach.
Well-built bungalows with good facilities and simple decor. Some a/c. Set in large grounds with plenty of trees for shade. Friendly staff. A bit pricey at the upper end but excellent value at the lower end. Right next to the Pearl Village and a hop over the road to the beach.

Garden Cottage $$
53/1 Moo 1, T076-327293, gardencot@yahoo.com.
Close to the airport and walking distance from the beach, charming cottage-style bungalows, friendly owners willing to show you the island. Excellent value with a masseur and attractive restaurant and communal areas.

Mai Khao
Marriott's Phuket Beach Club $$$$
T076-338000, marriott.com.
Take the turn-off at the sign on the main road (402) travelling north from the airport. There are also airport pick-up services for the hotel. More than 200 rooms and 2 pools, spa, fitness centre, tennis courts, shops, gallery and playground. Traditional boats (*korlae*) are dotted throughout the resort. The rooms are elegant and spacious. Sea turtle nesting grounds are close and the hotel has donated a large sum to the Thai World Wildlife Fund to start up a turtle conservation fund. Watersports are banned, and guests are asked to use the pools rather than the sea to avoid disturbing turtles.

Mai Khao Beach Bungalows $$$-$
T08-05228392 (mob), mai-khao-beach.com.
Tucked away in a grassy clearing shaded by large casuarina trees and shrubs right on the beach. There are 2 ranges of bungalows, smaller bamboo and palm roof huts with shared bathrooms and larger en suite concrete and wood rooms. It is also possible to pitch a tent for ฿150. The owners seem to enjoy getting to know their guests and set up a regular campfire to chat during the night. Contact the bungalows in advance to organize transport.

Phangnga Bay

Phangnga Town
Phangnga Inn $$$-$$
2/2 Soi Lohakit, Petkasem Rd, T076-411963.
A beautiful family house converted into a cosy hotel with a range of contrasting, immaculately clean en suite rooms. It is off the main road, and clearly marked by a purple sign. It is by far the quietest, most comfortable place to stay in town. There is a smart kitchen, spacious communal areas and the more expensive rooms have stylish furniture and elegant wooden floors.

Phangnga Guest House $$-$
99/1 Petkasem Rd, next to Rattanapong, T076-411358.
Excellent value, fan and a/c, fastidiously clean small rooms, tiny sparkling café downstairs.

Thawesuk $
79 Petkasem Rd, T076-412100.
Clean rooms, thin walls, basic, run by an eccentric family. Mr Thawesuk is an amiable character with a sharp eye for anyone who's not a guest, so the security is excellent, despite having to walk through what feels like an open garage to get to the rooms. A narrow stone staircase leads to a roof terrace at the back of the building where you can view the surrounding limestone mountains. Rooms have been recently renovated.

Koh Yao Noi
Koyao Island Resort $$$$
24/2 Moo 5, T076-597474-6, koyao.com.
Operated by a Frenchman. 15 villas incorporating traditional thatched Thai architecture mixed with the latest in French style. All villas are set around a garden in a coconut plantation, and look out on to an island-spotted stretch of the Andaman Sea and the only non-rocky beach on the island. Villas have small private gardens, satellite TV, phone and fax, minibar, etc. A largely outdoor spa offers sauna, jacuzzi and traditional Thai massage in a relaxed and airy setting.

Six Senses Hideaway Yao Noi $$$$
56 Moo 5, T076-418500, sixsenses.com.
Over the last few years the luxury Six Senses resort chain have been developing their portfolio of properties in Thailand and this is probably their finest example to date. Set amid the trees are 56 luxurious wooden villas, all complete with private pool, sunken tubs and *sala*. If you get one of the hill-top villas the sunrise will leave your jaw on the floor. Eating here is unforgettable as well – they have an in-house deli stocking the best cheeses and charcuterie you'll find anywhere in Thailand. The bakery is excellent and the spa probably the best on the island. Prices are high but you

get a lot for your money. Six Senses also donate a percentage of their revenue to carefully selected local projects.

Sabai Corner Bungalows $$-$

T076-597497, T08-1892 1827 (mob), sabaicornerbungalows. com.

Run by an Italian woman and her Thai husband. 10 romantic bungalows set among cashew and coconut trees with views over Pasai Beach. Attached toilets. Motorbikes, mountain bikes and canoes for rent, and the restaurant serves up tasty fare. Between them the management speak Italian, Spanish, French, English, German and Thai. A popular option, often full so ring ahead.

Ban Tha Khao Bungalows $$-$

T076-212172.

Several decently sized bamboo and wooden structures with chairs, table, wardrobes, Western toilets and mini balconies. No a/c. Near a deserted cove up a rough road in the centre of the island so a bit of a hike. This is a picturesque choice and the Mut family who runs it can arrange for a pick-up by motorcycle taxi.

The owners also manage the Sea Canoe company.

Coconut Corner Bungalows $$-$

T076-597134.

A handful of bungalows, all basic but charming, with attached toilets, presided over by the friendly and knowledgeable Mr Bean. The restaurant serves excellent food, and eating with the family is often the norm. Attracts returnees for the hospitality and Mr Bean's verve.

Koh Yao Yai

The choice on Koh Yao Yai isn't as great as on its smaller neighbour, and much of it is overpriced, although the lack of visitors does make bargaining more possible.

The Paradise Koh Yao Boutique Beach Resort and Spa $$$$

24 Moo 4, T08-1892 4878, theparadise.biz/.

48 superior studios, 16 de luxe studios and 6 pool villas on the beach in the north of Koh Yao Yai. Has its own passenger transfer boats and you can even get here by seaplane.

Yao Yai Island Resort $$$-$$

Moo 7, Ban Lopareh, T08-947 19110, yaoyai resort.com.

Located on a beach that's decent even at low tide, this western facing resort means you'll actually get to enjoy the setting sun. Good bungalows complete

with eccentric wood furnishings, everything is en suite though there is the choice of fan and a/c. If you can help it don't get suckered into taking the resort's overpriced transfer boat.

Thiwson Bungalows $$-$

58/2 Moo 4, Ko Yao Yai Rd, T08-1956 7582 (mob).

Clean little rooms in the usual bamboo and wood style, with bedside lights, Western toilets, deckchairs on the verandas and a pleasant garden over-looking one of the nicest beaches on the island, with Koh Yao Noi visible.

Khao Lak & around

Prices out of season can be very low.

Meridien Khao Lak Beach and Spa Resort $$$$

9/9 Moo 1, Khuk Kak beach, T076-427500, starwoodhotels.com.

Huge, well-managed resort beside a beautiful stretch of sand about 8 km north of Khao Lak town. It has superb kids' play area and all the usual spa and swimming pool facilities you'd expect, plus a range of accommodation from standard rooms through to stunning villas complete with private pools. The food is also top-notch.

Khao Lak Palm Hill Resort and Spa $$$-$$
4/135 Moo 7, Khuk Kak, T076-485138, khaolakpalmhill.com.
Friendly, well-run small resort set on a back *soi*, 5 minutes' walk from the beach. The rooms are large, cooling affairs all backing out on to a large pool. Decent food make this place one of the nicest away from the beach.

Father and Son Bungalow $$
T076-48527.
The friendly Nom family are planning to add to their 10 fan bungalows spread around a charming, shaded garden where the road is barely audible. The more expensive en suite rooms are good value at ฿500.

Motive Cottage $$
21/16 Moo 5, Khuk Kak, T076-486820, motivecottage resort.com.
Elegant minimalist rooms, each with own little balcony and surrounding a bijou pool make this an uplifting place to stay. All rooms have a/c, en suite facilities and hot water. Set beside the main road it's a 5-minute walk from the beach.

White Sand Bungalows $$
Ao Thong Beach.
Excellent little bungalow operation on this stunning stretch of sand just north of the main Khao Lak hub. Some of the neat and tidy bungalows – all

en-suite, with a/c and fans, hot water – are set right on the beach while the rest are placed in a compound in the trees a short walk away. Has a bar and restaurant attached so you never need to leave.

Khao Lampee-Had Thai Muang National Park

Accommodation is available in 4 fan-cooled bungalows in the Thai Muang part of Khao Lampee-Had Thai Muang National Park. Prices range from ฿800 for a 6-person bungalow to ฿1000 for a bungalow for 10 people. Bookings can be made at the central Forestry Department office in Bangkok (Reservations office, Marine National Parks Division, Royal Forest Department, Chatuchak, Bangkok, 10900 – T02-579 7047/8) or at the park HQ in Thai Muang. Call ahead to see if the bungalows are in operation. Camping is allowed and food and drinks can be purchased at the canteen.

Ranong & around

Jansom Hot Spa Hotel $$$$-$$$
2/10 Petkasem Rd, T077-811 5103, jansomhotspa.com.
In places this is a slightly shabby spa hotel with charming pretensions of grandeur. There have been some improvements over the years and the rooms,

pool and a huge jacuzzi are all supplied with mineral water from the nearby hot springs. The rooms remain a good deal with bathtubs, linen, fridge and TV. Breakfast included.

Khao Nanghong Resort and Spa $$$-$$
123/6 Moo 5, T077-831088, khaonanghongresort.com.
A beachside boutique resort with large, airy, luxury thatched villas set in gardens overlooking Burma's Victoria Point. Stylish design, spa and a romantic restaurant with sea views.

Royal Princess Ranong $$$-$$
41/144 Tamuang Rd, T077-835240-44, dusit.com.
A 4-star hotel (part of the long-established Dusit chain) with excellent service, good facilities including a mineral spa, and comfortable. One of the best hotels in Ranong. Has a pool and offers babysitting. It also pumps mineral water into the jacuzzi. Still very corporate with a suburban feel to the rooms.

Rim Than Resort $$-$
Chon Rau Rd, T077-833792
A little out of town, just past the hot springs on the road up to Ranong Canyon, this small, eccentric family-run resort offers a range of simple, clean fan and a/c bungalows set in a pretty garden with balconies right over the river. The choice of en suite

rooms includes cosy doubles and a large family villa with 2 bedrooms, bathtub, fridge, TV, veranda and private garden. Also has a restaurant.

Bangsan (TV Bar) $
281 Ruangrat Rd, T077-811240.
Cheap, basic rooms with fan above the trendiest cocktail bar in town. Hip with the young Thai and backpacker crowd.

Dahla House $
323/5 Ruangrat Rd, T077-812959, dahla.siam2web.com
Nice clean bungalows set in a private compound in easy walking distance of the town centre. All have hot water, are en suite etc and the owners are friendly and speak good English. They also have an internet café and sell reasonable food.

Laem Son National Park

Hat Bang Baen
Wasana Resort $$-$
T077-828209.
This Dutch/Thai operation is on the left before the main park entrance. It has 10 smart concrete bungalows tastefully decorated, attached Western toilets and verandas arranged around a garden with badminton net, ping-pong, children's pool and good restaurant. The proprietors are helpful and arrange day trips.

Andaman Peace Bungalows $
T077-820239.
A handful of smart concrete bungalows at the northern end of the long beach with fridge, fan and TV on slightly sparse land beyond the beach. Although it isn't a white- sand beach, trips to nearby paradise isles are popular and the excellent restaurant is the best in the area. Commands fantastic sunset views and attracts a mainly Thai clientele.

Koh Chang
The number of guesthouses here has more than doubled over the past couple of years. Most are in the budget range and offer simple bamboo huts. Many guesthouses shut down during monsoon season. There is limited electricity in most resorts. Many can be booked through travel agents in Ranong.

Cashew Resort $
T077-820116.
The granddaddy of the resorts and the largest with a variety of bungalows, pool table, travel services, credit card facilities, money exchange and attached yoga school. The resort has its own boat for fishing.

Lae Tawan $
T077-820179.
Tucked away in a slightly out-of-the-way spot this cosy place is one of the few open all year round. Thai restaurant.

Sabai Yai $
T08-6278 4112 (mob).
Swedish and Thai owned with good Western food, excellent service and well-kept rooms including dorms and bungalows. Home-baked bread.

Koh Phayam
Ao Yai Bungalows $$
Ao Yai, T077-821753, gilles_ phatchara@hotmail.com.
The original operation on this strip, this pretty, immaculately kept place in a secluded spot is run by a French/Thai couple, Gilles and Phatchara, who know the island intimately and have a range of wood and concrete bungalows on stilts. Some are surrounded by lovely gardens and set among pine and coconut trees. West facing, it makes for an ideal spot to watch the wildlife and the sunsets. Tasty restaurant.

Bamboo Bungalows $$-$
Ao Yai, T077- 820012, bamboo-bungalows.com.
A beach-side idyll and probably the most popular place on Ao Yai – booking is recommended during high season – although it is one of the few operations open year round. Bungalows range from new luxurious wooden villas with sprung mattresses, sofas, marble floors, sliding balcony doors and woven gables, through to pretty A-frame shell-covered bungalows. All have romantic outdoor bathrooms. There are

Eating

also a few cheaper bamboo huts. The landscaped communal areas, large dining table, small yoga space, beach campfires and volleyball sessions create a community vibe. The excellent restaurant with huge portions and home-baked bread attracts visitors from neighbouring bungalows. Kayaks, surfboards and snorkelling equipment are available.

Hornbill Hut $$-$
Ao Yai, T077-825543, hornbill_hut@yahoo.com.
Fantastically friendly family-run place with a great reputation and several styles of basic bamboo bungalows with concrete bathrooms set among the trees, along with a few excellent-value concrete villas with high ceilings and windows which allow the sea breeze to whistle through.

Baan Suan Kayoo Cottage $
Ao Yai, T077-820133, gopayam.com.
At the northern tip of the beach, with cottages and large restaurant set in a charming tropical garden – 'suan kayoo' means cashew nut garden in Thai. A choice of sturdy wooden superior en suite cottages with king-size beds and upmarket interior or budget thatched cottages with attached Thai-style toilet. Mosquitoes can be a problem.

Phuket City

There are quite a few reasonably priced Thai restaurants in the old town. The food in Phuket is highly rated throughout Thailand, for the range of dishes and the invigorating and sophisticated spices and herbs used in Southern Thai cuisine.

Ka Jok See $$$
26 Takua Pa Rd, T076-217903.
Excellent Thai restaurant. The success of the restaurant is leading to some pretty sharp pricing but the atmosphere, character, style and first-rate cuisine make it worth paying extra. Booking is essential.

Kanda Bakery $$$
31-33 Rasada Rd.
This spotlessly clean a/c restaurant with art deco undertones, serves breakfast, Thai and international dishes and cakes like cinnamon rolls, croissants and brownies.

La Gaetana $$$
Phuket Rd, T076-250253, T08-1397 1227 (mob).
The best Italian food in Phuket. Owners Gianni Ferrara and Chonticha Buasukhon offer impeccable service. There is also a decent wine list. Booking is recommended as the restaurant is rather small and fills up early.

Raya Thai Cuisine $$$
This restaurant is in a 70-year-old Macao-style house with a garden. It is well preserved with original tiling, windows, lighting and ceiling fans, and with a selection of photographs of old Phuket. The airy room upstairs is a pleasant place to eat. It serves Thai dishes and local specialities; if you like spicy food, try the *nam bu bai cha plu* (crab curry with local herbs served with Chinese rice noodles).

Santana Coffee $$$
54/8-9 Montri Rd
A nicely decorated European-style café that serves Thai food, steaks and European food as well as an excellent selection of coffees. Brews range from Jamaica Pea to Kilmanjaro.

Farang Restaurant $$
Off Chaloem Kiat Rd, next to Index, T08-6946 3142 (mob).
Amazing little restaurant that serves cheap, quality fusion dishes. Sausages, steaks, pasta, pizza, it's all here. There is also a second branch at 120/6 Cherngtalay, Thalang, T08-1620 7429 (mob).

Natural Restaurant $$
Soi Phutorn, T076-224287, T076-214037.
A long-time favorite in Phuket City, with fish swimming in televisions and all manner of plants everywhere. The oysters

are perhaps the best in Phuket. The sushi is average, but the Thai food is exceptional. Check out the range of curries for some spicy excitement.

Baan Talang Restaurant $
65 Thalang Rd
Tasty Thai and Islamic food (the lamb curry is excellent but hot). As with most places in this part of town, the walls are lined with photographs of old Phuket and there is an old-world feel.

Fine Day $
Chumphon Rd,
fineday- phuket.com.
Fine Day is an institution in Phuket. It's a hip hotspot where people hang out, eat and drink. Stays open until about midnight and is always busy. The staff are friendly and although there isn't a menu in English, there is always someone on hand to help out.

Food Court $
4th floor, around the corner from the cinema, Central Festival Phuket.
An excellent food court serving cheap Thai nosh. You can get everything from *kao man gai* (boiled chicken meat on a bed of rice and a side of spicy, ginger sauce) to noodles. Much better than most of the restaurants at Central Festival.

Kow-Tom-Hua-Pla (Boiled Fish Rice) $
Opposite Caramba Bar and Restaurant on Phuket Rd past Thalang Rd.
Popular with locals, this simple noodle café is open 1700- 2400 and is run by Chinese-Thai Mr Pinit. It serves an eclectic mix of noodles, including *Yen-ta-Foa* seafood noodles coloured a blood-red by a sweetish slightly hot sauce. Other noodle soups include fish skin and fish stomach noodles.

Nong Jote Café $
16 Yaowarat Rd.
This 100-plus-year-old building looks like a café in Lisbon with high ceilings, and, along one side, ceiling-to-floor antique glass cabinets in teak. On the other side there are banners for English football clubs; it's a sociable spot to watch Premiership matches. Tables are large enough to read a newspaper on and the service is admirably unrushed. The owner lived in New Zealand and has excellent English. You can find some of the best southern Thai food here, certainly in Phuket. Try the yum tour plu but remember it is hot. Some dishes have a Chinese edge.

Foodstalls
There is a late-night **khanom jeen vendor** on Surin Rd (towards Damrong Rd, just up the road from the Shell garage). Choose your curry, throw in a few condiments and enjoy some of the best Thai food on offer. Look for the large brown pots at the side of the road.
The best place to browse on the street is around the **market on Ranong Rd**. Just round the corner from Robinson on **Ong Sim Phai Rd**, is a lively collection of night-time street food vendors serving cheap Thai dishes to locals.

Patong Beach
Many of the sois off Patong Beach Rd sell a good range of international food.

Floyd's Brasserie $$$
Burasari Resort, 18/110 Ruamjai Rd, T076-370000.
Who better to open a restaurant in Phuket than acclaimed TV chef Keith Floyd? As you'd expect, the wine list is top class with 52 labels on the menu. There is some great food available, too. Floyd may now be cooking in that great kitchen in the sky, but even in his absence this is a restaurant worth checking out.

White Box $$$
247/5 Prabaramee Rd,
T076-346271,
whiteboxrestaurant.com.
A simple concept: it's white and it looks like a large box. The setting is ideal, far enough away from the madness of Patong, but with decent views over Patong Bay. The food is good, with a range of Mediterranean and Thai dishes. Children are welcome. Although not the cheapest place to drink (฿150 for a beer), there are usually parties at weekends with dancing until after midnight.

Lim's $$$-$$
Soi 7, Kalim Bay.
This opened in a small house in 1999 and now has a vast dining room with high ceilings and outdoor courtyard. Also features abstract paintings by one of the owners, 'Gop'. The food concentrates more on the quality of the ingredients rather than overwhelming with spices. Suits an exhausted palate. Choices of dishes range from grilled pork ribs to Vietnamese spring rolls.

Joe's Downstairs $$
223/3 Prabaramee Rd, Kalim Beach, near Patong, T076-344254, T076-344927.
A cool place to watch the sun set while sipping on a cocktail and enjoying the view of Kalim Bay. They have some great tapas.

Woody's Sandwich Shoppe $
Aroonsom Plaza, T076-290468, khunwoody.com.
Woody's Shoppe, run by local computer guru Woody Leonhard, is something of an institution in Phuket. For about ฿100 to ฿150, you can get a sandwich that puts Subway to shame. Woody also offers free Wi-Fi access.

Karon & Kata Beaches
Al Dente $$
Beach Rd close to Karon Circle, T076-396569.
You can't miss it, this is the traffic island decorated with mythical creatures. Try their meat and cheese fondues and Italian dishes while listening to classical music.

Drunken Monkey $$
Viset Rd, T08-1787 1184 (mob).
A favourite with Phuket's British contingent, Drunken Monkey does an awesome Sunday roast as well as the best bangers and mash on the island.

JaoJong Seafood $$
4/2 Patak Rd, Katanoi Beach, T076-330136.
Unpretentious sea- shanty feel to this spacious open-fronted seafood restaurant. Good selection of freshly caught seafood and well executed. The menu is illustrated with pictures. Low-key atmosphere.

The Green Man $$
82/15 Moo 4, Patak Rd, T076-281445, the-green-man.net.
Claims to be the only Tudor-style pub in Asia. In terms of pub grub, it's all very British and it's all very tasty. They even have pickled eggs.

Cape Panwa
Panwa House $$$-$$
Cape Panwa, on the beach.
Everything is in place here for the perfect meal: the 2-storey Sino-Portuguese house perched on the edge of a beach with indoor and outdoor dining, the serenading guitarist and singer, excellent service and deliciously executed dishes. Try their beef salad in lime juice or the lobster with shavings of caramelized shallot, palm sugar and tamarind. The desserts are superb too, for example the stuffed rambutan with vanilla custard.

Surin Beach & Pansea Beach
Amanpuri $$$
T076-324394.
Considered one of the best Thai restaurants on the island and the setting is sensational. At least 48 hrs advance booking needed during peak season.

Nai Yang & Nai Yang National Park

Nai Yang Seafood $$
Nai Yang beach.
One of several charming spots next to the empty beach, all of which serve excellent seafood.

Mai Khao

There is a full range of restaurants in the Marriott and a simple in-house restaurant at the Mai Khao Beach Bungalows.

Rivet Grill $$$
Indigo Pearl Resort, indigo-pearl. com/dining-rivetgrill.html.
Yes, it's expensive, but this is the restaurant to go to for the best steaks in Phuket and probably the whole of Southern Thailand. The restaurant is well designed with countless touches that reflect the overall tin-mining theme at the resort.

Phangnga Bay

Phangnga

Ivy's House $$-$
38 Petkasem Rd, next door to a dental clinic.
A tiny European-style café with a gas-fired oven for pizza, Italian wines and liquors and decent pastries. A little pricey but then the owner 'Ivy', who is from Switzerland, has to get all her imports from Phuket – including cheese from Italy. All her food is to a high standard. For many years she had a business in Koh Phi Phi but got tired of 'smiling all

the time', so came to Phangnga. Good source of information.

Open-air cinema eaterie $
Petkasem Rd and around Soi Bamrungrat.
This no-name eatery (the sign in Thai script simply describes what it sells) is not to be missed. There is a 100-year-old-plus tree that grows through part of it and a gigantic screen that can be heard along Petkasem Rd as it blares Southeast Asian martial arts flicks and straight-to-video Western horror movies. Outside this open-air restaurant and cinema, nocturnal stalls also sell sweet pastries. The food is of good quality. Popular with the locals, this Cinema Paradiso is a magical treat.

Ran Ja Jang $
Soi Bamrungrat on a corner opposite another café.
Superb seafood soup with egg and Tom Yee sauce swimming in tiger prawns and squid. This operation is run by 2 ladies wearing reassuring hair-nets as they bustle over an open kitchen. They also do home-made ices.

Koh Yao Noi & Koh Yao Yai

Most people eat at the restaurant attached to their bungalows, although there is Tha Khao Seafood right next to the pier. Otherwise a good option is to pick your choice of fish from the fishermen's huts on Tha Tondo Pier to the northwest of the

island, and take it to the local restaurant just by the pier for cooking while watching the best sunset the island can offer. For a local delicacy on Koh Yao Yai, it is worth trying/buying the *pla ching chang* dried anchovy paste which is used with rice and noodles to liven things up.

North towards Khao Lak & Ranong

Khao Lak

There are plenty of *farang* orientated restaurants on the main drag around Nang Thong, though most of them aren't very special. Most resorts and guesthouses will also offer food of some kind.

Mr Indian $$
26/22 Moo 7, T08-6593 5542 (mob).
Friendly little Indian place that sells a good range of food – they have a proper tandoori oven so the flat breads and meat dishes are cooked authentically. Also do an awesome *chai*.

Sun Star Siam $$
26/27 Moo 7, Khuk Kak, T076-485637.
Friendly Thai-Swiss run place serving up excellent Thai food.

Find plenty of seafood in Koh Yao Noi.

Ranong & around

The markets on Ruangrat Rd offer some of the best eating opportunities in town with specials worth sampling including the roast pork and duck. Also worth seeking out for its delicious dhal lunches is the Muslim roti shop (no English sign) on Ruangrat Rd, opposite TV Bar and guesthouse. Look for the roti/pancake stand outside.

Somboon Restaurant $$-$
Opposite the Jansom Thara Hotel.
Delicious Thai and Chinese seafood much of which is displayed in tanks at the front.

D&D Coffee $
Ruangrat Rd.
Where Ranong's café society congregate to discuss the day's issues, eat delicious Thai dishes over rice and sample a wide selection of good coffees.

J&T Food and Ice $
Also centrally located on Ruangrat Rd.
Excellent and serves a range of delicious but very reasonably priced Thai food and ice creams; popular place with locals and visitors, friendly owners.

Taxi Restaurant & Pizzeria $
Opposite the cinema with balcony seating overlooking Ruangrat Rd.
Inexpensive Thai, Italian and fusion dishes of a surprisingly good standard.

Laem Son National Park

Koh Chang
All the bungalow operations serve the usual spread of backpacker fare and watered down Thai food – there are few other options on the island.

Koh Phayam
Most guesthouses have cheap restaurants and guests have been known to be asked to leave resorts during the high season if they fail to eat where they are staying.

Middle Village $
On the road to Ao Yai.
Renowned for its excellent Isaan (northeastern Thai) dishes and rowdy karaoke nights.

Oscar's Bar $
Also in the village, turn right from the pier.
Run by the infamously affable Englishman Richard, a self-proclaimed food buff who offers a wealth of information about the island and its politics. The bar serves great, unexpected Western and Thai dishes to a sociable crowd.

Entertainment

Phuket City

Bars & Clubs

Phuket's club scene has experienced a resurgence and is now attracting the attention of DJs and promoters who have previously favored Koh Phangan and Koh Samui. International DJs such as Louie Vega, Judge Jules and Brandon Block have passed through. Whether you want house, electro, hip hop, rock, pop or reggae – you'll find somewhere to go in Phuket.

Blue Marina
Phuket Merlin Hotel, 158/1 Yaowarat Rd, T076-212866-70.
Offers up standard Thai hits and other random treats from bands and DJs. Fri and Sat are always very busy.

Kor Tor Mor
Chana Charoen Rd, near Nimit Circle, T076-232285.
Large, incredibly popular Thai club that gets ludicrously busy on Fri and Sat. Get there early or else you may be turned away. Buy a bottle of whisky, drink, kick back, dance and enjoy.

O'Malleys
2/20-21 Montri Rd, T076-220170.
An Irish-style pub that serves pints as well as a killer all-day breakfast (฿99). Upstairs there is free pool, darts, table football and some PS2s. There are usually a few friendly faces around if you fancy a chat about football or island life.

Oasis
Mae Luang Rd.
A small venue that doesn't attract too big a crowd so you've always got a bit of space to drink and dance in. As usual, expect bands singing Thai favorites and the occasional Green Day number. The in-house DJ usually closes the night with dance music. The Thais will be surprised to see you, but you'll be welcomed as long as you join in.

Timber Hut
118/1 Yaowarat Rd, T076-211839.
Something of an institution in Phuket, Timber Hut has been around for about 20 years. The crowd is a mix of Thais and foreigners. Arrive early on Fri and Sat because once midnight comes, you won't be able to move. A standard selection of Thai songs and odd Western classics is the order of the night. It's fun, but there are better places to choose.

Around Phuket Island

Bars & clubs
Patong Beach
BYD Lofts
Rat-U-Thit Road, Club Andaman Resort, T076-3430247, bydlofts.com.
In Patong, but sufficiently away from the madness of Soi Bangla. This restaurant doubles as a bar. The food is average but for pre-club drinks it's a chilled affair.

Club Lime
On the beach road, T08-5798 1850 (mob), T08-5798 8511 (mob), clublime.info.
The music ranges from electro and house to tribal and techno. Expect to pay a cover charge of up to ฿300 with 1 or 2 drinks included. Alcohol is on the pricey side but the club has a good vibe and you'll look out of place in sandals and a Beer Chang vest.

Paradise Complex
Ratuthit Rd.
Paradise Complex is like the gay community's version of Soi Bangla. The complex comprises gay bars, hotels, cafés and restaurants. There are endless cabaret shows to be watched. It can get pretty raunchy, but you won't come across any trouble. Visit gaypatong.com for info about the gay scene.

Tip...

Watch out for scams on Patong Beach – the Aussie Bar has a reputation for mysterious 'beer mat thefts' whereby ฿2000 Aussie Bar beer mats are found in drunk patrons' bags by police and staff who then demand bribes to secure release.

Listings

Safari
Located on the hill between Patong and Karon.
Where most people go after the other clubs have closed. There's a climbing wall that drunk tourists try to scale, not recommended if you've had a few. There are also opportunities to drench ladyboys by dunking them in large pools of water. You have to see it to believe it.

Seduction Discotheque
Soi Bangla, seductiondisco.com.
Has been around for a while and provides reasonably priced drinks and 2 floors of hip hop and dance beats. Doesn't get busy until later, but is worth a look if you fancy a dance. They sometimes have international guest DJs playing, but usually it's the residents taking you into the early hours of the morning. Happy hour is between 2300 and midnight.

Karon & Kata Beaches
Ratri Jazztaurant
Kata Hill, T076-333538, ratrijazztaurant.com.
The perfect spot for a romantic dinner or to kick back and enjoy the view. As the name suggests, this place is all about jazz. It isn't the cheapest spot around, but it can't be beaten in terms of setting and ambience.

Nai Harn & Promthep Cape
Reggae Bar
Nai Harn Lake.
Definitely worth a visit. This is about as real a reggae bar as you'll find in Thailand, complete with Rastafarians. It's chilled and peaceful next to the lake. Usually stays open later than regular closing times.

Cape Panwa
Baba Dining Lounge
Sri Panwa, T076-371006, sripanwa.com.
Hip, happening and with killer views of the sea at sunrise and sunset. The food and drinks are priced at the upper end of the Phuket scale, but are high quality. When they have special events the venue becomes a hive of nocturnal activity with lots of dancing. Requires a trip to the southernmost point of Phuket.

Phangnga Bay

Phangnga Town and the islands in the bay are mainly Muslim so nightlife is thin on the ground.

Koh Yao Noi

Reggae Bar
On the non-beach side of the road between Sabai Corner and Long Beach Village Bungalows.
Offers beer and cocktails and consists of a few tables set outside.

Pyramid Bar
A nice beachfront bar offering beer and cocktails.

North towards Khao Lak & Ranong

Many of Khao Lak's resorts and restaurants will have bars attached but there is little in the way of definitive nightlife. The same is true of the islands near Ranong and the town itself.

Cabaret Shows
Sphinx Restaurant and Theatre
Rat Uthit Rd, Patong Beach
Gaining popularity among the gay scene, this upmarket set-up offers Thai classical performances as well as Broadway hits and comedy. The food isn't bad – a mix of Thai and European cuisine.

Phuket Fantasea
99 Moo 3, T076-385111, Kamala Beach, phuket-fantasea.com.
For a long time this has been a firm favourite with visitors. It's billed as the ultimate in nightlife entertainment. The entire complex is huge and includes a carnival village, a restaurant and Las Vegas-style shows involving lots of animals, lighting effects and acrobatics.

Festivals & events

Old Phuket Town Festival
During the first weekend of February, the locals close off Thalang Rd, Krabi Rd and Soi Romanee to celebrate Old Phuket Town with foodstalls, music, plays and exhibitions.

Phuket Blues Festival
Feb
phuketbluesfestival.com.
One of the few music festivals held in Phuket. Great bands, a good crowd and lots of booze.

Phuket Food Festival
Held every March in Saphan Hin over a period of about 10 days. Enjoy Thai food accompanied by the world's most out-of-tune brass band, some karaoke singing and carnival games where you can win fish.

Thao Thep Kasattri and Thao Sisunthon Fair
13 Mar
Celebrates the 2 heroines who saved Phuket from the Burmese.

Fish Releasing Festival
Apr
Timed to coincide with Songkran or Thai New Year. Baby turtles are released at Phuket's beaches.

Chao Le Boat Floating Festival
Involving the Rawai, Sapan, Koh Sire and Laem Ka. This festival is held at night as boats are set adrift to ward off evil. Between the 6th and 11th lunar months.

Por Tor Festival
22 Aug-3 Sep.
Phuket City.
This means 'hungry ghosts' and is a time when ancestors are honoured. Ghosts are supposedly released into the world for the whole month. To keep them quiet, they are given food, flowers and candles at family altars. Bribes include cakes in the shape of turtles – the Chinese symbol of longevity.

Chinese Vegetarian Festival
Ngan Kin Jeh, lasts 9 days and marks the beginning of Taoist lent in October (movable). No meat is eaten, alcohol consumed nor sex indulged in. Men pierce their cheeks or tongues with sharp objects and walk over hot coals and (supposedly) feel no pain. The festival is celebrated elsewhere, but most enthusiastically in Phuket, especially at Wat Jui Tui on Ranong Rd in Phuket City. This must be one of the star attractions of a visit to Phuket. Visitors are made to feel welcome and encouraged to take part in the event. For more information, see page 183.

Shopping

Phuket

Most souvenirs are cheaper here than anywhere else in Thailand.

Weekend Market
Located on the outskirts of Phuket City, just off Chao Fa West Rd, opposite Wat Naka.
Sat-Sun from 1600.
A mass of cheap T-shirts, shoes and knick-knacks. Worth a visit.

Art galleries
DGallery
63/501 Moo 2, Thepkrasatri Rd, Koh Kaew, www.dgallery.co.th.
Tue-Sat 1100-1900, Sun 1200-1800.
Trendy gallery with regular exhibitions by Southeast Asian artists. Artwork can be bought.

Vichen Gallery
Bzenter Mall, Saiyuand Rd, Rawai.
Catch a glimpse of what Thai artists can do. There is usually an exhibition at the gallery.

Antiques
Ban Boran Antiques
39 Yaowarat Rd (near the circle), recently moved from Rasada Rd.
Arguably the best antique shop on Phuket; interesting pieces from Thailand and Burma.

Chan's Antiques
Thepkrasatri Rd, just south of the Heroines' Monument.
Not many 'antiques', but a selection of Thai artefacts.

Listings

Activities & tours

Food
Methee Cashew Nut Factory
9/1-2 Tilok Uthit Rd,
T076-219622/3.
The Methee experts have been around for more than 40 years. Stock up on a weird and wonderful range of cashews, including garlic, chilli and palm sugar flavour.

Handicrafts
Dam Dam
Rasada Rd, interesting selection; Rasada Centre, Rasada Rd; Prachanukhao Road
Numerous stalls leading to Karon which sell hand-painted copies of great artists, including Gauguin, Van Gogh and Da Vinci.

Khao Lak

All the usual stalls are here with more stylish shops opposite the Khao Lak Youth Club including the **Book Tree** bookshop, which sells international magazines and newspapers.

Ranong

Ranong's retail opportunities have expanded along with the tourist industry and cater for the crowds, with camping and outdoors shops lining Ruangrat Rd, ideal for pre-island purchases of tents, hammocks, mosquito nets and sturdy combat clothing. There are fashion boutiques and even a hip 60s-style hairdresser, Dichun Hair.

Phuket

Canoeing
John Gray's Sea Canoe Thailand
124 Soi 1 Yaowarat Rd,
T076-254505/6,
johngray-seacanoe.com.
John Gray has had 20 years' experience and is the man for day trips and overnights with the advantage being the limited number of expedition guests.

Diving
Most diving companies are to be found along Patong Beach Rd, on Kata and Karon beaches, at Ao Chalong and in Phuket City.

Santana
222 Thanon Sawatdirak Rd Patong Beach, T076-294220, santanaphuket.com.
A 5-star PADI instructor training centre with 25 years' experience. Does live-aboards to the Similan Islands, Surin and Hin Daeng.

Scuba Cats
94 Thaweewong Rd, Patong Beach, T076-293120, scubacats.com.
5-star PADI Instructor Development Centre offering live-aboards to the Similan Islands, Koh Bon, Koh Tachai and Richelieu Rock as well as fun dives. Phuket's first National Geographic Dive Centre, it is also a Go-Eco operator and is involved in marine clean-up.

Muay Thai (Thai boxing)
Tiger Muay Thai and MMA Training Camp
7/6 Moo 5 Soi Tad-ied, Chalong, T076- 367071, tigermuaythai.com.
One of Phuket's most famous camps. Anyone is invited to attend for serious training.

Bangla Boxing Stadium
T086-940 5463, T089-724 1581, 198/4 Ratuthit 200 Pee Rd, Patong, banglamuaythai.com/ bangla_ stadium. Php.
A decent place to watch a fight.

Phangnga Bay

The 3 main tour companies in town are **Sayan**, 209 Bus Terminal City, T076-430348, sayantour.com; **Kean**, bus terminal, T076-430619; and **MT Tours**, Muang Tong Hotel, 128 Petkasem Rd. All run similar tours. The tours are worthwhile and good value. Mr Hassim, who operates MT Tours grew up in Koh Panyi and comes from a long line of fishermen. He can also arrange overnight stays in fishermen's villages.

Koh Yao Noi

Tour operators
Reggae Tour, next to Reggae Bar, see Bars and clubs, page 212. Rents a long-tailed boat (฿800 for ½-day, or ฿1200 for a full day), and kayaks (฿250 for ½-day, ฿500, full day).

Transport

Khao Lak

Diving

Khao Lak Scuba Adventures
13/47 Moo 7, Khuk Kak,
T076-485602,
khaolakscuba adventures.com.
Well-run 5-star PADI dive resort
located in central Khao Lak,
offering all the usual PADI
courses and live-aboard trips to
the Koh Similans.

Sea Dragon

9/1 Moo 7, Khuk Kak,
T076- 420420,
seadragondivecenter.com.
A well-established operation
organizing day trips or live-
aboards to Richelieu Rock,
Similan and Surin Islands.
Teaches PADI dive courses.
European-managed.

Tour operators

Khao Lak Oasis Tour
Just down the road from Khao
Lak Scuba Adventures,
T076-485501,
T08-7271 4326 (mob).
One of the best and most
affordable tour operators in Khao
Lak. The owner, Su, works hard to
keep her customers and has a lot
of returnees. Private cars,
minibus tickets, train and flight
reservations and packages for
Khao Sok can be arranged here.

Ranong

Diving

A-One-Diving
Has branches at 256 Ruangrat Rd
as well as a dive school on Koh
Phayam (opposite the pier),
T077-832984, a-one-diving.com.
Organizes trips all over the
Andaman Sea including the
Similans, Surin and Burma.

Tour operators

Pon's Place Travel Agency
By the new market on Ruangrat
Rd, T077-823344.
Run by the affable Mr Pon who is
an excellent source of
information on the islands and
areas surrounding Ranong and
can help with tours, travel
information, guesthouse/hotel
bookings, and car and bike
rental.

Ranong Travel

37 Ruangrat Rd.
Probably a better source of
information than the tourist
information office. It can book
bungalows on Koh Chang,
arrange fishing trips and advise
on visiting Burma.

Phuket

THAI (thaiair.com) and **Nok Air**
(nokair.com) fly from Bangkok as
do **Air Asia** (airasia.com) who
connect with Singapore too and
Kuala Lumpur and **Bangkok
Airways** (bangkokair.com) who
fly to Samui and Pattaya as well.
Several international charters
also fly here.

Regular bus connections with
Bangkok as well as destinations
towards Ranong and in the
south. There is no railway line
though it's possible to take a
train to Phun Phin near Surat
Thani and then catch a
connecting bus (6 hrs).

Phangna

There are regular bus
connections with Phuket, Krabi
and towns south to the Malaysian
border and north to Bangkok.

Khao Lak

Many of the Phuket to Ranong
buses run through Khao Lak.
There are also a few buses each
way to Bangkok.

Ranong

There are regular bus
connections to Bangkok, Surat
Thani, Chumphon and Phuket.
You can also take the train from
Bangkok to Chumphon and the
bus from there.

Contents

South Andaman Coast & Islands

Macaque monkeys play on the beach.

Introduction

I t's with good reason that the islands and beaches of this stretch of Thailand's coast are gaining in popularity. Krabi has long been a stopover for travellers in search of that perfect beach and as a staging post to visit the sands near Ao Nang or the beauty of Koh Phi Phi. More recently climbers and divers have arrived, sampling the splendid cliffs around Rai Leh and some excellent dive sites.

Head even further south and quieter beaches and remoter, more authentic touches greet the visitor. While the island of Koh Lanta is home to upmarket resorts and tourist trinkets it is still an engaging place to absorb miles of beaches and gorgeous sunsets. Trang is a friendly rootsy spot whose charms grow on anyone who gives it a chance – it is also the gateway to the deep south of the country. The highlight of the south is the remote Tarutao National Park, home to dozens of beautiful, magical islands that are the source of myth and tales of pirates. Unfortunately, due to rough seas Tarutao is only accessible from October to April.

What to see in...

...a weekend
You could possibly squeeze a visit to **Koh Phi Phi** into a long weekend though **Koh Lanta** might be a better bet. **Trang** also makes for a great couple of nights – don't forget to sample the famous bbq pork (see page 229).

...a week or more
During high season this is a perfect stretch to island hop – start in **Krabi** or **Phuket** then take a boat via **Phi Phi**, **Lanta, Trang** before ending up at the magical **Tarutao** archipelago.

A long-tail boat at Phi Phi island.

Krabi & around

The provincial town of Krabi provides visitors to southern Thailand with an important hub of transport and facilities. There are beaches nearby at Rai Leh and the resorts of Ao Nang while the town itself is a perfect place to either prepare for, or recuperate from, island-hopping. From here travellers can connect with buses and planes and easily reach the popular islands of Koh Lanta and Koh Phi Phi – the latter, while firmly in the grip of mass tourism, is still one of the most beautiful islands in the country. Back in Krabi town you can stock up on bread – it has excellent bakeries – fetch your newspapers and get a decent caffe latte before heading back to the nature reserve for some more hammock swinging.

Sunset over the river at Krabi.

Essentials

❶ **Getting around** Plenty of places to rent motorbikes, cars and jeeps. *Songthaews* run regularly to/from the bus station at Talaat Kao, 5 km from town. White *songthaews* leave regularly 0600-1800 from Maharat Rd next to the 7-11 and from Phattana Rd for Ao Nang. Krabi Airport is 17 km south of the town. A bus runs into town and on to Ao Nang; taxis cost about ฿400-500.

❸ **ATM** You'll find branches of all major banks with ATMs scattered around the town.

❷ **Post office** Uttarakit Rd (halfway up the hill, not far from the Customs Pier).

❶ **Tourist information** There is a small TAT office on Uttarakit Rd, across from Kasikorn Bank, 0830-1630.

Boat tours from Krabi.

Krabi Town

Since the mid to late 1980s tourism in Krabi has boomed. It wasn't always like that – in the early 1970s communist bandits operated roadblocks along the only surfaced road in the area – Highway 4. Only those motorists who knew an ever-changing password would be allowed to travel. Travellers today don't have to suffer such travails as Krabi has excellent transport connections. There are not many sights in Krabi town itself but it is exceptionally well served with decent cafés, quirky bars and restaurants, catering for both tourists and locals. Many visitors to Krabi are using it primarily as a stop-off point and hub for visiting nearby islands, the beaches at Ao Nang and the cliffs at Rai Leh.

There is a **night market** close to the **Chao Fah Pier** that's full of food stalls frequented mainly by locals and a **general market** on Srisawat and Sukhon roads. **Wat Tham Sua** – the Tiger Cave temple – is 8 km northeast of town, hire a motorbike or get a tour operator to take you out there. It's home to dozens of *kutis* (monastic cells) set into the limestone cliff. Tiger Cave is so called because a large tiger apparently lived there leaving his pawprints as proof – some visitors find this claim dubious as the pawprints are not at all paw-like.

Take the 1237 steps up to the top of a 600-m-high karst peak for fantastic views. Mangroves line the river opposite Krabi town. This is a protected area and it is worth visiting for the birds, monitor lizards and macaques. Long-tailed boats can be hired for a trip into the mangroves at the Chao Fah Pier (rates are negotiable and depend on the time of year, length of time and number of passengers).

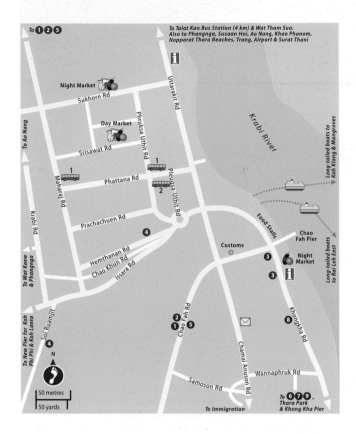

Krabi listings

① Sleeping

1 Bai Fern Guesthouse *24/2 Chao Fa Rd*
2 Ban Chaofa *20/1 Chao Fa Rd*
3 Blue Juice *1/1 Chao Fa Rd*
4 Europa Café & Guesthouse *1/9 Soi Ruamjit Rd*
5 K Guest House *15-25 Chao Fa Rd*
6 Khong Kha Guest House *Khongkha Rd*
7 Krabi River *73/1 Khongkha Rd*
8 Star Guest House *Khongkha Rd*
9 Thara Guesthouse *79/3 Khongkha Rd*

① Eating & drinking

1 Boathouse *Soi Hutangkonn*
2 Chao Sua *Maharaj Rd*
3 Kwan Coffee Corner *Khongkha Rd*
4 May & Mark's *Ruen-Ruedee Rd*
5 Ruen Mai *Maharaj Rd*

Ao Nang beach.

Tip...

The area around Ao Nang is predominantly Muslim – avoid topless bathing and both men and women should try to cover up away from the beach.

Ao Nang & around

Regular *songthaew* connections with Krabi, 30 mins, ฿40, or ฿80 after dark. For Krabi, *songthaews* leave from the eastern end of the beach road. The service runs regularly 0600-1800.

The road to the coast from Krabi winds for 15 km past limestone cliffs, a large reclining Buddha, rubber stands and verdant forest. Arriving at the coast in the evening, with the setting sun turning the limestone cliffs of **Ao Nang** a rich orange and the sea interspersed with precipitous limestone crags, is a beautiful first impression. Despite the glorious setting, the beach at Ao Nang is not particularly special with coarse sand and a concrete wall – also one end is filled with kayaks and long-tailed boats for transporting tourists to Rai Leh and other beaches. The town itself is a generic collection of souvenir shops, small resorts and bad restaurants. There are pleasant features in spite of all this – the beach front is lined with

coconut palms and mango trees with limestone walls at one end and lovely views of the islands on the horizon. Ao Nang is also good at providing facilities including diving, windsurfing, fishing and tours. But it is really the surrounding beaches, coves, caves and grottoes that make the place bearable, particularly at **Hat Nopparat Thara**, about 3 km northwest of Ao Nang. Here you'll find a deliciously long stretch of soft, pale beige sand covered in tiny seashells and shaded by tall casuarinas. To the back are paperbark forests. Locals used to call this place 'Hat Khlong Haeng' or dried canal beach because at low tide the canal dries up, leaving a long beach. Khlong Haeng is also the name of the village closest to the beach – around 900 m away. This 5-km-long beach is divided by a river with the side closest to Ao Nang being the most developed as it is bordered by a main road. The other side, which is lousy with sandflies, can only be accessed by boat.

Towards Rai Leh headland.

Rai Leh

Many Krabi guesthouses can arrange transport to Rai Leh. The other route is to take a *songthaew* to Ao Nang and then jump on a long-tailed boats to Rai Leh.

Located on **Phra Nang** peninsula to the south of Ao Nang, there are no roads to Rai Leh lending it a secret-hideaway ambience. The place consists mainly of **Rai Leh West** and **Rai Leh East**. Over the last few years Rai Leh has become something of a mecca for rockclimbers. This is partly because limestone is porous so that the water cuts into it and makes the natural grips ideal for climbers.

The best beach is on the west side – a truly picture-postcard affair. However, the east coast beach is still amazing at low tide in a sci-fi end-of-the-world way as the landscape transforms into a 300-m stretch of sinister shining mud. When Rai Leh East is not a mudbath, there are still the mangroves lining the beach so that it is fairly impossible to get any swimming in here. Rai Leh East also acts as a pier for taxi boats to and from Krabi and you will often spy tourists slogging across the mud with luggage over their heads. Pretty Rai Leh West, also knows as 'Sunset Beach', is about 10 minutes' walk away from the other beach – this means there is no escaping the daytime noises of the long-tailed boats although the evenings are delightful. There is also good snorkelling and swimming in archetypal crystal-clear water. The limestone rock formations are spectacular, and there are interesting caves with stalagmites and stalactites to explore though they require patience and fortitude as the paths are not always straightforward nor easygoing. At the southern extremity of the bay is a mountain cave (Outer Princess Cave) on **Phra Nang Beach** that is dedicated to the goddess of the area and considered 'her summer palace'. Here, you may be delighted to find an abundance of wooden and stone penises, many in wonderful colours of candy pink, lime green and pillar box red. It is believed local fishermen put the penises there to bribe the goddess into granting them plenty of fish on the sea. Be that as it may, many non-sailors also like to drop by a penis or two and the cave is suitably endowed. Near the penis cave are lots of monkeys that are rather friendly and several beachside stalls selling trinkets, clothes, beer and snacks like barbecued corn on the cob. There is also one outrageously priced bar that looks out of place.

If you feel you must make an effort, there is Sa Phra Nang (Princess Pool) to explore. This is a pond inside the cliff that can be accessed along a cave trail at the side of the mountain. You can get to the top of the mountain if you keep climbing. There's a walkway to Rai Leh east from Ao Phra Nang if you care to visit yet another Princess cave called the Inner Princess cave which is three caverns, one of which has a waterfall of quartz-like frozen amber.

There are several climbing schools (see Activities and tours, page 254), as the tower karst formations offer some truly outstanding climbing opportunities along with spectacular views.

For most arrivals on **Koh Phi Phi** it seems like you've reached paradise. Anvil-shaped and fringed by sheer limestone cliffs and golden beaches, Koh Phi Phi – the setting for the Leonardo Di Caprio film *The Beach* – is stunning. A quick walk along the beach, heaving with masses of pink, roasting flesh, or through Ton Sai village, which is filled with persistent touts and standardized tourist facilities, soon shatters the illusion of Nirvana. The Asian tsunami completely devastated the island on 26 December 2004 and over the last years has picked up the beaches in quite dynamic fashion. Whether Phi Phi can encourage enough sustainable tourism to survive the future is debatable – what is certain is that it has very quickly reached the same levels of development that existed pre-tsunami.

The island of **Koh Jum** is Phi Phi's smaller and much more low-key sister. While it isn't blessed with the same natural beauty as Phi Phi, Jum has managed to maintain a much quieter and more relaxed vibe – there's not much in the way of upmarket accommodation here and the island is home to Chao Ley sea gypsies and plenty of jungle.

Koh Phi Phi

During the high season there are regular, daily boat connections to/from Phuket, Krabi, Lanta and on to Koh Lipe. There are ATMs on the island and a pharmacy in Ton Sai near the pier.

Kho Phi Phi was one of the sites worst-hit by the tsunami – there is an aerial photograph on display in the Amico restaurant in **Ton Sai** village which shows the apocalyptic dimensions of the devastation. Both Ton Sai and Loh Dalem Bay were almost wiped out by the impact of the killer waves overlapping simultaneously on either side of this thin stretch of island. Today, Phi Phi is back to rude health. Tourists are streaming in and the dive shops, hotels, restaurants, shops and bars are now fully up and running. It should also be pointed out that large parts of the island were also completely unaffected by the tsunami. **Phi Phi Le** is a national

Tip...

It is possible to travel to Koh Phi Phi all year round but during the rainy season (May to October), the boat trip can be very rough and not for the faint-hearted.

park, entirely girdled by sheer cliffs, where swiftlets nest. It found fame as the location for the film *The Beach* starring Leonardo Di Caprio and Tilda Swinton. It is not possible to stay on Phi Phi Le but it can be visited by boat. The best snorkellin off Phi Phi is at Hat Yao (Long Beach) or nearby **Bamboo Island** and most boat excursions include a visit to the **Viking Cave**, which contains prehistoric paintings of what look like Viking longboats, and the cliffs where birds' nests are harvested for bird's nest soup.

Koh Phi Phi's beaches include **Loh Dalam**, which faces north and is on the opposite side to Ton Sai Bay, so is still under recovery. **Laem Hin**, next to Ton Sai Bay, has beautiful fine sand. **Ton**

Long-tail boat, Phi Phi island.

Tip...

Hire a long-tailed boat to take a trip around Phi Phi. Boats seat eight people and a day trip snorkelling is particularly worthwhile, with Bamboo Island, Hat Yao and, on Phi Phi Le, Loh Samah and Maya Bay, being good spots. Diving is also possible, with a chance of seeing white-tip sharks. Areas of interest include the Bida Islands, south of Phi Phi Le, where the variety of coral is impressive. There is a 50-m underwater tunnel here for more experienced divers. The best visibility (25-40 m) is from December to April.

Dao beach is a small and relatively peaceful stretch to the east of Laem Hin, hemmed in with the usual craggy rocks and vegetation.

Hat Yao (Long Beach) has excellent snorkelling offshore and is touted as having the cleanest water in Koh Phi Phi. Early in the morning (the best time being before 0930) black-tip sharks are a regular fixture before they swim further out to sea as the temperature rises. A walk to Hat Yao along the beach from the former Ton Sai Village takes about 30 minutes. You can also get a boat for around ฿100.

Loh Bakao is one of the larger of the minor beaches dotted around this island. Phi Phi Island Village is the only resort on this stretch of wide golden sand and is now fully operational. **Laem Tong** (Cape of God) boasts a wonderful sweep of white sandy beach that's relatively quiet and empty. There are only a few upper range resorts here, where many guests prefer poolside sunbathing, or the privacy of their own verandas, to the beach. The resorts also offer day trips, diving, snorkelling and cave-exploring expeditions. Increasingly, resorts are also conducting cultural workshops in skills such as Thai cookery, batik-painting and language courses.

Koh Jum

The boat from Krabi to Koh Lanta goes via Koh Jum, 1½ hrs, ฿350. There are connections with Koh Phi Phi and with Laem Kruat, on the mainland.

The island itself, with its beige-yellow beach and shallow waters, is not one of the most beautiful in the Andaman Sea. Its main attraction is as an escape from the crowds on other islands, a slightly rough-hewn edge and enough variety in accommodation and restaurants to keep things interesting. Recently, the island, which only has around a couple of hundred residents – mostly Chao Le and Muslim fishing families – has seen a flourishing of cheap bungalows and there are now over 20 places to choose from. There is also still a sense of being in the jungle, with pythons making slithering debuts in resort kitchens from time to time and the island has a undeniable quirky charm, both in terms of the locals and expats who have set up a semi-permanent base here. There is a working fishing village with a mosque on the other side of the island from the resorts. The village has a superb restaurant with sophisticated seafood dishes that would not be out of place in a metropolis. You can also watch fishermen at work here or have a cool beer away from the resorts.

Koh Jum.

Tip...

The island largely shuts its tourist industry down during the wet season May to October – the size of the waves makes swimming very difficult and dangerous.

Essentials

❶ **Getting around** *Songthaews* are the main form of public transport around the island – prepare to be overcharged with even a short journey costing upwards of ฿100. Motorbikes and mountain bikes are available for hire from guesthouses, some shops and tour companies. Long-tailed boats can be chartered for coastal trips. There is also a smattering of tuk-tuks in Sala Dan but prices are high.

❸ **ATM** You will find ATMs and currency exchange in Sala Dan and scattered around the island.

⊕ **Medical services** There is a health centre at Sala Dan.

❶ **Tourist information** There is no official tourist information office on the island.

Fisherman at Koh Lanta.

Koh Lanta

The story of Koh Lanta can be applied to most of the popular islands in Thailand: transformed in a generation from comatose tropical idyll without telephones, electricity or roads into a thrusting parade of generic resorts, all eager to separate visitors from their cash. But that's not the whole story – there are still great beaches and cheap backpacker bungalows, perfect places to lose yourself for weeks. If you're energetic enough to venture beyond the beaches you'll find a gorgeous interior crammed with luxuriant forests and a jungle-filled National Park. There's even Lanta's capital town of Ban Koh Lanta Yai, should you want to experience something a tad more authentic than just the usual run of beach resorts and bungalows. These days the island is also on the island-hopping route south from Phuket and Krabi and on to the pleasures of Tarutao and Lipe.

Around the Island

The two-street town of **Sala Dan** on the northern tip of the island is most arrivees' introduction to Koh Lanta, as the majority of ferries and boats dock here. There's not much of note but it does provide numerous facilities, including banks, ATMs, internet, bars and restaurants, though most are overpriced.

Ao Khlong Dao, which starts on the southern edge of Sala Dan, was one of the first beaches to open to tourism in Koh Lanta and as little as eight years ago had only about six small bungalow resorts and a couple of independent restaurants, not to mention the occasional buffalo family going for a paddle in the sea. While it is a lovely bay with soft sand and views over to Deer Neck Cape, development here has been rapid and unplanned. The bay is now heavily developed with most resorts encroaching on to the beach, each separated by high walls. Khlong Dao itself is a relatively safe place to swim and good for families and with the number of 'proper' hotels, it is often booked via travel agencies offering package tours to Lanta.

Keep going south from Khlong Dao along Lanta's west coast and you'll reach **Ao Phra-Ae**, also known as **Long Beach** – a lovely spot with soft white sand and a very long, gently sloping stretch that allows for safe swimming at both low and high tides. This beach is catering increasingly to well heeled retirees and families, particularly the Scandinavians although there are still remnants of its earlier days as a backpacker haven with restaurants and bars. The resorts here are no longer owned by local families and the bungalow resorts make their most lucrative profits through restaurant and bar sales.

Coconut palms at Koh Lanta.

local community. All that has changed with the arrival of the Pimalai Resort. This luxury resort has completely altered the feel of this bay. Nearby **Ao Khlong Jaak** is one of the most peaceful bays on Koh Lanta, a relatively small bay with sloping hills to the north and south and coconut plantations and grassland in the middle. **Ao Mai Phai** is the last bay before the national park and one of the few on the west coast of Lanta with good snorkelling opportunities. Again, it is a relatively small bay with steeply sloping hills leading down to the bay on the north and south and with a more extensive area of flatter land in the middle.

The **Moo Koh Lanta Marine National Park** (entry ฿200) covers much of the southern part of the island and extends over numerous islands in the area including Koh Rok, Hin Muang and Hin Daeng. The national park headquarters is at Laem Tanod and involves either a boat trip or a long and painful drive. The road to the park is in bad condition and practically impassable during the rainy season. There are two bays; one has fine soft sand and is great for swimming, the other, which faces west is rocky and a good place to explore if you like rock pools. Beyond the visitor centre is a nature trail which takes you up a fairly precipitous path into the forest. Take plenty of water and snacks with you. The bay is surrounded by forested hills and filled with forest sounds. It is a beautiful spot to spend a day swimming and walking, and then watching the sunset from the viewpoint on Laem Tanod.

The only real place of note on Lanta's east coast is **Ban Koh Lanta Yai**, the old administrative centre and port on Koh Lanta, now known simply as '*nai talad*' (in the market). It is developing its own tourism niche, with stunning views across to the islands of Koh Bubu, Koh Po, Ko Kum and Koh Tala Beng, and with most of its original old wooden shophouses/fishing houses still standing, this micro-town, which is actually only a couple of streets, has buckets of charm. Here, local entrepreneurs have opened galleries and souvenir shops, there are bed and breakfasts and the closest thing to family stays available on the island. Ban Koh Lanta really comprises one main street that

Hat Khlong Khoang is advertised by some as the 'most beautiful beach on Lanta'. But the beach is fairly steep down to the sea and the sand not as fine as that at Long Beach. The views along the bay are pleasant, but not spectacular. Behind many bungalow resorts is a canal which is treated as a dump for all sorts of waste from construction debris to coconut husks. In many parts of the beach it smells and is a mosquito trap and consequently best avoided if you are offered a room anywhere near. That said, there are a handful of establishments with real character and charm and, offshore, there are coral reefs that are increasingly attracting snorkellers and divers.

Ao Khlong Nin is a bit of a mixed bag in terms of accommodation, ranging from basic backpacker places through to the top-of-the-range resorts. There is, as they say, just about something for everyone. The beach itself is picturesque with rocks dotted about and not just a single sweep of sand. The downside is that this means that swimming, in places, can be tricky. Usually, though, it is possible to find a safe place to swim.

Ao Kantiang was once the cheap and secluded hideaway for many Europeans who spent months resting in bungalows overlooking the bay. With golden sand, steeply sloping hillsides and only a small village, the only accommodation was locally owned and operated and set well back from the

doesn't even go on for that long. The end of this road is indicated by an extraordinary ancient tree rather like a banyan and a tiny canal rivulet. There is a distinct Thai-Chinese ambience with rows of busy shophouses, each with its own exotically plumed bird in a wooden cage. Trade on this main street is largely fishing tackle shops and general goods stores, indicating the locals' overruling occupations. There are excellent restaurants offering either good working men's fare or more sophisticated seafood dishes.

Trang & around

On first sight, Trang looks like a somewhat drab but industrious Chinese-Thai town, filled with temples and decent schools, in other words, a good place to raise your children. Everything shuts down at around 2230 in the evening and even the traffic signals seem to go to sleep while early morning is filled with bustling tradespeople, eager to make their fortunes and provide for their families. But there is an underlying cranky charm and no-nonsense energy to this town which is famous for its char-grilled pork, sweet cakes and as the birthplace of former Prime Minister Chuan Leekpai. Its unique entertainments include bullfights (bull to bull) and bird-singing competitions (bird to bird) while the people are hugely friendly and exceptionally helpful the minute they realize that you like Trang too. Finally, Trang has a nine-day **Vegetarian Festival** in October, similar to that celebrated in Phuket. Vegetarian patriots, dressed all in white, parade the street, dancing through clouds of exploding fireworks, with the revered few shoving various objects through their cheeks. Trang is also an excellent jumping-off point for Koh Lanta, Krabi and the exotic coral islands of Kohs Muk and Ngai just off the coast

Trang Town

The town was established as a trading centre in the first century AD and flourished between the seventh and 12th centuries. Its importance rested on its role as a relay point for communications between the east coast of Thailand and Palembang (Srivijaya) in Sumatra. It was then known as Krung Thani and later as Trangkhapura, the 'City of Waves'. The name was shortened in the 19th century to Trang. During the Ayutthaya period, the town was located at the mouth of the river and was a popular port of entry for Western visitors continuing north to Ayutthaya. Later, during King Mongkut's reign, the town was moved inland because of frequent flooding. The arrival of the Teochew (Chinese) community in the latter half of the 19th century was a boon to the local economy which, until the introduction of rubber from Malaysia, was reliant on tin mining. Trang's rubber plantations were the first in Thailand (the first tree was planted just south of the city) and its former ruler, Phraya Rasdanupradit Mahitsara Phakdi, is credited with encouraging the spread of its cultivation. He also built the twisting road from Trang across the Banthat Range to Phattalung. There is a statue of him 1 km out of town on the Phattalung road. Trang has retained the atmosphere of a Chinese immigrant community, many of whom would be descendants of those who fled the corrupt and oppressive Manchu government.

There are good Chinese restaurants and several Chinese shrines dotted throughout the town that hold individual festivals. The **Kwan Tee Hun** shrine, dedicated to a bearded war god, is in Ban Bang Rok, 3 km north of Trang on Route 4. The Vegetarian Festival centres around the **Kiw Ong Eia Chinese Temple and Muean Ram**. There is also the **Rajamangkala Aquarium,** T075-248201-5, open daily during 'official hours', which lies 30 km from the city on the road to Pakmeng and is housed in the Fishery Faculty of the Rajamangkala Institute of Technology. The aquarium has 61 tanks of freshwater and marine life. Former Prime Minister Chuan Leekpai's house (ask locally for directions) has also become a pilgrimage spot of sorts and is open to visitors.

Approaching Koh Muk island.

Beaches & islands near Trang

Trang's embryonic tourism industry has so far escaped the hard sell of Phuket and Pattaya – excellent news for nature lovers, reef divers and explorers. The strip of coast running south from **Pakmeng** (38 km west from Trang) round to **Kantang,** boasts some of the south's best beaches. Unfortunately, it is also a relatively expensive place to stay with frankly exorbitant rates charged at some of the more popular beaches and islands and very ordinary food. Pakmeng and **Chang Lang** beaches are the most accessible – 40 km west of Trang town. The sea is poor here for swimming but it's a nice place to walk, although scarcely as scenic as the beaches of Koh Lanta or Krabi.

Trang's **Andaman Islands** number 47 in total and spread out to the south of Koh Lanta. More tourists are visiting the islands, and the beauty, rich birdlife and the clear waters that surround them make upmarket future development highly likely.

Koh Ngai is a 5-sq-km island cloaked in jungle and fringed with glorious beaches. It also enjoys fabulous views of the limestone stacks that pepper the sea around it. A coral reef sweeps down the eastern side, ending in two big rocks, between which rips a strong current – but the coral around

Tip...

The best time to visit Trang's islands is between January and April. The weather is unsuitable for island-hopping from May to December; the seas are rough, the water is cloudy and you may be stranded by a squall or by the boatmen's incompetence. There is a also a tendency to overbook these boats.

these rocks is magnificent. Koh Ngai is the clichéd resort island retreat where you wake up, eat and sleep at the same place. There are only three resorts on this island and no local community.

On the western side of **Koh Muk** is the **Emerald Cave** (Tham Morakot) – known locally as **Tham Nam** – which can only be entered by boat (or fearless swimmers) at low tide, through a narrow opening. After the blackness of the 80-m-long passage it opens into daylight again at an inland beach straight out of Jurassic Park – emerald water ringed with powdery white sand and a backdrop of precipitous cliffs that look as if they are made of black lava frozen over the centuries. The cave was only discovered during a helicopter survey not very long ago and is thought to have been a pirates' lair. Be warned, you can only leave the pool at low tide. The best way to visit is to hire a long-tailed boat privately and go at an early hour although the tide does dictate when it is safe to swim in. You may need your boatman to guide you. The island's west coast has white beaches backed by high cliffs where swallows nest. There are also beaches on the east coast facing the craggy mainland. There are a few places to stay on the island.

Tarutao National Park & the far south

While some say that Tarutao is merely a mispronunciation of the Malay words *ta lo trao*, meaning 'plenty of bay', when first spying this ominous humped island rising out of the sea, it is far easier to believe a second interpretation. That is, that Tarutao comes from the Malay word for old, mysterious and primitive. Resonating with a murky history of pirates, prisoners and ancient curses, it is no wonder the island was picked for the reality television series *Survivor* in 2002. Despite dynamite-fishing in some areas, the island waters still have reasonable coral, and provide some of the best dive sites in Thailand – particularly around the stone arch on Koh Khai. Adang Island has magnificent coral reefs. These are part of Thailand's best-preserved marine park, where turtles, leopard sharks, whales and dolphins can be spotted.

Inland, however, is a different story. Over half of Koh Tarutao is dense dark rainforest with only a single 12-km road cutting through the length of the island and scant paths leading into a potentially lethal jungle filled with poisonous snakes and volatile beasts like the wild boar. Created in 1974, the marine national park comprises 51 islands – the main ones being Tarutao, Adang, Rawi, Lipe, Klang, Dong and Lek. Tarutao Park itself is divided into two main sections– the Tarutao archipelago and the Adang-Rawi archipelago.

In the far south, there is the Muslim town of Satun with its preserved shophouses – there is a pier here with connections to Langkawi island in Malaysia.

Around the region

Koh Tarutao

To reach the mysterious island of **Koh Tarutao** nearly all visitors will pass through the mainland town of **Pak Bara**, see page 257. There's not much to keep you in Pak Bara but it is a good transport hub with connections to Satun and Trang (take a *songthaew* from the pier into the town), plus plenty of minibuses run by tour companies linking to all points in the south.

The mountainous island of Tarutao is the largest of the archipelago's islands, 26 km long and 11 km wide and covering 151 sq km. A mountainous spine runs north–south down the centre of the island, with its highest point reaching 708 m. The interior remains largely forested, cloaked in dense semi-evergreen rainforest. The main beaches are **Ao Moh Lai, Hin Ngam, Ao Phante, Ao Chak and Ao Sone**, mostly on the west of the island which has long sweeps of sand punctuated by headlands and mangrove. Ao Sone, for example, is a 3 km-long stretch of sand fringed with casuarina trees. (Much of the mangrove was cut for charcoal during the early 1960s before the national park was finally gazetted in 1974.) Notorious as the beach where a lone pirate killed a camping tourist in the 1980s, this eerie strip has quite a physical presence, unlike any of the other beaches along the west coast. The water is aggressive and choppy while Tarutao looms out from the water. This haunting beach, while it does have refreshments at one end, is not as busy as the others. Well worth the visit to Tarutao for the feeling that not everything has been tamed. You can also spot the electric kingfisher here.

Tae Bu cliff, just behind the park headquarters on **Ao Phante**, has good sunset views. You climb up an imaginative route which includes a path cut into the hill, rickety wooden plank steps and extraordinary rock formations, all the while hearing the sound of monkeys, mouse deer, hornbills and perhaps wild boar. Finally you reach the top and a lookout point over the beach and surrounding forest, which is not as satisfying as the walk itself. You may also find it taken over by groups of young park staff – especially in the early morning.

Essentials

❶ Getting around On Tarutao a pick-up truck runs a couple of times a day. There are also bikes for rent and you might be able to rent kayaks and a long tail by the pier. On the other islands walking and long-tail are likely to be the only means of transport.

❺ ATM There are no ATMs or banks on the islands though a couple of the bigger resorts on Lipe may offer cash advances on credit cards at extortionate rates.

⊕ Medical services There are small health clinics with basic facilities on each of the islands.

❶ Tourist information The office near the pier on Tarutao is quite informative – the entrance fee to Tarutao is ฿200 for adults. There is also a national park headquarters close to the ferry port at Pak Bara, T074-781285, which books accommodation on Tarutao and Adang (messages are radioed to the islands). At weekends and during public holidays the island is often full. Camping spaces are usually available.; Koh Lipe and Koh Bulon-Leh are the only islands where the private sector has a presence, meaning the resorts are better and activities more varied. The kohlipethailand.com website is an excellent source of local information.

❶ Safety Off-limits all year, at least for the moment, are the southern provinces running along the Malaysian border – Muslim insurgents are active here and we don't recommend travel to this region. Travellers should also be reminded that when such warnings are issued, if you choose to ignore them, insurance companies may withdraw their cover. This situation and warnings are also subject to change and visitors should check the present situation before they make plans to travel. Check with the UK Foreign and Commonwealth Office (fco.gov.uk) and the US State Department (state.gov). It is however possible to pass through should you wish to cross into Malaysia.

Tip...

November to April are the best months to visit; the coolest are November and December. The park is officially closed from the end of May to 15 October, but it is still possible to get there. Koh Bulon-Leh is accessible year round, although most resorts are closed for six months of the year so it is wise to ring ahead.

Boat to Pak Bara.

The prison at **Ao Talo U-Dang**, in the south, was established in 1939 and was once used as a concentration camp for Thailand's political prisoners; the graveyard, charcoal furnaces and a fish fermentation plant are still there. The other main camp, at **Ao Talo Wao** on the east side of the island, was used for high-security criminals. During the Second World War, when communications were slow and difficult, the remoteness of the island meant it was cut off from supplies of food. After 700 out of the 3000 prisoners died, the desperate inmates and some of the guards became pirates to stay alive. The prisons have been partially restored as historical monuments. Today the only people living on the island are the park wardens and other staff.

Coconut plantations still exist on Tarutao but the forests have barely been touched, providing a habitat for flying lizards, wild cats, lemur, wild boar, macaques, mouse deer and feral cows, believed to have bred when the prisoners were taken from the island. Crocodiles once inhabited Khlong Phante and there is a large cave on the **Choraka** (crocodile) water system known as **Crocodile Cave** (bring a torch). The best way to see wildlife on Koh Tarutao is to walk down the 12-km road during the dry season when animals come out in search of water. There are also many species of bird on the islands including colonies of swiftlets found in the limestone caves – mainly on **Koh Lo Tong** (to the south of Tarutao) and **Koh Ta Kieng** (to the northeast). Large tracts of mangrove forest are found here, especially along

Tip...

Bring plenty of cash as there are no banks on the islands, and only the dive centres accept credit cards.

Khlong Phante Malacca, on Tarutao. The islands are also known for their trilobite fossils, 400 to 500 million years old, found not just on Tarutao but all over the national park.

Koh Bulon Leh

Koh Bulon Leh has only developed into a beach resort fairly recently and only in the past 50 years or so has the island had year-round residents of any description: a Muslim population of around 50. The reason for this is down to the superstition of the Moken fisher people who believed the island was cursed and that everyone who lived there met an untimely end. The lifestyle here is laid-back and in the more expensive resorts – boho-chic. Development is still low-key but land speculation has been going on since the 1990s and investors are no doubt hoping that Koh Bulon-Leh will develop, especially as it is relatively near the pier at Pak Bara. While it is part of the same archipelago as Tarutao, the island is outside the boundaries of the

Tip...

While the waters around Tarutao are home to four species of turtle (the Pacific Ridleys, green, hawksbill and leatherback), whales and dolphins are also occasionally seen; the sea is clearer further west in the waters of the Adang-Rawi archipelago.

Pirates and political prisoners

Tarutao boasts the remains of the prison that held around 10,000 criminals and political prisoners, some of whom became pirates during the Second World War to stave off starvation. Island rumour also has it that somewhere on Koh Tarutao a tonne of gold dust looted from a French ship still remains buried along with the murdered pirates that attacked the vessel. Not all of the prisoners on this island were pirates, with some esteemed political prisoners also being incarcerated here. It is now believed that the political prisoners received the best of the treatment on Koh Tarutao, where the general criminals may even have served them. Certainly the two groups did not mix, with the criminals held in the eastern part at the present-day Taloh Woa Cove and the political prisoners detained at Udang Cove in the southern tip. But all suffered during the Second World War when the island was completely cut off – along with essential food supplies. In cahoots with the guards, prisoners took to ambushing passing ships, originally for food and then for anything of value. This only came to an end in 1947 when the British, who had retaken Malaya, sent in the Royal Navy to quell the pirates. Afterwards, the island was left in total isolation with the prison gradually reduced to the remains of the prison director's house on top of a dune along with a sawmill below and a mysterious hole indicating a torture cellar. Legend has it that, centuries ago, a princess of Langkawi who had been accused of misdeeds declared that the island would never be discovered.

national park. Furthermore, it has two caves of interest: **Bat Cave**, which houses a colony of fruit bats, and **Nose Cave**, where it's possible to dive in from one side, swim under the rocks and among thousands of fish (but beware the moray eel) and come up on the other side.

Koh Adang & Koh Rawi

Adang and Rawi lie 43 km west of Tarutao and are the main islands in the archipelago of the same name. They offer a stark contrast to Tarutao. While Tarutao is composed of limestone and sandstone, the rugged hills of Adang and Rawi are granite. Adang's highest mountain rises to 703 m while Rawi's is 463 m in height. Koh Adang is almost entirely forested and there is a trail that leads up to the summit, Chado Cliff, for good views over Koh Lipe and the Andaman Sea. There are also trails through the vegetation; to spot the inhabitants – including squirrels, mouse deer and wild pigs – it is best to wait half an hour or so in silence. The main beaches on Adang are **Khai, Laem Son, Ao Lo Lae Lae** and **Lo Lipa, and Sai Khao** on Rawi.

Koh Lipe

Koh Lipe is a beautiful island that attracts many returnees, mainly because of the laid-back and gentle populace, excellent snorkelling in some of the clearest waters in the Andaman Sea, blindingly white sand beaches and terrific seafood. The island is also extremely popular with young families. While much of the accommodation is poorly thought out, the island is still a delightful getaway with an unspoilt charm and snorkelling that is highly rewarding. Among the marine life that can be spotted in coral reefs only 60 m out are trumpet fish, sergeant majors, blue-spotted ribbontail rays, angel fish and anemones. The combination of a tiny island and rampant tourist bungalow expansion creates a dilemma as the accommodation along both sides hems in the resident Chao Le and intrudes on their privacy. Some resorts even back directly on to villages with the unfortunate effect that tourists in bikinis can too easily stroll into a communal shower occupied by the modest Chao Le, as few of their homes have running water and bathrooms. It is also true that while certain resorts have a surface aura of cleanliness and order, this is quickly dispelled by the smell of burning plastic as rubbish disposal here is largely accomplished on a chaotic and sporadic basis.

Koh Lipe.

The Chao Le areas are clearly at shanty town level which makes one wonder what benefits they are receiving from unchecked tourism. Indeed, it was only in 1940 that Koh Lipe officially became Thai territory – up to then it was unclear whether the Chao Le here were Malay or Thai. Locals maintain that the Thai authorities encouraged them to plant coconut trees to show that they had settled, presumably on the basis that occupation is as good as ownership.

Satun & the far south

Back on the main land and approached through towering karst peaks and bordered by limestone hills, Satun is a pleasant town with friendly, mostly Muslim inhabitants. Surrounded by mountains, it is cut off from the Malaysian Peninsula and the eastern side of the Kra Isthmus and while few towns in Thailand have escaped thoughtless redevelopment, Satun, though, has done better than most. It has an attractive, low-key centre with preserved shophouses and is Malay in feel; 85% of the population are thought to be Muslim. Few tourists include Satun on their itinerary. Instead, they make a beeline for Pak Bara, 60 km or so north of town and catch a boat to the Tarutao islands (see page 257). But perhaps Satun deserves a few more visitors.

The province seems to have spent the last century searching for an identity separate from that of its neighbours. In the early years of the last century it was administered as part of Kedah, in Malaysia. In 1909, following a treaty between Thailand and Britain, it came under the authority of Phuket. Fifteen years later it found itself being administered from Nakhon Si Thammarat, and it was not until 1932 that it managed to carve out an independent niche for itself when it was awarded provincial status by Bangkok.

The town's main mosque, the **Mesjid Bombang**, was built in 1979 after the previous mosque – also in the shape of a pyramid – fell prey to rot and was torn down. The mosque is on Satunthani Road. More interesting perhaps are the preserved **Chinese shophouses on Buriwanit Road**. They are thought to be around 150 years old. Ku Den's Mansion, on Satunthani Road, dates from the 1870s. It was originally the governor's residence. The windows and doors share a Roman motif while the two-storey roof is in Thai Panyi style.

Malaysia & Langkawi

Many visitors to the Southern Andaman Coast also carry on heading downwards into Malaysia – with the beautiful island of Langkawi being the most accessible port of call. In fact, a visit to the island could be considered the last stop in a giant island hopping route that starts with Phuket.

The Langkawi group is an archipelago of 99 islands around 30 km off the west coast of Peninsular Malaysia. Pulau Langkawi itself, by far the largest of the group, is a mountainous, palm-fringed island with scattered fishing kampongs, paddy fields and sandy coves. It has seen significant development in recent years and is home to some of Malaysia's most upmarket resorts. Other islands are nothing more than deserted limestone outcrops rearing

out of the turquoise sea, cloaked in jungle, and ringed by coral. The main settlement of locals is in the dusty town of Kuah. There are plenty of top-end resorts, while Pantai Cenang and Tengah also have a smattering of cheaper guesthouses.

The main town, Kuah, is strung out along the seafront and is the landing point for ferries from Satun (Thailand), Kuala Perlis, Kuala Kedah and Penang. The jetty is 2 km from Kuah itself. The town is growing fast and developers have reclaimed land along the shoreline to cope with the expansion. The old part of Kuah has several restaurants, a few grotty hotels, banks, plenty of coffee shops and a string of duty-free shops, which do a roaring trade in cheap liquor, cigarettes and electronics. There is also an attractive mosque.

Most of the new beach chalet development is along the 3-km stretch of coast from Pantai Cenang to Pantai Tengah, at the far southern end around a small promontory. Pantai Tengah is less developed and quieter than Pantai Cenang. The sea at Pantai Cenang and Pantai Tengah will come as a disappointment to those who have experienced the Thai islands to the north or the beaches on Malaysia's east coast. Unfortunately, plastic and rubbish from tour boats and larger vessels has dirtied the sea, which can be a little murky anyway. It is best to swim at high tide, and give the sea a miss at low tide. Zackry's guesthouse has a weekly tide chart posted at their reception. The road west leads past the airport to Pantai Kok, on the magnificent Burau Bay. Once unspoilt, it is now spotted with upmarket resorts and a fancy marina. There are several isolated beaches along the bay, accessible by boat from either Pantai Kok itself, Pantai Cenang (12 km away) or Kampong Kuala Teriang, a fishing village en route. On the west headland, the Telaga Tujuh waterfalls are not as impressive as they used to be thanks to a pipeline running next to them to Berjaya Langkawi Beach Resort.

Listings

Sleeping
Berjaya Langkawi Beach Resort $$$$
*Burau Bay, T04-959 1888,
berjaya resorts.com.my.*
Malaysian-style chalets in rainforest, some on stilts over water, some on jungled hillside. Excellent facilities, white sand beach, restaurant.

Zackry $
Right at the south end of Pantai Tengah.
Rooms are a jumbled assortment of a/c and fan, some with attached bathroom. Runs on a trust system, with payment for beers and internet done by guests at the end of their stay. Great communal bar area, and a communal kitchen where travellers cook up a storm each evening. It's across the road from the beach.

Eating
Langkawi's speciality is *mee gulong* – fried noodles cooked with shredded prawns, slices of beef, chicken, carrots, cauliflower rolled into a pancake and served with a potato gravy.

Oriental Pearl $$$
Berjaya Langkawi Beach Resort, Burau Bay.
Upmarket but simple Chinese, ocean views, good steamboat.

Nam $$
inside the Bon Ton Resort just north of Pantai Cenang.
Beautiful restaurant overlooking a lake serving funky fusion food. Try the rock lobster and baked snapper on mango rice.

Getting there

During high season (November to May) boats run direct from Koh Lipe to Langkawi – see kohlipethailand.com for more details. Boats also run from Tammalang pier south of Satun to Langkawi three times a day.

Listings
Sleeping

Krabi River Hotel $$
73/1 Khongkha Rd,
T075-612321.
Fairly new, 5-storey white-fronted hotel with splendid view of the river, the mangroves and the hustle and bustle of the boats. Rooms are bright and simply decorated if uninspiring. Concrete and tiles throughout. Spotless with all the facilities you need, and the restaurant is ideal for breakfast. There is also a rooftop terrace. Good value, especially if you can get a room with a small veranda overlooking the river. Suitable for families.

Bai Fern Guesthouse $$-$
24/2 Chao Fah Rd, T075-630339,
baifern-mansion.com.
Clean rooms in this well-run guesthouse Some attempt has been made to personalize the entrance with an aquarium by the stairs but overall the establishment craves a more intimate touch. However, it is safe, secure and clean with trustworthy family staff who try to help and, if you choose your room carefully, it is decent value. Excellent advice on tours and travel.

Thara Guesthouse $$-$
79/3 Kongkha Rd, T075-630499.
Next to the Krabi City Sea View Hotel. The rooms are bright and airy, they have fridges and TVs with some overlooking the river.

The staff are considerate and everything is well maintained. Good for this price range.

Ban Chaofa $
20/1 Chao Fah Rd, T075-630359.
Mix of a/c and fan, 2-storey hotel edging to 2-star. Japanese/Ikea feel – clean, chic and minimalist. Rooms overlooking street have small balconies. The owner speaks fairly good English and has put care into his venture. Internet and laundry. Restaurant on ground floor.

Blue Juice $
1/1 Chaofa Rd, T075-630679.
Just before the pier, where the boats leave for Raleh, this concrete building houses several different fan rooms. The cheaper ones have a shared clean bathroom. The teak floors and whitewashed walls makes this place bright and airy. There's a PADI dive shop and restaurant on the ground floor.

Europa Café and Guesthouse $
1/9 Soi Ruamjit Rd, T075-620407,
cafe europa-krabi.com.
Under Thai and Danish management, the Europa Café has 5 rooms above the restaurant. All rooms are nicely decorated and clean but the smallest lack windows. Shared spotless bathroom with hot water. The restaurant is cosy and inviting, rather like a Danish café, and serves good quality

northern European food (imported meats and cheeses). The owners are entertaining sources of information – all speak excellent English, German and Danish. The guesthouse closes at 2300 and security is excellent.

K Guest House $
15-25 Chao Fah Rd, T075-623166.
Mainly fan rooms with mosquito nets. 2-storey building with a long wooden veranda balcony along the first floor. Views over town. Potted foliage along the front intensifies the feeling of being in a hideaway. Wooden floor and ambient lighting. Get a room in the wooden part and not the airless ones with shared bathroom at the back. Restaurant, laundry service and internet. Good bargain.

Khong Kha Guest House $
Khongkha Rd.
Small guesthouse with great views over the mangroves, looking across to Koh Klang. To reach it, walk along the promenade past the pier to Phi Phi and away from the town. A converted house, all rooms have windows. Clean and simply furnished, most rooms are spacious with views over the water. One of the better locations in Krabi. Easy access to the night market and tour agency. Friendly, helpful owner. The only downside is the noise of long-tailed boats during peak season.

Star Guest House $
Khongkha Rd, T075-630234.
A charming wooden guesthouse over the top of a small convenience store and tour office, the 7 rooms are tiny, leaving little space for more than a bed, but there is a pleasant balcony with tables and chairs overlooking the night market and the river. Separate bathrooms are downstairs near a small bar in a garden at the back.

Ao Nang

High-season (Nov-May) room rates may be as much as double (or more) the low-season (Jun-Oct) rates. Most of the places here are populated with package tourists.

Golden Beach Resort $$$$
254 Moo 2, T075-637870-4, goldenbeach-resort. com/beach.
This has one of the best locations on the beach with good views across to the islands. Rooms are in cute green-roofed- white-bungalow style and low-rise hotel blocks. Pool and well-tended gardens. The Thai restaurant (Thai Thai) is probably the best in Ao Nang.

Pavilion Queen's Bay $$$$
56 Moo 3, T075-637612, pavilionhotels.com/queensbay.
This huge hotel of more than 100 rooms is luxurious and has very friendly staff, but is hampered with some silly design flaws, and lack of attention to detail. International, Thai and Japanese restaurants (the last highly exclusive with top-class sushi on offer), very large spacious rooms but somewhat cramped bathrooms. Luxurious spa – one of the best features of the hotel and open to non-residents too. All the other facilities expected from a hotel like this, including a 3-layered swimming pool. Good views. Big discounts online.

Royal Nakara $$$$-$$$
155/4-7 Moo 3, T075- 661441, royalnakara.com.
Built on the edge of a steep drop, the rooms are reached by descending several flights of stairs. All rooms are very light and spacious, with modern furniture, TV and DVD player. Premium rooms have pantry kitchen and dining area. Infinity pool. Interesting design. Very accommodating staff.

Ao Nang Beach Home $$$
132 Moo 2, T075-695260, aonangbeachhome.com.
Offers large, well appointed a/c rooms, with spacious bathrooms and nice touches such as beach mats in the rooms. Laminate teak furniture, modern and comfortable. Restaurant overlooking the beach. Recommended for price (includes breakfast) and location.

Blue Village $$$
105 Moo 3, T075-637887, bluevillagekrabi.com.
Ignore the goofy name, this is a fantastic layout with huts and palm trees growing through the roofs – beds on floor futon-style, sunken bathrooms. Run by a Canadian (Richard) a former diving instructor who has lived in Thailand for 19 years. Good cheap food. Impossible not to relax here.

Harvest House $$
420/18-19 Moo 2, T075-695256, harvest-house@hotmail.com.
Spanking new rooms, comfortably furnished with balcony, a/c, cable TV, bath tub. It is quite a walk to the beach from here but these rooms are very good value.

Hill Side Village $$
168/10 Moo 2, T075-637604, krabidir.com/hillsidevillage. Opposite the Lai Thai Resort.
Converted concrete row of a/c rooms. 19 rooms come in sets of 2 (double at back, twin at front) and would make good family rooms. Rooms to the back are smaller and cheaper, with shower only and no hot water. Rooms at the front are twin beds with a bath and hot water. All rooms come with TV (satellite) and a fridge. Friendly staff provide information on tours, and will take guests to and from the beach.

Leela Valley $$-$

262/1 Ao Nang, T075-635673, krabidir.com/leelavalley.
Some simple bamboo bungalows on the ground that need repairs, and some smarter fan and a/c houses on stilts with balconies, set in spacious grounds rather lacking in shade. Good views of the mountains. Rooms are clean. Discounts for long stays. Quite a distance from the sea, but excellent value.

Nopparat Thara
Emerald Bungalow $$$

Catch a boat from Nopparat Thara pier across the estuary, westwards, T08-1892 1072 (mob).
This place is very peaceful with around 40 large, fan bungalows and some a/c rooms. Restaurant. Location is the high point; it is south facing so you get a good sunset and there is also a river to swim in at the end of the beach. Can arrange transfers for you. Friendly staff.

Jinnie's Place $$$

101 Moo 3, T075-621042, aonangks@hotmail.com.
The red brick a/c bungalows have bags of character and charm. The bathrooms are possibly the largest around Krabi and have bathtubs and even a garden. There's a children's pool and a main pool.

Na-Thai Resort $$$-$

Near Nopparat Thara and Phi Phi Island National Park Head-quarters and the Montessori School, T075-637752.
It's 5-10 minutes by motorbike or car from Hat Phra Ao Nang and Hat Nopparat Thara. Free pick up. Surrounded by oil palms and rubber trees, this is a husband and wife set-up – Gerard and Walee who have more of an eco-friendly approach to running things. There are 5 evenly-spaced bungalows set around a small pool that you can swim in at night and a restaurant where they can trot out Western favourites or excellent Thai food. Not the most imaginative bungalows but great attitude and good for a more isolated getaway. Prices depend on the month.

Rai Leh

Rai Leh West is a beautiful beach but huts have been built too closely together, making for overcrowded conditions and basic (but not cheap) accommodation.

Rayavadee $$$$

T075-620740, rayavadee.com.
There are 98 2-storey pavilions and 5 villas set amid luscious grounds studded with coconut palms in this luxurious, isolated getaway. Every service imaginable is provided in the beautifully furnished pavilions, including lovely, exclusive bathrooms and bedtime chocolates. Some rooms have private pools. The strikingly large main pool faces Rai Leh beach. Restaurants include the Krua Phranang, on the renowned Phra Nang beach. Indulge in the magnificent spa and the Rayavadee signature massage, including a hot herb compress. Excursions are offered. Due to its location, bordering 3 beaches and caves, it feels more like an adventure than just a hotel. Price includes airport transfer.

Railei Beach Club $$$$-$$$

Phra Nang, T08-1464 4338 (mob), raileibeachclub.com.
On its own section of beach (opposite end to the Rayavadee), is one of the most stylish places to stay at Rai Leh. Traditional Thai-style houses have been sold as holiday homes. Their owners let them whenever they are not in residence. Fully equipped with kitchens and bathrooms but no a/c. Electricity goes off after 2400. Prices depend on size. Houses for 2 to 10 guests are available. Maid service can be provided as there is no restaurant.

Rai Leh Viewpoint Resort and Spa $$$-$$

Rai Leh East, T075-621686-7, viewpointresort 66.com.
Large upgraded resort. Friendly, well run, clean and well-

maintained rooms. Good restaurant, minimart, internet and pool. The least accessible of all the places at the far end of Rai Leh East, but some of the best bungalows, especially given the rates. Cheaper ones are far from the water.

Koh Phi Phi

Zeavola $$$$
Laem Tong, T075-627000, zeavola.com.
Set on the beachfront, close to the swimming pool or on the hillside among gardens of the flowering plant after which the resort is named (*Scaevola taccada*). Some of the beautifully furnished wooden suites have outside showers and bathrooms with coloured ceramic sinks. Outside living areas with chairs and minibars are also a feature, although the mosquitoes can be horrific. The food is decidedly average though you can dine on the beach by candlelight or under the fabulous striped awning at the Tacada restaurant or enjoy Italian cuisine at Baxil, the covered restaurant. Excellent spa. There's a PADI dive centre and excursions are arranged. Staff are friendly, helpful and courteous. Transfers from Phuket ฿1750 and Krabi ฿1700 per person.

Viking Resort $$$$-$$
T075-819398, ppvikingresort.com.
All of these huts have been individually designed with Balinese influences. Most sit on the cliffside with seaviews, all have bags of character, with homely, warm touches such as floor rugs, paintings, lamps and 2 person hammocks. The cheapest share a bathroom and are possibly overpriced, the rest, for Phi Phi, are good value especially considering the attention given to creating a unique atmosphere. Quiet and secluded sandy beach.

Koh Jum

All of the accommodation on Koh Jum is listed on kohjumonline.com. Accommodation is mostly simple bamboo bungalows or other basic A-frame bungalows.

Joy Bungalows $$$-$
T075-618199.
Best known and most established resort; still the most imaginative in terms of variety. There are more than 30 wooden family chalets with balconies on the beachfront, bamboo huts on stilts at the back, wooden bungalows throughout, and treehouses – some of these set-ups even come with attached bathrooms (hot and cold water) and mosquito nets. Tour counter and an average restaurant. The bungalows at the

back are not particularly well-kept and are too close together but the de luxe wooden chalet ones at the front are usually taken by families. Also has hammocks slung along the beachfront which become more essential as the days wear on.

Woodland Lodge $$-$
Next to Bodaeng Beach Resort, T08-1893 5330 (mob), rayandsao@hotmail.com.
Run by Englishman Ray and his Thai wife Sao, reliable concrete bungalow set-up. Some of the bungalows, which are nicely spaced from each other, can be too hot as they lack the necessary electricity for day-time fans. But they are kept clean and staff are helpful. What makes this place stand out is a marooned Gilligan's Island feel as it acts as a meeting spot for expats on the island. The food is generally buffet but if you want anything special, Ray can fetch it at the markets in Krabi. Do be firm about how you want it cooked.

Koh Lanta

Most bungalow operations are scattered down the west coast of Koh Lanta Yai and usually offer free pick-ups from the pier at Sala Dan. There is considerable variation between high season (Nov-May) and low season (Jun-Oct) rates.

Ao Khlong Dao

Costa Lanta $$$$
Moo 3, T02-6623550, costalanta.com.
Tranquillity and privacy are the order of the day at this exclusive resort. Whilst modernism may not be to everybody's taste, this resort has succeeded in creating a very different ambience, somewhere between modern urban living and beach hideaway. Standard rooms have huge, floor to ceiling teak doors that concertina back to completely open 2 sides to the elements, flooding the rooms with natural light. As you would expect there is a swimming pool and restaurant.

Lanta Sand Resort and Spa $$$$
Ao Khlong Dao edging to Ao Phra-Ae, T075-684633, lantasand.com.
Excellent reports from this luxury resort next to Sayang Resort. Spacious rooms plus amazing bathroom with glass wall so that the monkeys can peer in while you are taking a bath. The tubs are also a good size. Good service, fine food. Prices double during high season.

Golden Bay $$$$-$$$
22 Moo 3, T075-684161, goldenbaylanta.com.
There are 3 styles of room, all with TV, fridge, a/c and hot water. Hotel room ambience. Friendly, helpful owners and an easy place to get to. Awesome restaurant serving some of the best Thai and Isaan food on the beach.

Lanta Sea House $$$$-$$$
15 Moo 3, Sala Dan, T075-684073-4, lantaseahouse resort.com.
Bungalows near beach, and pool. Consistently well-kept establishment. 2 grades of room, both are clean and well supplied, the more expensive have spacious balconies and their own bathroom. Very good value in the low season.

Sayang Beach $$$-$$
Situated just south of the Lanta Villa between Khlong Dao and Ao Phra-Ae, T08-1476 6357 (mob), sayangbeachlanta.com.
This operation is run by a local family that took care to protect the environment while constructing their bungalows (unlike many), leaving trees to provide necessary shade and ambience. Excellent food cooked by one of the daughters, with fresh fish nightly. The bungalows are large; the ones towards the beachfront are better quality, while the others at the back are rather too close together.

Ao Phra-Ae

Chaw Ka Cher Lanta Tropicana Resort $$$$-$$$
352 Moo 2, T08-1895 9718 (mob), lantatropicanaresort.com.
Set on a hill just off the main road at the far southern end of Ao Phra-Ae, this is a very friendly and beautifully set out resort. The gorgeous bungalows have open-air bathrooms and are much bigger than anything in a similar price range on the beach. Pool, excellent restaurant, free internet, huge library. 500 m from the beach; owners supply bicycles to get you there.

Relax Bay $$$$-$$$
111 Moo 2, T075-684194, relaxbay.com.
48 large bungalows, some basic, some VIP, raised high off the ground and scattered through a beachside grove, unusual angles to the roofs and comfortable verandas. Very quiet, all rooms have glass and/or mosquito panels in the windows, fans and shower rooms in the open air adjoining. Spartan decor – airy. 2 beach bars and café, French owned and managed. Excellent service and layout.

Mook Lanta $$$$-$
343 Moo 2, T075-684638, mooklanta.com.
Both the bungalows and rooms have been built with considerable attention to detail. All rooms, even fan, come with hot water and Wi-Fi access. Beautifully designed with nice finishes such as silk throws, mood lighting and curtains. The management go out of their way to be helpful. Also offers massage and spa services.

Blue Sky Resort & Restaurant $$-$

238 Moo 3, T075-684871, krabidir.com/ blueskylanta.
Bamboo huts, very clean and surprisingly spacious. Good mix of nationalities stay here. Check for discounts if you are staying for a while. Super friendly staff.

Last Horizon Resort $$-$

175 Moo 2, Baan Phu Klom Beach, lantalanta.com/last_ horizon_resort/index.html. last_horizon@ hotmail.com.
25 stone bungalows in a coconut grove with attached showers, 24-hour electricity, restaurant and beach bar. Friendly management, motor-bikes for hire, tours arranged. The beach here is only suitable for swimming at high tide.

Hat Khlong Khoang
Nice and Easy $$$

315 Moo 2, T075-667105.
It's easy to spot this resort as the owner's art deco house-cum-spaceship, fronts on to the beach. The a/c bungalows resemble Swiss chalets inside, very quaint with frilly curtains. There is a pool and the staff are friendly.

Where Else Resort $$$-$

Next to Bee Bee, T075-667173.
This place has bags of character and a lot of thought has gone into the design of the bamboo bungalows. These rustic huts are half hidden in the jungle garden, just back from the beach. All have bathrooms, mosquito screens and hammocks on the balcony. The ones at the back are a little cramped together.

Fisherman's Cottage $$

190 Moo 2, Klong Khong Beach, T08-1476 1529 (mob), krabidir.com/fishermanscottage.
Collection of 11 moody, atmospheric bungalows, all with sea views, on a steep bend of the main island road before the turn-off to the national park. Decorated with style, most of the many owners and staff appear to be artists. Trendy, though there is a family cottage, and the staff are very family friendly – so is the beach area which is gently shelving and a safe place to swim. Good music at the bar.

Ao Khlong Nin
Sri Lanta $$$$

Moo 6, T075-662688, srilanta. com.
Spacious, well-designed bamboo and wood bungalows with a/c (but no mosquito screening or ceiling fans) and hot showers. The bathrooms are semi-outdoors. Beautiful pool right on the beach. Fan-cooled restaurant in similar style and a spa in garden area adjacent to the pool and other facilities. Beautiful spot on the bay with rocks adding character to the area, but still with access to a sandy beach for swimming.

Narima Bungalow Resort $$$$-$$$

98 Moo 5, Klong Nin, T075-662668, narima-lanta.com.
Large bungalows with wooden floors overlooking a quiet part of beach. Wall of sliding glass doors. Doctors own this place. The restaurant here also serves a greater variety of Thai dishes than most places. Pool, exercise bicycle, DVDs, CDs and a mini-library. Good reductions if you stay for 7 or 14 nights.

Atcha Hut $

70 Moo 6, T094-704607, atchahut.com.
This area has a bohemian arty feel to it. The concrete bungalows have been finished to resemble an adobe finish and for this price, right on the beach, they are a steal. The owner has tried to create an artistic vibe rather than just a business, although the party atmosphere might be a too much for those seeking tranquillity and solitude. Beachfront bar and yoga classes. There are more good value bungalows further down.

Ao Kantiang
Pimalai Resort $$$$

99 Moo 5, Ba Kan Tiang Beach, T075-607999, pimalai.com.
Yet another resort to make big claims about the pristine nature of its setting with the implication that staying here will not be causing damage to the environment or local culture.

Listings

Huge resort, beautifully designed rooms, although parts of the garden look very sparse and there's an awful lot of concrete used in creating terraces, steps and roads. The resort also encroaches on to the beach – something which undoes its avowed eco-aims in one fell swoop. All facilities are on offer as one would expect for a resort of this type.

Lanta Marine Park Resort $$$
58 Moo 5, krabidir.com/ lantampv/index.htm.
Set up high on the hill overlooking Ao Kantiang with great views of the bay from the bungalows in the front. Several styles of bungalows: the small bamboo ones set back from the view are the cheapest; the larger concrete ones with views from the balconies are the most expensive. Rooms are spacious and comfortable. The walk up to the bungalows will keep you fit. Free pick-up from Sala Dan.

Ao Khlong Jaak
Andalanta Resort $$$$-$$$
T075-612084, discoverythailand.net/ kohlanta/waterfall_bay.html.
Well-run resort set amid trees and by the beach. Variety of wood bungalows, good facilities. Boat trips are organized to nearby islands and other places of interest.

Ban Koh Lanta Yai
Mango House $$$
Middle of the main street, T075-697181, kolanta.net/south ern lantaresort.htm.
Very nicely restored old wooden house overlooking the sea. Rooms are nicely decorated and some have views over to Bubu island. No a/c and shared facilities throughout. Was once, allegedly, a government-run opium den. The owners also have a number of villas and houses for rent ($$$-$). Certainly one of the most original places to stay on the island.

Trang & around

Trang town
Wattana Park $$$-$$
315/7 Huay Yod Rd, T075-216216.
A little way out from the town centre on the road in from Krabi. A modern hotel with good rooms – probably the best value business-class hotel in Trang. Does not have a pool.

My Friend $
25/17 Sathani Rd, T075-255447, myfriend-trang.com.
All rooms in this guesthouse are en suite with TV and a/c. Convenient location near the station – they'll let you check in early, if they have availability; good news for those arriving on the sleeper train from Bangkok. Internet, lots of local information, staff are helpful but don't speak much English. Free hot drinks.

Only For You $
Patalung Soi 1, T08-13974574 (mob).
Breezy, cool house, 5 mins' walk from the centre of town, with 2 bedrooms, bathroom and a kitchen. Ideal for those wanting to stay in Trang for at least a week (minimum). Rate includes utilities. Very good value.

Beaches & islands near Trang
Amari Trang Beach Resort $$$$
199 Moo 5, Had Pakmeng, Changlang Beach, T075-205888, amari.com.
Newly opened spa and 138 seafront rooms in a contemporary, minimalist low-rise. The Amari also has a speedboat shuttle to the exclusive private day resort of Koh Kradan which you may need as the beach here is poor and not particularly clean. For entertainment in this isolated spot the Amari offers 5 restaurants and a pool.

Pakmeng Resort $$
Pakmeng, T075-274112, pakmengresort.com.
Turn left after reaching the main seafront and continue on towards the national park. The resort is on the left and is well marked. Wooden bungalows with attached bathroom and fan and some a/c. The resort backs on to the main *khlong* leading to

Trang makes a good alternative to Krabi if you want to explore the south; most places to stay are situated between the clock tower and the railway station.

the river. Good restaurant. Motorbikes (฿350 per day) and bicycles (฿100 per day) for rent.

Barn Chom Talay – Seaview Guest House $$-$
Hat Yao.
Dormitory room and bungalows all clean and well-furnished. The daughter of the owners speaks excellent English. Also offers every type of tour, including kayak rental, trips to the nearby caves and boat tours to the islands. A pleasant out-of-the-way place to stay.

Koh Ngai
Koh Ngai Fantasy Resort and Spa $$$$-$$$
Next door to Koh Ngai Villa, T075-206923, kohhai.com.
A/c bungalows and family suites. Obscured in the foliage of this island. Pool. Stately rooms. Has been upgraded since its early days and now has decent food.

Koh Muk
The majority of the accommodation here shuts 6 months of the year.

Rubber Tree Bungalows $$$-$
T075-215972, mookrubbertree.com.
Across from Mayow, up a long wooden staircase cut into the hill are these marvellous family-run bungalows. Attached toilet and bathroom. These are set in a working rubber tree plantation so that you may be woken early in the morning by the lanterns of the rubber tree tappers. You are welcome to observe them at work. The attached restaurant has easily the best food on the island – cooked by a northern Thai native. Let her choose what to cook if you can't decide.

Sawadee Bungalows $$
Next to Charlie's, T075-207 9645, sawadeeresort64@ yahoo.com.
Basic wooden bungalows on stilts set into hill. Own bathroom. Romantic spot as it is at the end of the beach where it is rather rocky and private. Attached restaurant serves bland portions of Thai food but is OK for morning coffee and fruit salad. Electricity only 4 hrs a day.

Mookies $
Down the lane/dirt path towards the sea gypsy village (there is only one path on from Rubber Tree), T08-727 56533 (mob), mookiebrian@yahoo.com. Open all year.
Cross over a wooden bridge and follow the disco music to Mookie's Bar, where you are likely to find Aussie Mookie reading pulp fiction and drinking in the mid-afternoon. This is a completely eccentric set-up. Rooms are large with spring mattresses and 24-hr electricity with light and fan inside. While the toilet and shower is shared, they are kept clean to military standards. The shower outside also has hot water. See also Eating, page 251.

Pak Bara
Best House Resort $
T074-783058/783568.
Close to the pier, 10 a/c and clean bungalows with comfortable beds, friendly owners and a good restaurant.

Listings

Koh Tarutao

Book through the National Park office in Bangkok, T02-579052, or the Pak Bara office located next to the pier, T074-783485. Accommodation is in the north and west of Tarutao. There are 3 choices: multi-occupancy bungalows that can accommodate families or groups, longhouses and tents. The 3 main beaches – Ao Pante, Ao Molae and Ao Sone offer some or all of these types, with Ao Pante, the one closest to the pier and where the park warden offices are, offering the most selection. The rooms may also have shared outside toilets. The bungalows are sparsely furnished wooden structures, set along the side of the road against the cliffs. Tents are on the beach with a public shower and toilet. Check your tent for size and condition. If you intend to stay for more than 2 nights it's best to buy a tent from the mainland; it will pay for itself and be clean and in good condition. The treatment given to tent visitors varies. Hired tent cost ฿100-200; own tent ฿60. Best spots for camping are on Ao Jak and Ao Sone. You can also camp on the beach close to the national park bungalows (฿30 per night per person, as in other Thai national parks). At all beaches the rates are the same – a small, 2-person bungalow costs ฿600 and the larger 4-person, ฿1000. There are big dormitory-type buildings too that are hired out to large Thai families or students.

Koh Bulon Leh
Pansand Resort $$
T08-1397 0802 (mob), or First Andaman Travel (Trang), T075- 218035.
Well-maintained and welcoming bungalows with attached bathrooms and dormitories. The views are good, and the garden pleasant. Watersports, camping, snorkelling and boat trips. Has an evening internet service. Set in from main beach but this is a plus as it makes it feel more exclusive. Closed July-September.

Chaolae Food and Bungalows $$
Run by a Chao Le family. 8 raised brick and bamboo bungalows set up hill further on from Bulon Viewpoint Resort. It has sunken bathrooms with squat toilet and shower but no fans. Restaurant with shell mobiles and lined with cacti and brightly hued flowers in pots. You can choose your fish from the daily catch for beautiful cooking with herbs and spices. Excellent reports from guests.

Bulon Le Resort $
T08-1897 9084 (mob).
Well positioned where the boats dock overlooking a beautiful beach. A wide range of bungalows from pleasant, spacious, almost colonial options to the more basic, single rooms with spotless shared bathrooms. All in good shape and run by friendly and helpful management. Electricity 1800-0200. Good restaurant and the island's best breakfast.

Panka Bay Resort $
T074-711982/783097.
Up the hill and down on the Panka Bay side of the island, this is the only resort here. There are 21 bungalows at this Muslim Malay/Thai family-run establishment. They are arranged along the beach and in tiers up a hill with handmade steps. The beach is not great as it has a rocky shore, but you can walk to the other beach in 20 mins and see some bird and lizard life on the way. They offer a free pick-up from the Bulon-Leh Resort. Another perk is electricity until 0500. Huge restaurant with superb food.

Koh Adang & Koh Rawi
Accommodation is all on the southern swathe of Adang island, with longhouses offering $$$-$$ rates, where some rooms can accommodate up to 10 people.
Tents are available on Adang: big ฿200, small ฿100, own tent ฿60 at Laem Son. There is a simple restaurant. The island closes down during the rainy season. The bungalows here differ in terms of the perks offered (eg hot showers).

Laem Son, ฿400. 4 people per bungalow.
Big tents (8-10 people), ฿300,
Medium/ middle tents
(3-5 people), ฿300
Small tents (2 people), ฿150
Rawi Long House, ฿400. 4 people per room. Toilet outside.

Koh Lipe

Prices on Lipe can vary dramatically according to which point of the season you arrive. Also new accommodation is opening – and sometimes closing – all the time. Our pick here are the most reliable and long-term businesses.

Varin Resort $$$-$
Pattaya Beach, T074-728 080/ T081-598 2225.
The most upmarket spot on the beach, these 109 exceptionally clean bungalows, suites and villas are set in an attractive, if fairly cramped and regimental layout facing each other. Still, it offers the highest standard of accommodation on Lipe. The operation is run by a Muslim Thai/Malay family. The restaurant is a little characterless but service is excellent and attentive.

Andaman Resort $$-$
Sunlight Beach, T074-728017.
A mix of 40 concrete, log and bamboo bungalows spaced along a quiet beach. The best rooms are the white-and-blue concrete row on the beach near the restaurant, although they lack some of the other huts' character. Clean, quiet, bright rooms popular with families.

Mountain Resort $$-$
Bay to west of Sunlight Beach, T074-728131, mt- resort.com.
One of Lipe's best resorts with spacious grounds and corrugated-roofed bamboo bungalows. The rooms have electricity, verandas and basic bathrooms. The restaurant is set on a shaded cliff high above idyllic views over the sandbanks with great sea breeze. Steep steps down the cliff lead to a shallow beach and the Karma beach bar. Fan and a/c rooms.

Pooh's $
Sunlight Beach, T074-722220.
Has 6 clean fan bungalows set in Pooh's excellent, family-run complex of bar, internet, restaurant, travel agency and dive shop. Nice enough bungalows but they are not on the beach. Breakfast and 10 mins on the internet are included. Convenient for morning coffee and everything else at this 1-stop operation run by the affable Mr Pooh ('crab' in English). Guests get a discount at the dive shop.

Porn Bungalows $
Sunset Beach, T08- 9464 5765 (mob).
A Chao Le run operation headed by Mr Gradtai (Rabbit). Fairly self-contained resort with simple woven bamboo huts on a beautiful beach; incredibly popular with return visitors – especially families with small children. The staff can take time to warm to newcomers but it's worth the work. The restaurant is a bit overpriced but the menu of the nearby Flour Power bakery is an excellent alternative.

Satun

Sinkiat Thani $
50 Buri Wanit Rd, T074-721055.
A hotel with a modicum of style. 108 large, well-kept rooms. Great views from the upper floors; guesthouse annex across the road with cheaper but spotless fan rooms. Satun's best hotel with low-season discounts. Claims to have the first disco in Satun.

Eating

Krabi Town

Chao Sua $$
Maharaj Rd, along the road from the Ruen Mai (the sign, with a leopard on it, is in Thai).
Considered by many locals to be one of the best restaurants in Krabi. The restaurant itself has a rambling feel and service is sometimes a little haphazard. Excellent Thai food. Barbecued seafood, crispy duck salad and virtually anything that is fried is especially good; the *pad pak pung* is delicious. An original menu with lots of house specialities.

Ruen Mai $$
Maharaj Rd well beyond the Vogue Department Store up the hill on the left-hand side as you leave the town.
Excellent Thai food in a quiet garden. Popular with locals, with good English-language menu and helpful staff. Has a number of southern specialities. Fish dishes are particularly good, as are the salads.

The Boathouse $$-$
Soi Hutangkonn.
A restaurant in a real wooden boat set in a garden with a fake moat around it. Even more bizarre, the street appears largely residential. What keeps the whole affair from looking like a theme restaurant nightmare is the romantic glory of the gleaming golden boat with its chandeliers and perfectly executed main courses, like steamed bass and plum sauce. This is the perfect place for couples though it also popular for intimate business meetings.

Europa Café $$-$
1/9 Soi Ruamjit Rd, T075-620407.
A favourite with locals and expats. Serves tasty northern European food – including pickled fish and Danish pork. Excellent helpings and always fresh. Possibly the best Western breakfast in town. Leonardo Di Caprio ate here while filming *The Beach*. Japanese tourists are keen on sitting in the star's seat and scoffing the Leonardo Special which is a banana milkshake, meatballs with mashed potatoes, mixed salad and bread and a pancake with strawberry ice cream.

Kwan Coffee Corner $
Khongkha Rd, T075-611706, kwan_café_kbi@hotmail.com.
Delicious fresh coffee, sandwiches, milk-shakes, ice creams, cheap and tasty Thai food, good breakfasts of fruit and muesli, almost everything. A good place to acclimatize to Krabi, with chatty owners. Kwan has become so much of an institution that they have their own T-shirts for sale.

Tip...
A night market sets up in the early evening on Khlong Kha Road, along the Krabi river, and serves good seafood dishes.

May and Mark's Restaurant $
Ruen-Ruedee Rd.
Good information, friendly atmosphere and attracts expats so the conversation goes beyond predictable backpacker chat. However, this tiny and well-loved hang-out seems to be resting on its laurels. It's not as clean as it could be and the much-touted bread needs to appear more often. Thai, Italian, Mexican and German food, along with the traveller usuals.

Ao Nang

The Roof Restaurant $$$
Ao Nang.
Attractive building with a flower-filled dining room and setting, although not on the beach. Good extensive menu which offers organic steak and Swiss-German specialities as well as Thai dishes. Expensive, but worth it.

Tip...
Food in Rai Leh can be found at hotels and guesthouses and is the usual mix of grills, seafood and watered down Thai dishes.

Koh Phi Phi

Nearly all the food on the island is aimed at tourists and so few of the culinary delights found in the rest of the country are available here. There are some good Western restaurants though, and Ton Sai is packed with bakeries and all manner of seafood.

Le Grand Bleu $$$
Ton Sai.
French- and Thai- run restaurant near the pier. Excellent wine list and seafood make this one of the best places to eat on the island. Good atmosphere and service.

Amico Italian Restaurant $$$-$$
Ton Sai, T08-1894 0876 (mob).
Great little pizza and pasta place near the pier. Perfect pit stop if you're jumping on the ferry. Friendly with good service.

Jasmin $$-$
Laem Tong beach.
A tiny little Thai eatery set next to the sea gypsy village. Tak, the owner, is a friendly character who serves up excellent Thai food. The seafood is great. It is full every night with guests from the nearby luxury resorts.

Pee Pee Bakery $$-$
Ton Sai.
In the heart of Ton Sai this bakery and coffee house sells donuts, choc-chip cookies and anything else you need for a sugar rush.

Koh Jum

Koh Jum Seafood $$
On a mini pier next to the actual working pier. Choose fine fresh seafood directly from traps. Cooked to perfection with a sophisticated range of ingredients – do not be surprised to find them cooking the shellfish in a broth of around 15 different ingredients. You can watch the birds following the boats for fish and all the activities of a working pier while taking in the islands opposite.

Bodaeng Beach Resort $
Between Woodland Lodge and Andaman Beach Resort.
Excellent fare from the owner here, especially the salads and soups. But take a mosquito coil or repellent as the restaurant is open and set in a little from the beach.

Koh Lanta

All the guesthouses and hotels provide restaurants with fairly similar menus.

Sala Dan
Seaview 1 $
(aka Monkey in the Back)
Slow service, good seafood, no electricity, cheap. Also Seaview 2 Larger menu, Thai and seafood, friendly, cheap. The enormous scones are tasty and filling.

Ao Khlong Dao
Sayang Beach Resort Restaurant $$$
Khlong Dao Beach by Lanta Sand Resort and Spa.
Excellent Malay-Thai fusion cuisine here – among the best along the west coast, cooked with real flair and precision.

Costa Lanta Restaurant $$$-$$
Northern stretch of the beach.
Lunch and dinner, served in exquisite surroundings. This spacious building mixes concrete, wood and fabrics to create a very special ambience. Delicious Thai food and a decent wine list. The bar is perfect to relax with a drink, after a hard day on the beach; this isn't the place to lounge about in a bikini or Speedos.

Golden Bay $$$-$$
See Sleeping, page 242.
Beachside restaurant in the bungalow operation of the same name. Excellent Thai and Isaan food on sale here. They also BBQ a fresh catch of seafood daily and offer discounts in low season. Reasonably priced in comparison to other places.

Danny's $$
Southern end of Khlong Dao beach.
Huge menu of seafood, Thai and international, Sun evening Thai buffets are popular.

Ao Phra-Ae
Retro Restaurant & Bar $$
On the main road, located behind Red Snapper.
Rustic restaurant made from natural local materials, touches most bases on the culinary spectrum: Thai, pizza, pasta and the usual, other European fare.

Hat Khlong Khoang
Bulan Lanta $$-$
Opposite Sonya Homestay.
Impressive range of Thai food to satisfy your taste buds. Some Western food, such as chips and burgers. Also open for breakfast. Check out the specials board.

Ao Khlong Nin
Cook Kai $$-$
Just across the road from the beach, opposite the Apichayavee Residence.
This family-run restaurant serves a great range of Thai dishes including a comprehensive selection of vegetarian food. Food is served in a traditional Thai building with seashell chandeliers that tinkle in the sea breeze, making it a beautiful setting to enjoy lunch or dinner.

Green Leaf Café $
On the main road, opposite the entrance to the Where Else Resort.
A warm welcome awaits at this comfy café. The English and Thai owners offer up real coffees, generous baguettes, served on fresh multigrain bread and healthy salads.

Ban Koh Lanta Yai
Mango Bar & Bistro $$$-$$
Below Mango House guesthouse.
Decent Thai and Western food in this great little hang-out. Bar serves cocktails and whiskies.

Krue Lanta Yai Restaurant $$
At the end of 'town', T075-697062. Hours variable.
A restaurant on the pier along a walkway filled with plants. Good selection of fresh seafood.

Trang Town

Trang's BBQ pork is delicious and one of the town's few claims to national fame. It is made from a traditional recipe brought here by the town's immigrant Chinese community and is usually served with rice or dim sum. It's the speciality of several Chinese restaurants and can also be bought from street vendors and is usually only available from 0900-1500ish.

Koh Chai Pla Phrao $$
Rusda Rd.
Look for a bright yellow sign (Thai only) and a big open-plan eatery for one of the most popular places in Trang. Don't be fooled by the cheap plastic furniture, the Thai food here is awesome. House speciality is grilled fish – so fresh it will be staring back at you – or steamed fish with a mood altering chilli and lime sauce.

Tip...
There is an excellent, small night market, selling everything from seasonal fruit through to Isaan food, just off of Phraram VI Road past the town hall. Open every night 1800-2100.

Krua Trang $$
Visetkul Rd.
Excellent Thai food and draft Carlsberg beer. The stuffed steamed seabass is a specialty and is delicious, filleted, stuffed with shrimp and vegetables and then steamed. The entire range of food is impressive. Staff are friendly and helpful at recommending dishes.

BBQ Pork Shophouse $
Corner of a small soi on Kantang Rd.
This Chinese place is often packed with families queuing for either takeaway or a table. Only really sells one dish – BBQ pork smothered in a sweet gravy with leafy green vegetables on rice. You can also get chicken satay.

Kao Tom Pui Restaurant $
111 Phraram IV Rd, T075-210127.
Open since 1967. Family restaurant, very popular with the locals, an unpretentious café setting with Sino-Portuguese feel. Does cauldrons of seafood soup, excellent seafood dishes, including steamed seabass. Good vegetables – morning glory with garlic especially nice.

Ko Rak (Somrak) $
158-160 Kantang Rd.
Friendly shophouse-style eatery surrounded by a throng of stalls which sell tender duck and pork, rice and noodles. The family who runs this packed place is originally from the Chinese island of Hainan and first came to Trang over 70 years ago. Full of bustle and good grub.

Meeting Point Restaurant and Internet Café $
Right along from the railway station.
This does a good breakfast, decent coffees in an airy café with tiled ceramic floor and wooden benches. For some reason there are pictures of Native Americans on the wall. Also has a little bar.

Sam's Bar $
Opposite the railway station. Happy hour 1600-1800.
Does fantastic salads and sandwiches. The baguettes are loaded with fresh salad from the deli and are recommended if you are craving some *farang* food.

Beaches & islands near Trang

Mookies Bar $
Koh Muk.
Does spare ribs, hamburgers, grilled chicken, but you need to order ahead of time so he can get the supplies from the mainland. The entertainment

here is provided through the colourful tales of Russell who first came to Thailand in 1969.

Koh Tarutao

Each cluster of bungalows has it's own basic National Park-run Thai restaurant selling average Thai food at reasonable prices – there is also a shop selling snacks near the pier by the park entrance.

Koh Lipe

Pooh's $$$
T074-722220, on the path between Chao Le Resort and Pattaya Beach.
Usually the busiest place, offering music, a good bar and tasty meals in a well-decorated, relaxed airy setting. The bakery also serves up typically delicious goods.

Daya $$
West end of Pattaya Beach.
One of the best places for barbecued fish thanks to an exquisite marinade.

Banana Tree Restaurant $
In the village (take a left at Forra Dive Centre).
An off- beach setting with shady floor seating under the trees. A popular spot with an extensive Thai menu, it shows movies in the evenings.

Flour Power Bakery $
Sunset Beach, behind Sabye Sports.
It has expanded its seating area along with its repertoire to include a mouth-watering selection of Thai and Western dishes, such as lemon chicken, as well as its staple fruit pies, brownies, fresh bread and cinnamon rolls. The vegetarian selection is good and all meals are served with fresh bread or baked potatoes and salad.

Satun

Pretty much opposite the Sinkiat Thani are several restaurants serving Malay food and a roti shop selling banana, egg and plain rotis in the mornings.

Banburee $$-$
Buriwanit Rd.
1 of 2 places with English signs, modern establishment behind the Sinkiat Thani; and Kualuang, Satuntanee Phiman, the best in a group of small restaurants.

Entertainment

Stand-alone bars and clubs are thin on the ground – Krabi Town is the best destination for nightlife. Most restaurants, hotels, resorts and cheap bungalow places will also offer music and drinks usually in keeping with the style, clientele of the place.

Krabi Town

Bars & clubs
Bar Chaofa Rd
A laid-back vibe with lots of comfy places to sit and chill. There are also numerous other bars along this road worth checking out.

Kwan Fang Live Music
Sudmongkol Rd, next to Mixer Pub.
For a sense of weirdness and longing, there is always Kwan Fang with its staple of country and western bands. This out-of-place haunt looks a little like a western saloon with some of the space out in the wide open air. An older crowd than Mixer.

Mixer Pub
100 Sudmongkol Rd.
Pulls in a solid local crowd. At Mixer they prepare your poison all night with your choice of mixer. Mischievous staff will also videotape you through the stages of drunkenness, table-top dancing and singing. Doubling the fun (or horror), this is later played on a screen, so not a place for shrinking violets. Suits a younger crowd. Great for anthropological viewing and for the brave – unparalleled for shameless exhibitionism.

Nyhavn
Across from Europa, Soi Ruamjit.
Based on Nyhavn in Denmark. They only play jazz and sometimes have live performances. You also get sandwiches and baguettes with beef, imported cheese, salami, etc. It has a small garden too.

Festivals & events
Berg Fa Andaman Festival
November, Krabi.
In the gardens beyond the pier (coinciding with Loi Krathong). A showcase for traditional dancing and singing from around Thailand. Also features Andaman handicrafts.

Ao Nang

Bars & clubs
Plenty to choose from but they tend to open and close with great frequency. A 'bar-beer' scene has opened up off the beachfront in Hat Nopparat Thara behind the front row of dive and souvenir shops and is complete with massage services, pink lights, cocktails, etc.

Irish Rover and Grill
247/8 Moo 2, Ao Nang.
Theme pub but still, sometimes, Guinness is good for you. Good selection of draughts and have cider too. Well run, with fairly high standard of bar food here too including chilli con carne, toasties, pies and chops. Does roast dinner but can be heavy for a tropical climate. Live sports.

The Lost Pirate Bar
Beachfront Rd, down from La Luna, Ao Nang.
Slightly more adventurous crowd – good information about parties and alternative scenes.

Luna Beach Bar
Hat Nopparat Thara, Ao Nang.
Has fantastic cocktail prices (for Ao Nang anyway), and a very loose interpretation of closing hours. Can get raucous.

Koh Phi Phi

Bars & clubs
Carlito's Bar
East from Ton Sai Bay.
Well worth visiting just to get the atmosphere of the island and its people. It used to cater to largely Swedish clientele but has since become more international.

Sunflower Bar
At the end of Loh Dalum Bay.
This bar, made from flotsam and other debris, is a good place to chill out and enjoy a few cocktails. BBQ and live music.

Shopping

Bars & clubs

As the tourist trade picks up, more bars and clubs are springing up. On Pattaya Beach there's **Time to Chill** probably the pick of the bunch; **Monkey Bar,** Moon Light Bar, and **Peace and Love Bar**, all are relaxed with mats on the beach.

Jack's Jungle Bar

Up in the hills (follow the signs from the village). Has a more upbeat feel and is popular with the diving crowd. Make sure you bring a torch for the trek home.

Karma beach bar

On the charming bay below the Mountain Resort. A popular bar. The owners are friendly and it normally has a great atmosphere.

Pooh's

A favourite watering hole and is more upmarket than the beach bars with a stage for live bands.

Festivals & events
Vegetarian Festival

Oct (movable), Trang.
9-day festival in which a strict vegetarian diet is observed to purify the body. Mediums pierce their cheeks and tongues with spears and walk on hot coals. On the sixth day a procession makes its way around town, in which everyone dresses in traditional costumes. The same event occurs in Phuket.

Krabi Town

Clothes & tailoring

There is a tailor on the corner of Issara and Khongkha roads. Lots of clothes stores on Phattana, Prachachuen and Uttarakit roads, mostly selling beachwear.

Souvenirs

Khun B Souvenir, and other souvenir shops on Khongkha and Uttarakit Rd, sell a range of souvenirs from all over Thailand and Southeast Asia. Thai Silver, opposite Thai Hotel. Sells silverware mostly from Nakhon Sri Thammarat.

Ao Nang

Shops open on the beachfront at Ao Nang during the evening selling garments, leather goods, jewellery and other products made specifically for the tourist market. There isn't much that's unusual, except for batik 'paintings', usually illustrating marine scenes, which are made in small workshops here.

Koh Lanta

Hammock House

Main street, Ban Koh Lanta Yai.
A great little shop in an old wooden house. The owner is very friendly and provides visitors with a 'Lanta Biker Map' as well as trying to sell well-made hammocks and art.

Handicrafts

Huan Mae Khum Pan, on the main road near Lanta residence, huanmaek hampan-handicraft. com. Lanna style clothing, furniture and decorative pieces. The owner Pom, is friendly, helpful and speaks excellent English.

Trang Town

Best buys in Trang include locally woven cotton and wickerwork and sponge cake. Thaklang and Municipal markets are next door to each other in the centre of town, off Rachdamnern Rd.

Ani

Pattalung Rd, T08-1397 4574 (mob).
Huge range of jewellery, mostly made on the premises.

Fha Trang Collection

283 Radchadamnern Rd, T075-217004.
Posh and souvenirs reasonably priced. Embroidered shoes, scarves, artistic mobiles and folk craft. There is also a second-hand bookshop next door.

Activities & tours

Krabi Town

Canoeing
Europa Café
Krabi (see page 238).
Offers a mangrove/canoeing tour but with an English-speaking guide, which is necessary if you wish to learn about local history and why mangroves are so important. The tour, which goes near Bor Thor village close to Ao Luk, takes in caves and allows for swimming.

Sea Canoe
Ao Nang, T075-212252, seacanoe.net.
Provides small-scale sea canoeing trips (self-paddle), exploring the cliffs and caves, and the coastline of Phra Nang, Rai Leh and nearby islands.

Game fishing
Phi Phi Marine Travel Co
201 Uttarakit Rd, Krabi, T075-621297.
Arranges expeditions to catch marlin, barracuda and tuna.

Tour operators
Tour operators in Krabi are concentrated on Uttarakit and Ruen-Ruedee roads and close to the Chao Fah Pier. There are many tour and travel agents, and information is widely available, so it is not necessary to list numerous outfits here. Prices and schedules are all openly posted and a 30-minute walk around town will reveal all.

Ao Nang & around

Diving
Ao Nang Divers
On the main street, 208/2-3 Moo 2, T075-637246, aonang-divers.com.
Easily the best in town and is a 5-star PADI dive centre.

Muay Thai (Thai boxing)
There is a well-supported stadium for Thai boxing in the Ao Nang area. The old one was next to Ao Nang Paradise. This much larger stadium which attracts national standard boxers is set back from Hat Nopparat Thara beach by about 300 m.

Therapies
Tropical Herbal Spa
20/1 Moo 2, Ao Nang, tropicalherbalspa.com.
A glorious day spa, a little away from the beach but set in beautiful gardens and mostly open to the air.

Tour operators
Ao Nang Ban Lae Travel
Close to Krabi Resort.
Runs boat tours to various islands and beaches, including Rai Leh and Phi Phi.

AP Travel
Beachfront Rd, T075-637642.
Offers a range of tours to various temples and short 'jungle tours' – very helpful and friendly though not terribly exciting.

Rai Leh

Rock climbing
Tex's Rock Climbing Adventure
Rai Leh Beach, molon.de/galleries/Thailand/Krabi/Climbing/.
Mr 'Tex' is a bit of a local hero who also runs a kids adventure camp just outside town for orphans and street children.

Koh Phi Phi

Diving
There are currently around 15 dive shops operating on Koh Phi Phi. Most of the dive shops charge the same with 2 local fun dives coming in at around ฿1800. Open Water courses start from ฿11,900. Alternatively, you can book with one of the many dive centres on Phuket.

Phi Phi Scuba Diving
Main street in Ton Sai, T075-612665, phiphi-scuba.com; SSI (Scuba School International).
Offers a 5-day certificate course

Visa Diving
Main street in Ton Sai, T076-618106, visa diving.com.

Rock climbing
The limestone cliffs here are known internationally. There are 3 companies operating, including **Cat Climbers** and **Phi Phi Climbers**, krabidir.com/phiphiclimbers/index.htm.

KE Hang Out, main street down from the pier at Ton Sai Bay. Probably the best of the bunch. They are experienced climbers who have been here for 7 years. A ½-day costs ฿1000 for 4-5 hours, ฿1500 for 8-9 hours, and includes lunch, water and fruit. A 3-day course is ฿5000.

Therapies
Zeavola Spa
Zeavola, T075-627000. Open 0900-2100.
It is definitely worth stopping by here for some wonderful treatments. The signature massage is the Zeavola Body Brush Massage – a body brushing followed by a head massage then body massage with rice oil and lemongrass, kaffir lime and essential oils.

Ministry of Health Spa
Panthai Clinic, 32-34-36 Saingam Rd.
This superb spa does everything from ear candles to moxibusiton (Gwyneth Paltrow is a great fan of this detoxification process which involves hot suction caps). You can get acupuncture here and Chinese remedies, as well as Thai massage. Reasonable prices.

Tour operators
The North Star Travel
125/101 Moo 7, T075-601279, northpole_nts@hotmail.com.
Very helpful and friendly tourist information and booking centre. Not pushy, good level of English.

Koh Jum

Tour operators
Koh Jum Center Tour
Shop on the opposite side of Koh Jum Seafood and the pier at 161 Moo 3.
Native Koh Jumian Wasana Laemkoh provides tickets for planes, trains, buses and boats. She will also change money, make overseas calls, and arrange 1-day boat trips. Her husband is a local fisherman so you may end up going with him. You can also rent motorbikes here. Honest and reliable.

Wildside Tours
Along the road opposite Koh Jum Village School (signposted).
This set-up, operated by a German lady, offers kayaking and snorkelling expeditions, and some trekking.

Koh Lanta

Cookery classes
Time for Lime
T075-684590/08-947 45171 (mob), timeforlime.net.
Contact Junie Kovacs. Learn Thai cookery on the beach.

Diving
Blue Planet Divers
3 Moo 1, T075-684165

Lanta Discovery Divers
Long Beach Resort, T075-684035/08-1797 2703 (mob).

Scool Divers
T075-684654.
See also Tour operators, below.

Tour operators
The following are well run and friendly, and can offer motorcycle rental, and boat and bus tickets: **Makaira Tour Centre**, 18 Moo 1, Sala Dan; **Amour Travel and Tour**, Khlong Dao beachfront, T075-684897.

For long-tailed boat trips from Ban Koh Lanta including fishing and camping tours, contact Sun **Fishing and Island Tours**, main waterfront Rd, Lanta Old town, T087-8916619, lantalongtail.com.

Trang & around

Diving
Rainbow Divers
Koh Ngai Resort, T075- 206962. rainbow-diver.com.
Run by a German couple, they offer PADI courses and excursions, mid-November until the end of April.

Tour operators
Chao Mai Tour Ltd
15 Satanee Rd, contact Jongkoolnee Usaha, T075-216380, cha omai-tour-trang.com.
Reliable and trustworthy, they go out of their way to help, can make hotel reservations, offer information, airport reservations and a/c bus/van, and tours. English spoken. Recommended.

Listings

PJ Guesthouse
25/12 Sathani Rd.
A well-informed travel service that is as much about you getting to experience local life as making money. They can set you up with cars and also English-speaking tuk-tuk drivers who organize Trang tours (from ฿200 per hr) showing you all the nooks and crannies of this vibrant town.

Koh Lipe

Diving
Dang's Tours
A stone's throw from Pooh's on the way to Chao Le Resort. Arranges snorkelling for around ฿1000 per boat for 6 people.

Forra Dive Centre
Near Chao Le Resort.

Jack's Tours
On the beach at Koh Lipe.

Lotus Dive (Pooh's)
See Eating, page 251.

Ocean Pro Divers
Near Leepay Resort.

Sabye Sports
T08-94645884, T/F074-734 104, info@sabye-divers.com.
The island's first scuba diving centre, next to Porn Bungalows, offers diving and rents canoes (฿500 per day) and snorkelling equipment (฿200 per day).

Starfish Scuba
T074-728089, starfishscuba.com, next to the Leepay Resort on Pattaya Beach.
Also offers diving courses.

Satun & far south

Diving
Charan Tour
19/6 Satunthani Rd, T074-711453/01-9573908.
Runs boat tours every day to the islands between October-May. Lunch and snorkelling equipment are provided. Has a good reputation.

Transport

Krabi

The transport to and from Krabi varies greatly according to season.

Air
Air Asia (airasia.com) fly to Bangkok and Kuala Lumpur, **THAI** (thaiair.com) to Bangkok and **Bangkok Airways** (bangkokair.com) to Samui. Several charter airlines also fly into Krabi.

Boat
The monsoon season affects timetables as does the low season. There are 2 or 3 piers in the area (including Ao Nang) with services to Koh Lanta, Koh Phi Phi, Koh Jum, Koh Yao Noi/Yai and Phuket.

Bus
Numerous evening a/c, VIP and non-a/c connections with Bangkok's Southern bus terminal. Regular a/c and non-a/c connections with Phuket via Phangnga. Various minivans to other destinations and regular connections with Surat Thani and Trang. Tickets and information about bus connection (both public buses and private tour buses) available from travel agents. Also bus/boat connections to Koh Samui, Koh Tao and Koh Phangnan and international bus routes to Malaysia and Singapore.

Koh Lanta

Boat

Most visitors to Koh Lanta will arrive via either Krabi or Trang with minivans providing through links from/to both. During the high season boats run to/from Ao Nang (for Krabi) Phi Phi, Phuket, Koh Jum and even south to Koh Lipe. The frequency of these services change annually and according to demand.

Trang

Air

Daily connections on **Nok Air** (nokair.com) to Bangkok. An a/c minibus ฿100 goes to and from the railway station – tuk-tuks for ฿150.

Boat

Boats leave from Pakmeng, about 25 km west of Trang to Koh Ngai and Koh Muk, There are now also through services to islands in the Koh Tarutao archipelago, (Nov-May) and Phi Phi. You can buy tickets for combined minivan/boat service from tour operators in Trang near the railway station.

Bus

Buses to Bangkok leave from the bus station on Ploenpitak Rd. To Phuket, regular services from Ploenpitak Rd, from 0600-1800, normal a/c ฿290, VIP ฿340. These buses also stop at Krabi. To Satun

(for Pak Bara and Tarutao), non a/c ฿150, from the bus terminal on Huai Yod Rd. There is also a daily service to Singapore – book through a tour operator. Minibuses to Koh Lanta leave from outside KK Travel, opposite the train station, every hour in high season; to Nakhon Si Thammarat, from Wisekul Rd. To Pak Bara, organize a minivan from your hotel, or book through an agency. To Surat Thani, minivan from Thaklang Rd, near the fruit market.

Train

There are two sleeper trains a day in both directions between Trang and Bangkok – connects to Hua Hin, Prachuap Khiri Khan, Chumphon and Phun Phin (for Surat Thani). Advance booking is often necessary as the train is usually fully booked.

Koh Tarutao

One of the best routes to reach Tarutao is via Trang. From there minibuses and buses run to Pak Bara, the main pier for the entire archipelago. In high season October to April boat services regularly leave Pak Bara for all the islands – in the low season and during bad weather boats might not run at all. In high season there are now some boats that island hop from Phi Phi via Koh Lanta and Trang to Koh Lipe, from where there is a service to

Langkawi. During high season boats now link between all the islands meaning that you don't have to return to the mainland. Some boats stop a little offshore with smaller boats bringing people ashore – expect to pay 30 to ฿50 per person for this.

Contents

Practicalities

Buddha at Pattaya.

Getting there

Air

The majority of visitors arrive in Thailand through Bangkok's Suvarnabhumi International Airport, which opened in 2006 but has been plagued with problems. The city's old airport, Don Muang, still deals with a few short-haul domestic destinations. All of the national carrier THAI's, flights now leave from Suvarnabhumi. Phuket in the south also has an international airport – a few regional charter flights land at Krabi and Samui airports. More than 35 airlines and charter companies fly to Bangkok. Fares can inflate by up to 50% during high season.

From Europe

The approximate flight time from Europe to Bangkok (non-stop) is 12 hours. From London Heathrow, airlines offering non-stop flights include **Qantas**, **British Airways**, **THAI** and **Eva Air**. You can easily connect to Thailand from the UK via most other European capitals. **Finnair** flies daily from **Helsinki**, **KLM** via Amsterdam and **Lufthansa** via Frankfurt. **SAS** flies from Copenhagen and **Swiss Air** from Zurich. Further afield, **Etihad** flies via Abu Dhabi, **Gulf Air** via Bahrain and **Qatar** via Muscat and Doha. Non-direct flights can work out much cheaper, so if you want a bargain, shop around. Finnair, finnair.com, often offers some of the cheapest fares. It is also possible to fly to Phuket from Dusseldorf and Munich.

From USA & Canada

The approximate flight time from Los Angeles to Bangkok is 21 hours. There are one-stop flights from Los Angeles on THAI and two stops on Delta; one-stop flights from San Francisco on Northwest and United and two stops on Delta; and one-stop flights from Vancouver on Canadian.

From Australasia

There are flights from Sydney and Melbourne (approximately 9 hours) daily with Qantas and THAI. There is also a choice of other flights with **British Airways**, **Alitalia**, **Lufthansa** and **Lauda Air**, which are less frequent. There are flights from Perth with **THAI** and **Qantas**. From Auckland, **Air New Zealand**, **THAI** and **British Airways** fly to Bangkok.

Rail

Regular services link Butterworth (near Penang) in Malaysia to Bangkok, and the major southern Thai towns. You can connect at Butterworth to Kuala Lumpur and Singapore. Express air-conditioned trains take 24 hours from Butterworth to Bangkok and call at Surat Thani, Chumphon and Hua Hin. All tickets should be booked in advance. **Orient-Express Hotels** run the luxury **Eastern & Oriental Express** between Bangkok, Kuala Lumpur and Singapore. Reservations can be made at orient-express.com.

Getting around

Air

Budget carriers now offer cheap flights all over the country. **Air Asia** (airasia.com), **Bangkok Airways** (bangkokair.com), **Nok Air** are the present major players in this market. **Thai Airways (THAI)** is the national flag carrier and is also by far the largest domestic airline – they often offer promotions that will match the budget carriers.

THAI head office is found at 89 Vibhavadi rangsit Road, Jompol, Jatujak, Bangkok 10900, T02-2451000, thaiair.com. **Bangkok Airways** head office is at 99 Mu 14, Vibhavadirangsit Road, Chom Phon, Chatuchak, Bangkok 10900, T02-265 5678 (ext 1771 for reservations centre), bangkokair.com. **Thai Air Asia**, T02-515 9999, airasia.com.

Road

Bus

Private and state-run buses leave Bangkok for every town in Thailand; it is an extensive network and a cheap way to travel. The government bus company is called Bor Kor Sor, and every town in Thailand will have a BKS terminal. There are small stop-in-every- town local buses plus the faster long-distance buses (*rot duan* – express; or *rot air* – air-conditioned). Air-conditioned buses come in two grades: *chan nung* (first class, blue colour) and *chan song* (second class, orange colour). *Chan song* have more seats but less elbow and leg room, and will not offer hostess, food and drink services, or a toilet. *Chan nung* buses will have all of these as well as a maximum of 42 seats (adjustable to 70° recline). For longer/overnight journeys, air-conditioned de luxe (sometimes known as *rot tour*, officially Standard 1A buses, also blue like the *chan rung*) or VIP buses, stewardess service is provided with food and drink supplied en route and more leg room plus constant Thai music or videos. There should be no more than 24 seats (adjustable to

135° recline). Many fares include meals at roadside restaurants, so keep hold of your ticket. If you're travelling on an overnight air-conditioned bus bring a light sweater and some earplugs – both the volume of the entertainment system and cooling system are likely to be turned up full blast. The local buses are slower and cramped but worth it for those wishing to sample local life. The seats at the very back are reserved for monks, so be ready to move if necessary.

offering travel from popular spots like Khao San road in Bangkok or Surat Thani will advertise huge roomy seats but when you turn you will find a small seat is the only comfort you will have for a 14-hour overnight bus ride. Our advice is to always travel, just like Thais, from the official bus station.

Car hire

The average cost of hiring a car from a reputable firm is ฿1000-2000 per day, ฿6000- 10,000 per week, or ฿20,000-30,000 per month. Some companies automatically include insurance; for others it must be specifically requested and a surcharge is added. An international driver's licence, or a UK, US, French, German, Australian, New Zealand, Singapore or Hong Kong licence is required. The lower age limit is 20 years (higher for some firms). If the mere thought of competing with Thai drivers is terrifying, an option is to hire a chauffeur along with the car. For this service an extra ฿300-500 per day is usually charged, more at weekends and if an overnight stay is included. There are a few safety points that should be kept in mind: accidents in Thailand are often horrific. If involved in an accident, and they occur with great frequency, you – as a foreigner – are likely to be found the guilty party and expected to meet the costs. Ensure the cost of hire includes insurance cover. If you, as a foreigner are involved in an accident, call the Tourist Police (see page 272) to aid with translation.

Private tour buses

Many tour companies operate bus services in Thailand; travel agents in Bangkok will supply information. These buses are seldom more comfortable than the state buses but are usually more expensive. Overnight trips usually involve a meal stop (included in price of ticket) and stewardess service for drinks and snacks. They often leave from outside the company office, which may not be located at the central bus station. Many of the private bus companies

Motorbike hire

Motorbike hire is mostly confined to holiday resorts and prices vary from place to place; ฿150-300 per day is usual for a 100-150 cc machine. Often licences do not have to be shown and insurance will not be available. Riding in shorts and flip-flops is dangerous – a foot injury is easily acquired even at low speeds and broken toes are a nightmare to heal – always wear shoes. Borrow a helmet or, if you're planning to ride a motorbike on more than one occasion, consider buying one

fares, but can often be hired and used as a taxi service (agree a price before setting out). To let the driver know you want to stop, press the electric buzzers or tap the side of the vehicle with a coin.

Taxi

Standard air-conditioned taxis are found in very few Thai towns with the majority in the capital. In Bangkok all taxis have meters. Most Bangkok taxis will also take you on long-distance journeys either for an agreed fee or with the meter running. In the south of Thailand, shared long-distance taxis are common.

Tuk-tuks come in the form of pedal or motorized machines. Fares should be negotiated and agreed before setting off. It will not take long to discover what is a reasonable price, but don't expect to pay the same as a Thai. Drivers are a useful source of local information and will know most places of interest, plus hotels and restaurants (and sometimes their prices). In Bangkok, and most other towns, these vehicles are motorized, gas-powered scooters. Pedal-powered *saamlors* (meaning 'three wheels') were outlawed in Bangkok a few years ago and they are now gradually being replaced by the noisier motorized version throughout the country.

Sea

Boat

The boats and ferries that link the islands of Thailand can be everything from ships large enough to carry several trucks down to speed boats which can only hold 10 people. You can also rent *hang-yaaws* (long-tailed boats) in many places and they are loud, fast and fun.

There are numerous boats to and from the Gulf Coast Islands of Koh Samui, Koh Phangan and Koh Tao. Principal services run from Chumphon to Koh Tao and from Surat Thani and the port of Don Sak

– decent helmets can be found for ฿1500 and are better than the 'salad bowls' usually offered by hire companies.

In most areas of Thailand it is compulsory to wear a helmet and while this law is not always enforced there are now periodic checks everywhere – even on remote roads. Fines are usually ฿300; if you have an accident without a helmet the price could be much higher. Thousands of Thais are killed in motorcycle accidents each year and large numbers of tourists also suffer injuries (Koh Samui has been said to have the highest death rate anywhere in the world). Expect anything larger than you to ignore your presence on the road.

Motorbike taxis are becoming increasingly popular, and are the cheapest, quickest and most dangerous way to get from 'A' to 'B'. They are usually used for short rides down *sois* or to better local transport points. Riders wear coloured vests (sometimes numbered) and tend to congregate at key intersections or outside shopping centres for example. Agree a price before boarding – expect to pay ฿10 upwards for a short *soi* hop.

Songthaews are pick-up trucks fitted with two benches and can be found in many upcountry towns. They normally run fixed routes, with set

Rail

The State Railway of Thailand, railway.co.th/english, is efficient, clean and comfortable, with five main routes to the north, northeast, west, east and south. It is safer than bus travel but can take longer. The choice is first-class air-conditioned compartments, second-class sleepers, second-class air-conditioned sit-ups with reclining chairs and third-class sit-ups. Travelling third class is often cheaper than taking a bus; first and second class are more expensive than the bus but infinitely more comfortable. Express trains are known as *rot duan*, special express trains as *rot duan phiset* and rapid trains as *rot raew*. Express and rapid trains are faster as they make fewer stops; there is a surcharge for the service.

Reservations for sleepers should be made in advance (up to 60 days ahead) at Bangkok's Hualamphong station, T02-220 4444, the advance booking office is open daily 0700-2400. Some travel agencies also book tickets. A queue-by-ticket arrangement works efficiently, and travellers do not have to wait long. If you change a reservation the charge is ฿10. It is advisable to book the bottom sleeper, as lights are bright on top (in second-class compartments) and the ride more uncomfortable. It still may be difficult to get a seat at certain times of year, such as during festivals (like Songkran in Apr). Personal luggage allowance is 50 kg in first class, 40 kg in second and 30 kg in third class. Children aged three to 12 years old and under 150 cm in height pay half fare; those under three years old and less than 100 cm in height travel free, but do not get a seat. It is possible to pick up timetables at Hualamphong station (from the information booth in the main concourse). There are two types: the 'condensed' timetable (by region) showing all rapid routes, and complete, separate timetables for all classes. Timetables are available from stations and some tourist offices.

to Koh Samui and then on to Koh Phangan. Fast ferries, slow boats and night boats run services daily. On the Andaman Coast there are services to and from Phuket, Koh Phi Phi, Krabi, Koh Lanta, the islands off Trang and from Ban Pak Bara and Koh Tarutao National Park. The islands off the eastern seaboard are also connected by regular services to the mainland. Note that services become irregular and are suspended during certain times of year because of the wet season and rough seas. Each section details information on the months that will affect regular boat services.

Directory

Accident & emergency

Emergency services   Police: T191, T123. Tourist police: T1155. Fire: T199. Ambulance: T02-255 1134-6. Tourist Assistance Centre: Rachdamnern Nok Av, Bangkok, T02-356 0655.

Children

Many people are daunted by the prospect of taking a child to Southeast Asia and there are disadvantages: travelling is slower and more expensive and there are additional health risks for the child or baby. But it can be a most rewarding experience and, with sufficient care and planning, it can also be safe. Children are excellent passports into a local culture. Many Western baby products are available in Thailand.

More preparation is probably necessary for babies and children than for an adult, and particularly when travelling to remote areas where health services are primitive. A travel insurance policy which has an air ambulance provision is strongly recommended. When planning a route, try to stay within 24 hours' travel of a hospital with good care and facilities. For advice about common problems, see Health, page. Note– Never allow your child to be exposed to the harsh tropical sun without protection. A child can burn in minutes. Loose cotton clothing with long sleeves and legs and a sunhat are best. High-factor sun-protection cream is essential.

Children should already be properly protected against diphtheria, poliomyelitis and pertussis (whooping cough), measles and HIB, all of which can be more serious infections in Southeast Asia than at home. The measles, mumps and rubella vaccine is also given to children throughout the world, but those teenage girls who have not had rubella (German measles) should be tested and vaccinated. Hepatitis B vaccination for babies is now routine in some countries.

At the hottest time of year, air conditioning may be essential for a baby or young child's comfort. This rules out many of the cheaper hotels, but air-conditioned accommodation is available in all but the most out-of-the-way spots. When the child is bathing, be aware that the water could carry parasites, so avoid letting him or her drink it.

Customs

All narcotics are prohibited as well as obscene literature, pornography, firearms (except with a permit from the Police Department or local registration office) and some species of plants and animals (for more information contact the Royal Forestry Department, Phahonyothin Rd, Bangkok, T02-561 0777).

Duty free

The allowance for duty free is 500 g of cigars/cigarettes (or 200 cigarettes) and one litre of wine or spirits. No Buddha or Bodhisattva images or fragments should be taken out of Thailand, except for worshipping by Buddhists, for cultural exchanges or for research. However, it is obvious that many people do – you only have to look in the antique shops to see the abundance for sale. A licence should be obtained from the Department of Fine Arts, Na Prathat Rd, Bangkok, T02-224 1370, from Chiang Mai National Museum, T02-221308, or from the Songkhla National Museum, Songkhla, T02-311728. 5-days' notice is needed; take 2 passport-size photos of the object and photocopies of your passport. Most of the major department stores have a VAT refund desk. Go to them on your day of purchase with receipts and ask them to complete a VAT refund form, which you then present, with the purchased goods, at the appropriate desk in any international airport in Thailand. They'll give you another form that you exchange for cash in the departure lounge. You'll need to spend at least ฿4000 to qualify for a refund.

Disabled travellers

Disabled travellers will find Thailand a challenge. Buses and taxis are not designed for disabled access and there are few hotels and restaurants that are wheelchair-friendly. This is not to suggest that travel in Thailand is impossible for the disabled. On the plus side, you will find Thais to be helpful and because taxis and tuk-tuks are cheap it is usually not necessary to rely on buses. The Global Access – Disabled Travel Network website, globalaccess news.com, is useful and access-able. com has a specific section for travel in Thailand.

Electricity

Voltage is 220 volts (50 cycles). Most first- and tourist-class hotels have outlets for shavers and hairdryers. Adaptors are recommended, as almost all sockets are 2-pronged.

Embassies & consulates

Thai embassies worldwide, thaiembassy.org is a useful resource.
Australia 131 Macquarie St, Level 8, Sydney 2000, T02-9241 2542.

Canada 180 Island Park Drive, Ottawa, Ontario, K1Y 0A2, T613-722 4444.
Germany Lepsiusstrasse 64-66, 12163 Berlin, T030-794810.
Japan 3-14-6, Kami-Osaki, Shinagawa-Ku, Tokyo 14-0021, T03-3447 2247.
Malaysia 206 Jalan Ampang, 50450 Kuala Lumpur, T03-2148 8222.
New Zealand 2 Cook St, Karori, PO Box 17226, Wellington, T04-476 8616.
UK 29-30 Queens Gate, London, SW7 5JB, T020-7589 2944.
USA 1024 Wisconsin Av, NW, Suite 401, Washington, DC 20007, T202-944 3600.

Gay & lesbian travellers

On the surface, Thailand is incredibly tolerant of homosexuals and lesbians and the country's gay scene has flourished. However, overt public displays of affection are still frowned upon (see Local customs and laws, page 275). Attitudes in the more traditional rural areas, particularly the Muslim regions, are far more conservative than in the cities. By exercising a degree of cultural sensitivity any visit should be hassle free. The essential website is utopia-asia.com and Utopia Tours at Tarntawan Palace Hotel, 119/5-10 Suriwong Rd, T02-634 0273, utopia-tours.com, provides tours for gay and lesbian visitors. There's also a map of gay Bangkok. The main centres of activity in Bangkok are Silom Rd Sois 2 and 4 and Sukhumvit Soi 23. There is also a thriving gay scene in Pattaya and, to a lesser extent, on Phuket and Koh Samui.

Health

In Thailand the health risks, especially in the tropical areas, are different from those encountered in Europe or the USA. Malaria is common in certain areas, particularly in the jungle. There is an obvious difference in health risks between the business traveller who tends to stay in international class hotels in the large cities and the backpacker trekking through the rural areas. There are no hard and fast rules to follow; you will often have to make your own judgement on the healthiness or otherwise of your surroundings.

You should see your GP/practice nurse or travel clinic at least six weeks before your departure for general advice on travel risks, malaria and recommended vaccinations. Your local pharmacist can also be a good source of readily accessible advice. Make sure you have travel insurance, get a dental check (especially if you are going to be away for more than a month), know your own blood group and if you suffer a long-term condition such as diabetes or epilepsy make sure someone knows or that you have a Medic Alert bracelet/necklace with this information on it.

No vaccinations are specifically required for Thailand unless coming from an infected area, but tuberculosis, rabies, Japanese B encephalitis and hepatitis B are commonly recommended. The final decision, however, should be based on a consultation with your GP or travel clinic. You should also confirm that your primary courses and boosters are up to date (diphtheria, tetanus, poliomyelitis, hepatitis A, typhoid).

A yellow fever certificate is required by visitors who have been in an infected area in the 10 days before arrival. Those without a vaccination certificate will be vaccinated and kept in quarantine for 6 days, or deported.

Useful websites
nathnac.org National Travel Health Network and Centre.
who.int World Health Organisation.
fitfortravel.scot.nhs.uk Fit for Travel. This site from Scotland provides a quick A-Z of vaccine and travel health advice requirements for each country.

Internet

Apart from a few remote islands Thailand has an excellent internet network. Tourist areas tend to be well catered for with numerous internet shops offering a connection for between ฿30-90 per hour. Some guesthouses and hotels have free wireless while the more expensive ones charge extortionate rates of up ฿1000 per day. You might also be able to pick up wireless for free from office blocks, etc.

Insurance

Always take out travel insurance before you set off and read the small print carefully. Check that the policy covers any activities that you may end up doing. Also check exactly what your medical cover includes, ie ambulance, helicopter rescue or emergency flights back home. If diving in Thailand, it's worth noting that there are no air evacuation services, and hyperbaric services can charge as much as US$800 per hour so good dive insurance is imperative. It is inexpensive and well worth it in case of a problem, real or perceived. Many general travel insurance policies will cover diving but you have to ask for it to be included in your policy.

Media

Newspapers & magazines

There are two major English-language dailies – the *Bangkok Post* (bangkokpost.net) and *The Nation* (nationmultimedia.com). They provide acceptable international coverage. There are a number of Thai-language dailies and weeklies, as well as Chinese-language newspapers. The local papers are sometimes scandalously colourful, with gruesome pictures of traffic accidents and murder victims. International newspapers are available in Bangkok, Pattaya, Phuket and on Koh Samui.

Television & radio

CNN and BBC are available in most mid- or upper-range hotels. Local cable networks will sometimes provide English language films, while a full satellite package will give you English football and various movie and other channels. Programme listings are available in *The Nation* and *Bangkok Post*.

Online

Recent events in Thailand have exposed the vested interests hiding in the background of papers such as *The Nation* and they are no longer reliable news sources. Into this gap has sprung up a number of excellent blogs: bangkokpundit.blogspot.com; facthai.wordpress.com; rspas.anu.edu.au/rmap/newmandala; news.inbangkok.org; prachatai.com/english; khikwai.com; notthenation.com.

Money

Currency

Exchange rates: £1=฿53.4, €1= ฿48.7, US$1=฿33.5 (Nov 2009). For up-to-the-minute exchange rates visit xe.com.

The unit of Thai currency is the baht (฿), which is divided into 100 *satang*. Notes in circulation include ฿20 (green), ฿50 (blue), ฿100 (red), ฿500 (purple) and ฿1000 (orange and grey). Coins include 25 *satang* and 50 *satang*, and ฿1, ฿2, ฿5, and ฿10. The 2 smaller coins are disappearing from circulation and the 25 *satang* coin, equivalent to the princely sum of US$0.003, is rarely found. The colloquial term for 25 *satang* is *saleng*.

Exchange
It is best to change money at banks or money changers which give better rates than hotels. The exchange booths at Bangkok airport have some of the best rates available.

Credit & debit cards
Plastic is increasingly used in Thailand and just about every town of any size will have a bank with an ATM. Visa and MasterCard are the most widely taken credit cards, and cash cards with the Cirrus logo can also be used to withdraw cash at many banks. Generally speaking, AMEX can be used at branches of the **Bangkok Bank**; JCB at **Siam Commercial Bank**; MasterCard at **Siam Commercial** and **Bangkok Bank**; and Visa at **Thai Farmers' Bank** and **Bangkok Bank**. Most larger hotels and more expensive restaurants take credit cards as well. Because Thailand has embraced the ATM with such exuberance, many foreign visitors no longer bother with traveller's cheques or cash and rely entirely on plastic. Even so, a small stash of US dollars cash can come in handy in a sticky situation.

Notification of credit card loss: American Express, SP Building, 388 Phahonyothin Road, Bangkok 10400, T02-2735544; Diners Club, Dusit Thani Building, Rama IV Road, T02-233 5644, T02-238 3660; JCB, T02-256 1361, T02-256 1351; Visa and MasterCard, Thai Farmers Bank Building, Phahonyothin Road, T02-251 6333, T02-273 1199.

Cost of travelling
Visitors staying in the reasonable hotels and eating in decent restaurants will probably spend at least ฿3000 per day, conceivably much much more. Tourists staying in cheaper a/c accommodation and eating in local restaurants will probably spend about ฿1000-1500 per day. Backpackers staying in fan-cooled guesthouses and eating cheaply, should be able to live on ฿300 per day.

Opening hours

Banks Monday-Friday 0830-1530.
Exchange 0830-2200 in Bangkok, Pattaya and Phuket; shorter hours in other places.
Government offices Monday-Friday 0830-1200, 1300-1630.
Shops 0830-1700, larger shops 1000-1900/2100.
Tourist offices 0830-1630.

Safety

In general, Thailand is a safe country to visit. The majority of visitors to Thailand will not experience any physical threat whatsoever. However, there have been some widely publicized murders of foreign tourists in recent years and the country does have a high murder rate. It is best to avoid any situation where violence can occur – what would be a simple punch-up in the West can escalate in Thailand to extreme violence. A general rule of thumb if confronted with a situation is to appear conciliatory and offer a way for the other party to back out gracefully. It should be noted that even some police officers in Thailand represent a threat – at least 3 young Western travellers have been shot and murdered by drunken Thai policemen in the last few years. Confidence tricksters, touts, all operate, particularly in more popular tourist centres. Robbery is also a threat; it ranges from pick-pocketing to the drugging (and subsequent robbing) of bus and train passengers. Watchfulness and simple common sense should be employed. Women travelling alone should be careful. Always lock hotel rooms and place valuables in a safe deposit if available (if not, take them with you).

If you do get any problems contact the tourist police rather than the ordinary police – they will speak English and are used to helping resolve any disputes, issues, etc.

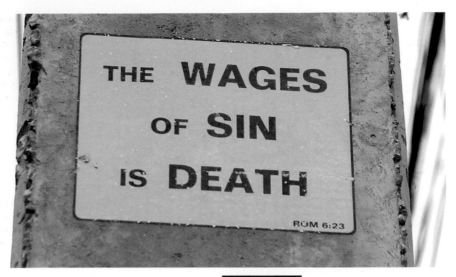

THE **WAGES** OF **SIN** IS **DEATH**

ROM 6:23

Foreign and Commonwealth Office (FCO), T0845-850 2829, fco.gov.uk/travel.
The UK Foreign and Commonwealth Office's travel warning section.
US State Department, travel.state. gov/travel_warnings.html. The US State Department updates travel advisories on its 'Travel Warnings and Consular Information Sheets'. It also has a hotline for American travellers, T202-6475225.

Many prostitutes and drug dealers are in league with the police and may find it more profitable to report you than to take your custom (or they may try to do both). They receive a reward from the police, and the police in turn receive a bonus for the detective work. Note that foreigners on buses may be searched for drugs. Sentences for possession of illegal drugs vary from a fine or one year in jail for marijuana up to life imprisonment or execution for possession or smuggling of heroin. The death penalty is usually commuted.

Tourist police

In 1982 the government set up a special arm of the police to deal with the demands of the tourist industry – the tourist police. Now, there is no important tourist destination that doesn't have a tourist police office. The Thai police have come in for a great deal of scrutiny over recent years, although most policemen are honest and only too happy to help the luckless visitor. Tourist Police, Bangkok, T02-281 5051 or T02-221 6206. Daily 0800-2400.

Telephone

Country code +66.
From Bangkok there is direct dialling to most countries. To call overseas, you first need to dial the international direct dial (IDD) access code, which is 001, followed by the country code. Outside Bangkok, it's best to go to a local telephone exchange if calling internationally.

with domestic call charges from ฿3 per min and international calls from ฿8 per min. GPRS data deals are also incredible cheap – the AIS network offers 100 hrs of mobile internet connection for ฿300 per month. Speeds are slow though the network is perfectly adequate for text emails, basic web-browsing and social sites such as Facebook.

Time

GMT plus 7 hours.

Tipping

Tipping is generally unnecessary. However, a 10% service charge is now expected on room, food and drinks bills in the smarter hotels as well as for any personal service. Increasingly, the more expensive restaurants add a 10% service charge; others expect a small tip.

Tour operators

STA Travel, statravel.co.uk.
Travelmood, travelmood.com.

Tourist information

Local offices are found in most major tourist destinations in the country. For the main office in Bangkok, see page 71.

UK, 1st floor, 17-19 Cockspur St, Trafalgar Sq, London SW1Y 5BL, T0870-900 2007, tourismthailand.co.uk.
USA, 1st floor, 611 North Larchmont Blvd, Los Angeles, CA 90004, T461-9814, F461-9834, tatla@ix.netcom.com.

Local area codes vary according to province. Individual area codes are listed through the book; the code can be found at the front of the telephone directory.

Calls from a telephone box cost ฿1.

Mobiles are common and increasingly popular. Coverage is good except in some border areas. A Thai sim card is very easy for visitors to acquire and highly recommended if you are staying for any period of time in Thailand. You will need an unlocked phone (cheap, unlocked second-hand phones are available throughout Thailand from about ฿700) and a valid ID when buying a sim card. AIS and Happy D Prompt sim cards and top ups are available throughout the country and cost ฿200

Visas & immigration

For the latest information on visas and tourist visa exemptions see the consular information section of the Thai Ministry of Foreign Affairs website, mfa.go.th. The immigration office is now at Building B, Bangkok Government Center, Chaengwattana Road (near Dept of Consular Affairs). To get there take bus 103 from Mo Chit BTS Skytrain station.

Thai immigration authorities will only issue 15-day visa-free entry permits if you enter Thailand by a land crossing from any neighbouring country. How long this will stay in force is unknown.

For tourists from 20 countries (all Western countries, plus most Arabic and other Asian states; see mfa.go.th for a full list) it is possible to have a special 30-day entry permit issued on arrival. These permits are not strictly visas and differ from 'visa on arrival' service signposted at the airports. Applicants must also have an outbound (return) ticket and possess funds to meet living expenses of ฿20,000 per person or ฿40,000 per family.

Tourist visas

If you intend to stay in Thailand for a period over 30 days you'd be best advised to get this 60-day visa before you travel from a Thai embassy. They can be extended for a further 30 days from the immigration office in Bangkok (see above) for ฿1900. Visas are issued by all Thai embassies and consulates.

Volunteering

Projects range from conservation and teaching English to looking after elephants. They vary in length from two weeks and beyond and generally need to be organized before you arrive. Consult individual organizations about visas and lodgings – most include basic shared accommodation in the price but not travel to and from Thailand. The following international organizations run projects in Thailand.

British Trust for Conservation Volunteers, UK, T01302-388888, btcv.org;
Cross Cultural Solutions, USA, T1800 380 4777 (US only), crossculturalsolutions.org.
Earthwatch, UK, T01865-318838, earthwatch.org.
Global Services Corps, USA, T415-7883666, ext128, globalservice corps.org.
Involvement Volunteers, Australia, T613-9646 5504, volunteering.org.au.
VSO, UK, T0208-780 7200, vso.org.uk.

Local customs

Thais are generally very understanding of the foibles and habits of foreigners and will forgive and forget most indiscretions. However, there are a number of 'dos and don'ts' that are worth observing.

Avoid wearing shorts and sleeveless tops in towns and at religious sights. Make sure your shoulders and knees are covered up and avoid wearing flip-flops.

It is important to keep calm in any disagreement – losing one's temper leads to loss of face and loss of respect.

Try to not openly point your feet at anyone – feet are viewed as spiritually the lowest part of the body. At the same time, never touch anyone's (even a child's) head, which is the holiest as well as the highest part.

Never criticize any member of the royal family or the institution itself. The monarchy is held in very high esteem and lese-majesty remains an offence carrying a sentence of up to 15 years in prison. You should treat coins and bank notes with respect as they bear the image of the king, as well as postage stamps which are moistened with a sponge rather than the tongue.

Remove shoes on entering any monastery building, do not climb over Buddha images or have your picture taken in front of one.

Smoking is now illegal in all air-conditioned areas. Fines are heavy, although not always enforced.

Bangkok police regularly fine people up to ฿3000 for discarding cigarette butts anywhere other than in official ashtrays.

Language

Polite particles

At the end of sentences males use the polite particle *krúp*, and females, *kâ* or *ká*.

Learning Thai

The list of words and phrases below is only very rudimentary. For anyone serious about learning Thai it is best to buy a dedicated Thai language text book or to enrol on a Thai course. Recommended among the various 'teach yourself Thai' books is Somsong Buasai and David Smyth's *Thai in a Week*, Hodder & Stoughton: London (1990). A useful mini-dictionary is the Hugo Thai phrase book (1990). For those interested in learning to read and write Thai, the best 'teach yourself' course is the Linguaphone course.

General words and phrases

Yes/no	*chái/mâi chái, or krúp (kâ)/mâi krúp (kâ)*
Thank you/no thank you	*kòrp-koon/mâi ao kòrp-koon*
Hello, good morning, goodbye	*sa-wùt dee krúp(kâ)*
What is your name?	*Koon chêu a-rai krúp (kâ)?*
My name is …	*Pom chêu …*
Excuse me, sorry!	*kor-tôht krúp(kâ)*
Can/do you speak English?	*koon pôot pah-sah ung-grìt*
a little, a bit	*nít-nòy*
Where's the …?	*yòo têe-nai …?*
How much is …?	*tâo-rài …?*
Pardon?	*a-rai ná?*
I don't understand	*pom (chún) mâi kao jái*
How are you?	*Mâi sa-bai?*
Not very well	*sa-bai dee mâi*

At hotels

What is the charge each night?	*kâh hôrng wun la tâo-rài?*
Is the room air conditioned?	*hôrng dtìt air reu bplào?*
Can I see the room first please?	*kor doo hôrng gòrn dâi mái?*
Does the room have hot water?	*hôrng mii náhm rórn mái?*
Does the room have a bathroom?	*hôrng mii hôrng náhm mái?*
Can I have the bill please?	*kor bin nòy dâi mái?*

Travelling

Where is the train station?	*sa-tahn-nee rót fai yòo têe-nai?*
Where is the bus station?	*sa-tahn-nee rót may yòo têe-nai?*
How much to go to…?	*bpai … tâo-rài?*
That's expensive	*pairng bpai nòy*
What time does the bus/ train leave for …?	*rót may/rót fai bpai … òrk gèe mohng?*
Is it far?	*glai mái?*
Turn left/turn right	*lée-o sái / lée-o kwah*
Go straight on	*ler-ee bpai èek*
It's straight ahead	*yòo dtrong nâh*

At restaurants

Can I see a menu?	*kor doo may-noo nòy?*
Can I have …?/	
I would like …?	*Kor …*
Is it very (hot) spicy?	*pèt mâhk mái?*
I am hungry	*pom (chún) hew*
Breakfast	*ah-hahn cháo*
Lunch	*ah-hahn glanhg wun*

Time and days

in the morning	*dtorn cháo*
in the afternoon	*dtorn bài*
in the evening	*dtorn yen*
today	*wun née*
tomorrow	*prôong née*
yesterday	*mêu-a wahn née*
Monday	*wun jun*
Tuesday	*wun ung-kahn*
Wednesday	*wun póot*
Thursday	*wun pá-réu-hùt*
Friday	*wun sòok*
Saturday	*wun sao*
Sunday	*wun ah-tít*

Numbers

1	*nèung*
2	*sorng*
3	*sahm*
4	*sèe*
5	*hâa*
6	*hòk*
7	*jèt*
8	*bpàirt*
9	*gâo*
10	*sìp*
11	*sìp-et*
12	*sìp-sorng … etc*
20	*yêe-sìp*
21	*yêe-sìp-et*
22	*yêe-sìp-sorng… etc*
30	*sahm-sìp*
100	*(nèung) róy*
101	*(nèung) róy-nèung*
150	*(nèung) róy-hâh-sìp*
200	*sorng róy … etc*
1000	*(nèung) pun*
10,000	*mèun*
100,000	*sairn*
1,000,000	*láhn*

Basic vocabulary

airport	*a-nahm bin*
bank	*ta-nah-kahn*
bathroom	*hôrng náhm*
beach	*hàht*
beautiful	*oo-ay*
big	*yài*
boat	*reu-a*
bus	*ót may*
bus station	*sa-tah-nee rót may*
buy	*séu*
chemist	*ráhn kai yah*
clean	*sa-àht*
closed	*bpìt*
cold	*yen*
day	*wun*
delicious	*a-ròy*
dirty	*sòk-ga-bpròk*
doctor	*mor*
eat	*gin (kâo)*
embassy	*sa-tahn tôot*
excellent	*yêe-um*
expensive	*pairng*
food	*ah-hahn*
fruit	*pon-la-mái*

hospital	rohng pa-yah-bahn
hot (temp)	rórn
hot (spicy)	pèt
hotel	rôhng rairm
island	gòr
market	dta-làht
medicine	yah
open	bpèrt
police	dtum-ròo-ut
police station	sa-tah-nee,
	dtum-ròo-ut
post office	bprai-sa-nee
restaurant	ráhn ah-hahn
road	thanon
room	hôrng
shop	ráhn
sick (ill)	mâi sa-bai
silk	mai
small	lék
stop	yòot
taxi	táirk-sêe
that	nún
this	née
ticket	dtoo-a
toilet	hôrng náhm
town	meu-ung
train station	sa-tah-nee rót fai
very	mâhk
water	náhm
what	a-rai

Index

Index

V

W

Tread your

Footprint Lifestyle guides

 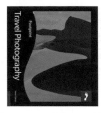 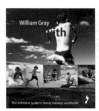 

Books to inspire and plan some of the world's most compelling travel experiences. Written by experts and presented to appeal to popular travel themes and pursuits.

A great book to have on your shelves when planning your next European escapade
Sunday Telegraph

Footprint Activity guides

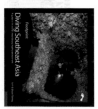   

These acclaimed guides have broken new ground, bringing together adventure sports and activities with relevant travel content, stunningly presented to help enthusiasts get the most from their pastimes.

This guide is as vital as a mask and fins.
David Espinosa, Editor of Scuba Diver Australasia

own path

Footprint Travel guides

Credits

Footprint credits

Editor: Alan Murphy, Alice Jell
Picture Editors: Kassia Gawronski,
Rob Lunn
Layout & production: Davina Rungasamy
Maps: Kevin Feeney
Proofreader: Carol Maxwell

Managing Director: Andy Riddle
Commercial Director: Patrick Dawson
Publisher: Alan Murphy
Publishing Managers: Felicity Laughton,
Jo Williams
Digital Editor: Alice Jell
Design: Mytton Williams
Sales & marketing: Liz Harper,
Hannah Bonnell
Advertising: Renu Sibal
Finance & administration:
Elizabeth Taylor

Print

Manufactured in Italy by EuroGrafica
Pulp from sustainable forests

Footprint feedback

We try as hard as we can to make each
Footprint guide as up to date as possible
but, of course, things always change. If
you want to let us know about your
experiences – good, bad or ugly – then
don't delay, go to footprintbooks.com
and send in your comments.

Every effort has been made to ensure that
the facts in this guidebook are accurate.
However, travellers should still obtain
advice from consulates, airlines etc about
travel and visa requirements before
travelling. The authors and publishers
cannot accept responsibility for any loss,
injury or inconvenience however caused.

Publishing information

FootprintAsia Thailand Islands & Beaches
1st edition
© Footprint Handbooks Ltd
December 2009

ISBN 978-1-906098-84-1
CIP DATA: A catalogue record for this
book is available from the British Library

® Footprint Handbooks and the Footprint
mark are a registered trademark of
Footprint Handbooks Ltd

Published by Footprint

6 Riverside Court
Lower Bristol Road
Bath BA2 3DZ, UK
T +44 (0)1225 469141
F +44 (0)1225 469461
www.footprintbooks.com

Distributed in North America by

Globe Pequot Press